Children's Television, 1947–1990

CHILDREN'S TELEVISION, 1947–1990

Over 200 Series, Game and Variety Shows, Cartoons, Educational Programs and Specials

by JEFFERY DAVIS

McFarland & Company, Inc., Publishers
Jefferson, North Carolina, and London

British Library Cataloguing-in-Publication data are available

Library of Congress Cataloguing-in-Publication Data

Davis, Jeffery, 1949–
    Children's television, 1947–1990 : over 200 series, game and
variety shows, cartoons, educational programs and specials / by
Jeffery Davis.
      p. cm.
    Includes bibliographical references and index.
    ISBN 0-89950-911-8 (lib. bdg. : 50# alk. paper) ∞
    1. Television programs for children — United States — Encyclopedias.
I. Title.
PN1992.8.C46D38   1995
791.45′75′083 — dc20   94-10808
                                                   CIP

Manufactured in the United States of America

McFarland & Company, Inc., Publishers
  Box 611, Jefferson, North Carolina 28640

To my wife, Tena,
and my children, Candice and Jeffery,
whose enthusiasm, patience, and
understanding helped guide me through

Acknowledgments

A book of this sort could not have been completed without the help and support of the people and institutions that shared with me their research and collections.

Especially appreciated are the contributions of Bob Clampett Productions, the Family Communications Corporation, Bob Keeshan Productions and Associates, Jack Mondrus and Associates, Charles Fries Productions, the Hanna-Barbera Studios, Norman Maurer Productions, Barry-Enright Productions, the Children's Television Workshop, Michael I. Silberkleit of Archie Comic Publications, Willy Tyler, Robert Shayne, David ("Mr. Trivia") Strauss, Vincent ("Mr. Television") Terrace, and James Robert ("Mr. Movies") Parish.

I also appreciated the help of many librarians from various film institutes who took the time to research reviews and articles from the original program pages of old *TV Guides*.

Deserving special mention are my wife, Tena, and two children, Candice and Jeffery, whose patience through those long nights of typing and hours of video viewing finally paid off.

Final thanks go to my mother, whose purchase long ago of a 21-inch black-and-white Zenith brought hours of joyful Saturday morning viewing to me and to my Kellogg's Sugar-Smacking buddy and sister, Donnie.

Contents

Introduction

As early as 1931, television's first screen images were projected with primarily a young audience in mind. Puppeteer Bernard H. Paul was the first to bring his company of marionettes to life over experimental stations such as W3XK in Wheaton, Maryland. Eight years later, another young puppeteer by the name of Burr Tillstrom displayed a soon-to-be-familiar bulb-nosed hand puppet over the television airwaves of the 1939 World's Fair.

It was not until 1947, however, that the new medium realized the great potential in children's television programs. Its first big success, came over the old Dumont network, on station WABD, New York City. "Big Brother" Bob Emery became the first children's show host in a 30-minute weekday series of fun, games, and prizes entitled "Small Fry Club." Its success led the way for future shows of its kind.

Before long, the term *children's television* became associated with the three larger broadcasting companies, NBC, CBS, and ABC, with each featuring its own variety of puppets and "kindly old uncle" figures, as well as anything available that might appeal to young children. This usually meant comedy, light action drama, and of course animation of all types.

Unlike today, the early children's programs were shown during the evening hours, since the average broadcast day lasted only a few hours and concluded no later than 7:00 p.m. Before long, however, Saturday mornings became a haven for live performances, dull government documentaries, and half-hour edited versions of Hollywood's "B" Western movies.

Before long the NBC network led the children's ratings with some of the most popular shows in the genre. Puppet shows "Howdy Doody" and "Kukla, Fran, and Ollie" ruled their daily time slots, while Western hero Bill ("Hopalong Cassidy") Boyd acquired the television rights to his feature films, which in turn led to an additional 52 episodes being made especially for television.

Then CBS and ABC came from behind, with two of the most

1

popular shows of all time premiering the same day. Each altered the course of children's daily programming. "Captain Kangaroo" premiered October 8, 1955, on CBS, just hours before "The Mickey Mouse Club" gave ABC the boost it needed to dethrone NBC's top-rated "Howdy Doody Show." The following year Howdy and all his Doody-Ville friends moved to Saturday mornings where they remained throughout the show's run.

During this period, kids' cereal and candy manufacturers realized the great influence that these early shows had on their viewers. So, they bought air time to sponsor some of the most popular of the new shows, despite outcries from teachers, parents, and other pressure groups. Wanting to satisfy both the child and the parent, producers began to develop other shows, like "Captain Kangaroo," which contained some elements of information and education. Eventually programs such as PBS's "Sesame Street" and CBS's "Fat Albert" would meet the standards of each group.

For baby boomers, the shows were influential. Most today still remember these early programs.

During my formative years, I became fascinated by the fact that there were so many different types of shows. "Howdy Doody," "Super-man," "Soupy Sales," and "Huckleberry Hound" were equally enjoyable, although each was different from the others. Although most of the shows were uncomplicated in structure, it was usually easy to see why some were more popular than others. Live performers such as Buffalo Bob Smith, Bob Keeshan, and Pinky Lee, playing friendly video uncles, served as role models who helped to shape children's lives. Their shows and others like them had value as terrific entertainment in a tiny industry that was soon to become a giant. Today, many producers of children's shows have been criticized time and again by advocacy groups for stifling creativity with either violent or toy-related animation. Nevertheless, there are still a few good shows. And of course there is the Public Broadcasting System, which has served as the greatest alternative to network children's programming since the late 1960s.

Unlike some other books that deal with the subject of children's television mainly from a psychoanalytical point of view, this is a reference book about the shows themselves. The reader will find not only the beloved classics of yesterday, but also some of the most popular of kids' video today, readily available at the turn of a dial. While to the browser some of the shows will be readily recognizable, others will seem less familiar and still others will be totally unfamiliar or forgotten.

Although the easiest part of compiling a book of this sort is watching and remembering the shows themselves, information from other sources with updated material was also required, as was information on the various dates and times of broadcast. As I researched with the help of videocassettes and cable and syndicated reruns, some of the older shows were more easily available to me than others. Some of the more inaccessible programs were reviewed at institutions such as the National Film Library and the St. Louis Museum of Broadcasting. Many programs were totally unavailable for reviewing, and information about them was obtained by researching such publications of organizations such as *Facts on File, Filmfax*, the American Broadcasting Co., the Columbia Broadcasting Co., the National Broadcasting Co., the International Communications Archives, and the television and motion picture film libraries of St. Louis.

1. Action-Adventure Shows

Many people who watched television as children in the 1950s can probably recall when at least 50 percent of their favorite characters from television were live dramatic figures. While law enforcement and family relationships provided the most common of backdrops for most of these shows, continuing characters in other forms of the genre were also presented.

As the medium expanded, so did the shows themselves. Studios such as Screen Gems, Ziv-TV, Hal Roach, Wrather, and Disney, as well as several networks themselves, were the ones most responsible for holding children's attention long enough to get their messages across. Messages remained consistent and repetitive: "Good guys always win, bad guys always lose" ("And be sure to tell Mom it's the label that says Ovaltine").

Although many such shows were confined to Saturday mornings, others became extremely successful weekday favorites, and still others were featured weekly during the prime-time hours.

Ironically, in an attempt to recreate the success of some of the most popular of these shows absent since the 1960s, bleak new Saturday morning productions appeared for a brief period during the 1970s; they quickly disappeared, though. They were no match for their largest competitor, the "big budget" cartoon show.

The ABC Weekend / After School Specials

This renowned series of live-action stories and occasional animated films for children is based on original stories adapted specifically for television. Unlike the similar "CBS Children's Film Festival," which focused primarily on foreign films, these shows deal with today's children facing real problems, both dramatic and documentary. Topics never before

Willie Tyler and Lester, hosts of the ABC Weekend Specials, 1977–78.

discussed on a children's program, such as child abuse, drug abuse, and dealing with the loss of a loved one, are splendidly portrayed, usually by child actors with whom most young viewers have become familiar. The series often changes pace and style, switching from serious issues to occasional comedy and fantasy. The award-winning story "The Runaways," for instance, tells of the relationship between two friends, a young boy and an escaped leopard. In a first for television, a February 1977 weekday episode entitled "My Mom's Having a Baby" actually televised a live birth.

Other titles and stars have included, over the years, "Me and Dad's New Wife," with Kristy McNichol, "The Secret Life of T.K. Dearing," with Jodie Foster, "Mighty Moose and the Quarterback Kid," with Brandon Cruz, and "Stoned," with Scott Baio, about the trials of a teenage alcoholic.

The series was designed to provide children with a well-balanced variety of quality programming to be shown occasionally during the week and on Saturday mornings. Except on the PBS network, live-action shows targeted at the 10–15-year-old had been limited in variety since the mid–1960s. Through the professional guidance of such organizations as the Children's Programming Workshop, in affiliation with the ABC Children's Programming Department, headed by Marilyn Olin, the "After School Specials" were consistent in bringing children's programming up to a level of high quality. Initially hosted by Michael Young, and occasionally by ventriloquist Willie Tyler and his dummy, Lester, the program is incorporated into the "ABC After School/Afternoon Specials" and children's selected novels for television. The former is often repeated on the Saturday morning show.

A winner of numerous citations over the years for excellence, the series initially appeared, on an irregular basis, in October 1972. It became a regular part of the Saturday lineup as a series of its own on September 10, 1977, appearing in the 12:00–12:30 time slot. It has won the approval of parents and critics alike. One possible explanation for the program's success may lie with the fact that most of the story lines are clear to young viewers while also sophisticated enough to intrigue the older children.

The Adventures of Robin Hood / Robin Hood

This prime-time adventure series starred the dashing English actor Richard Greene in the title role as the legendary bandit of Sherwood Forest who robbed the rich to feed the poor. The series was originally broadcast on Monday evenings, and then rerun on Saturday mornings after three seasons.

Episodes told the ancient tale of how Sir Robin of Locksley was forced to flee after being declared an outlaw by the evil Prince John (Donald Pleasance) when he objected to the illegal tax levied upon the poor Saxons of England. Sentenced to die, Robin retreated to the sanctuary of Sherwood Forest where he formed a band of resisters like himself whom he called his Merry Men. He and his men swore allegiance only to King Richard the Lion-Hearted (Ian Hunter), the imprisoned rightful ruler of the Kingdom of Britain. Subsequent episodes followed the familiar saga of Robin Hood's efforts to protect his fellow countrymen from the evil Prince John and the wily Sheriff of Nottingham Village (Alan Wheatley). Among Robin's Merry Men were Archie Duncan as Little John, Alexander Gauge as Friar Tuck, and Ronald Howard

(1955–56) and Paul Eddington (1956–58) as Will Scarlett. Bernadette O'Farrell (1955–57) and Patricia Driscol (1957–58) portrayed Robin's sometime romantic interest, the fair Maid Marian. Like most shows that attracted a huge children's audience, "Robin Hood" presented the usual battles of good versus evil, promoting strength and defiance in the face of injustice and inequality.

Sponsored in the United States by the Wild Root Hair Oil Company on CBS, the series was seen weekly by more than 30 million viewers, beginning on September 26, 1955, in the 6:30–7:00 P.M. time slot on Mondays. Remaining in this slot until September 22, 1958, the series was moved to Saturdays from 11:30 to noon beginning October 4, 1958. There it would remain until its final appearance on October 11, 1959. The series eventually inspired other programs based on popular literary characters, such as "Long John Silver" (syndicated, 1955), "Sir Lancelot" (NBC, 1956–57), "William Tell" (syndicated, 1958), and "Francis Drake" (NBC, 1962). Robin Hood, one of the most enduring legendary figures of any age, had been a screen favorite long before the premiere of the television series. Errol Flynn's breathtaking portrayal of the character in the 1938 *Adventures of Robin Hood* has become a film classic. Other popular films featuring the character have included *The Prince of Thieves* (1948), with Jon Hall in the title role, and Richard Todd's brilliant performance in *The Story of Robin Hood* (1951). The latter film served as something of a model for the television series. "The Adventures of Robin Hood" went into syndication in the 1960s under the new title "Sherwood Forest," also known as "Adventures in Sherwood Forest."

The series was among the few British imports at the time to become popular with American viewers. It paved the way for other such classic exports as "The Saint" (syndicated, NBC, CBS, 1966–80), "The Avengers" (ABC, 1966–69), and the comedy series "Fawlty Towers" (syndicated, 1980). Today, the legend still survives, more recently given the full-scale treatment, with actor Kevin Costner in the lead role, in the 1991 blockbuster movie *Robin Hood, Prince of Thieves*.

The Adventures of Superman see Superman

Batman

Considered by many a situation comedy without a laugh track, "Batman," produced by William Dozier, was a textbook example of a camp show. At no time since then has such sophisticated nonsense appeared any better than on this 30-minute 1966 midseason replacement series based on Bob Kane's action comic strip, "Batman, the Dark Knight."

Adam West starred in the title role as Gotham City's caped crusader against such diabolical forces as the Joker (Cesar Romero), the Penguin (Burgess Meredith), and the Riddler (Frank Gorshin/John Astin). Burt Ward costarred as Batman's youthful ward and sidekick, Dick Grayson, alias Robin, the Boy Wonder, whose biggest claim to fame in the series was his use of such exclamations as "Holy overacting, Batman!" Also featured were Neil Hamilton as Commissioner Gordon, Stafford Repp as Chief O'Hara, Madge Blake as Aunt Harriet, and Alan Napier as Alfred, the faithful butler of stately Wayne Manor and the only other person besides Dick Grayson to know that millionaire Bruce Wayne and Batman were one and the same.

Episodes always began with a message from the frantic Commissioner Gordon to the caped crusader via the private Batline regarding a dastardly deed currently being perpetrated by that week's special guest villain ("Bad news, Batman; the Penguin is up to his old tricks"). Operating from their secret Batcave crimelab, located just beneath Wayne Manor, Bruce and Dick assume their secret identities by sliding down the Batpoles from the Wayne library to their jet-propelled Batmobile, emerging from a secret exit onto the road to Gotham City and the office of Commissioner Gordon.

Batman's last known on-screen appearance prior to the television series was in 1949, when he was played by actor Robert Lowery in the Columbia movie serial "The New Adventures of Batman." This serial was the sequel to the original "Batman" (1943) serial in which Lewis Wilson portrayed the role. Any similarities between West's portrayal of Batman and that of the more serious Wilson or Lowery were strictly coincidental. In all fairness, however, the absurd quality was deliberate and something that fans began to look forward to. Scenes with stilted dialogue parodied their own sound effects, like any comic book hero who ever took a "POW!" or a hard "THUD!" Even the opening credits were amusing, with an animated version of the Dynamic Duo running and fighting throughout the theme song. The show's formula became a winning one; the show soared to the top of the ratings heap shortly after its broadcast premiere on January 12, 1966, over ABC. So successful was it, in fact, that two episodes were presented during the week, with the first ending on Wednesday nights in a cliffhanger and the second appearing on Thursday to resolve the story. This format lasted until August 22, 1967; then, beginning on September 7, 1967, the show moved to Thursdays only, still appearing in its original 7:30–8:00 P.M. time slot.

It wasn't long before guest starring on the show in the role of off-beat villains became the "in thing" among Hollywood's most celebrated stars. George Sanders, Eli Wallach, and Otto Preminger all took turns playing the role of Mr. Freeze. Art Carney became the Archer; Vincent Price, Egghead; Michael Rennie, the Sandman; Ethel Merman, Lola Lasagna; Tallulah Bankhead, the Black Widow; Liberace, Chadell the Magnificent; Victor Buono, King Tut; Zsa Zsa Gabor, Minerva; and, in one of his most laid-back performances, comedian Milton Berle was Louie the Lilac. Also, actress Julie Newmar and singer Eartha Kitt played the Catwoman at different times without anyone ever noticing the difference.

Adam West as Batman.

After two and a half seasons, "Batmania" appeared to have run its course, as viewers began to tire of the characters and their trite escapades. In an attempt to improve the ratings, Yvonne Craig joined the cast as Barbara Gordon, daughter of the commissioner and, secretly, Batgirl, who independently joined forces with Batman and Robin whenever help was needed. Unfortunately, on March 14, 1968, the once-popular series was canceled in midseason. What once ranked among the top ten shows was now almost forgotten by viewers.

Adam West and Burt Ward were never able to live down their roles, and eventually recreated the characters by lending their voices to an animated Saturday morning version that appeared on CBS in the fall of 1977.

Long before "Batmania" resurfaced with the premier of the 1989 blockbuster film starring Michael Keaton, reruns of the television series had been a children's favorite in syndication for many years.

Brave Stallion see *Fury*

The Buccaneers

Actor Robert Shaw starred as Captain Dan Tempest, an ex-pirate turned commander of the buccaneer ship *Sultana*, in this 30-minute action-adventure series set in the eighteenth century on the Caribbean island of New Providence. Along with his crewmen, Paul Hansard as Taffy and Brian Rawlingson as Gaff, Captain Tempest fought all sorts of evil doers who threatened the safety of the early Caribbeans. Among the most notorious were Blackbeard the Pirate and the invincible Jean Lafitte (actually Lafitte had become an American ally during the War of 1812). Episodes filmed in England followed the legendary exploits as well as the heroic side of the Buccaneers as they gallantly sailed the seas in search of adventure and excitement.

"The Buccaneers" was aimed at young audiences, after failing to attract much adult attention in the first few episodes during prime time. From September 22, 1956, through September 14, 1957, it ran Saturdays on CBS from 7:30 to 8:00 P.M. Mature audiences, expecting the heroics to which they had grown accustomed in such swashbucklers as Errol Flynn's *Captain Blood* (1935), were largely disappointed. Kids, however, found the robust action exciting, and episodes eventually became more oriented to juvenile audiences.

The show featured documentary footage throughout the program, which helped to provde an authentic feel for the period. And while the series as a whole consisted mainly of contrived situations, given a choice, children usually favored "The Buccaneers" to such adult favorites as Art Linkletter's "People Are Funny" on a different network.

When the series ended its first season on CBS, an additional 18 episodes were produced for the following season. It was then picked up by ABC, which was seeking replacements for the second half hour of "The Mickey Mouse Club," and appeared on Fridays from 5:00 to 5:30 P.M., beginning October 11, 1957, and lasting through September 26, 1958. Episodes of this underrated series have not been repeated since the 1960s, when it appeared briefly in syndication as "The Adventures of Dan Tempest."

The ship used in the series had been seen previously as the *Hispaniola* in Walt Disney's *Treasure Island* (1950) and as the *Pequod* in the 1956 film classic *Moby Dick*. "The Buccaneers" was a production of Sapphire films of England.

The son of an alcoholic physician, the Scottish actor Robert Shaw was drawn to his profession at a very early age. He made his debut on the British stage at 22 with the Shakespearean Memorial Company. He proceeded to early screen appearances in both the United States and

Great Britain, where he is best remembered for a variety of menacing villain roles. In the 1960s he emerged as one of the screen's best dramatic actors. He was nominated for an Oscar in 1967 for his role as King Henry VIII in *A Man for All Seasons*. After portraying the fearless sea captain on "The Buccaneers" for two seasons, Shaw was destined to ride the waves again, some 20 years later. In 1976 he again played an infamous pirate turned buccaneer, as Captain Ned in the film *Swashbuckler*. But it was the 1975 blockbuster hit *Jaws* that fans mostly remember him for; he played the role of Quint, the hard-headed skipper of the fishing boat *Orca*.

The CBS Children's Film Festival

Kukla, Fran, and Ollie became household names in the early years of television, but that is another chapter (chapter 8, "Puppets, Marionettes, and Dummies"). Here they simply ad-libbed while serving as hosts for this long-running, 60-minute program of child-oriented films developed for a young audience. The specials were first introduced in September 1967 over the CBS network on an irregular basis. The program was so well received that it was awarded a regular weekly place of its own four years later, in fall 1971. The show appeared on Saturdays from 1:00 to 2:00 P.M. from September 11, 1971, through September 13, 1977. The following week it was shifted 30 minutes later, but on April 9 it returned to its original time. There is remained until the final show aired on August 25, 1979.

The films were selected by a special panel of CBS television researchers from hundreds of award-winning programs shown at children's film festivals around the world since the early 1950s. Each film gave children a special opportunity to visit other youngsters in foreign lands with different customs and backgrounds. One of the outstanding films featured (and rerun in subsequent seasons) was Albert Lamorisse's poignant, award-winning tale, *The Red Balloon* (1956), retitled and televised in September 1972 as *Stowaway in the Sky*, about the enchanting friendship of a little boy and his large red balloon. *Circus Angel* (September 18, 1971), a 1965 prize-winning comedy from France, was about an angel who has difficulty entering the pearly gates because of his fascination with gold watches and clocks. One of the best films presented during the program's premiere season was a rare German version of the classic *Heidi*, presented in two parts on January 22 and 30, 1972.

The series received numerous awards and citations for excellence over the years, from parents and critics alike. Although many of the films were made years before the series actually aired, several, such as *The Angel and Big Joe* (September 17, 1977), and *Tony and the Tic Tock Dragon* (January 27, 1973), were produced especially for the program. Films ranged from comedy and fantasy to true-to-life experiences that expressed children's innermost joys and sorrows. In the 1965 award-winning film *Skinny and Fatty* (February 5, 1967), two young friends battle against peer pressure, cruelty, and personal hardships to remain good friends, despite their outward and inward differences.

Because the shows rarely focused on violent or harmful topics, younger children especially felt a bit more at ease when watching the program than they did with most other child-oriented films, leading to a huge and loyal following.

"The Children's Film Festival" proved to parents that children of all ages, regardless of race, creed, or color, had much in common, each in his or her own intelligent, proud, and resourceful way. Viewers also learned that problems can sometimes be solved by seeing how others solve them.

By the close of the 1970s, a variety of other live children's dramatic presentations were being shown on both a regular and an irregular basis. Among the most familiar were "The NBC Children's Theater" and "The ABC Afternoon Specials."

In the Saturday morning sea of animation, "The CBS Children's Film Festival" provided something very different: inspiring, worthwhile, and a joy to watch.

Captain Gallant of the Foreign Legion / Foreign Legionnaire

This 30-minute adventure series, shot on location in the Sahara Desert, featured actor Larry ("Buster") Crabbe, famous for his movie and serial roles as Buck Rogers and Flash Gordon. A former Olympic swimming champ, Crabbe was also featured as a Tarzan type in the film *King of the Jungle* (1933) before appearing as the actual character in *Tarzan the Fearless* (1933). In this program, Crabbe portrayed the daring commander of the North African headquarters of the French Foreign Legion, fighting whenever there was a cause, and righting wrongs.

The series, produced by Harry Saltzman, who later went on to produce the immensely successful James Bond films, closely resembled the traditional Westerns of the early television era, with camels and sabres instead of horses and six-shooters. With the scenes calling for lifelike desert enactments, a single season of episodes demanded dozens of extras in the roles of Arabs and legionnaires.

Captain Gallant was aided in every episode by his comical, bearded sidekick, Fuzzy Knight, an awkward, stuttering character who played himself in over 200 Westerns. Crabbe's real-life son, ten-year-old Cullen Crabbe, also appeared on the program, as Cuffy, a ten-year-old honorary member of the unit, who was placed in Gallant's care after his father, one of his men, was killed by Arabs. Typical episodes involved hunts for lost treasure, a search for kidnapped dignitaries, ancient curses, and the usual number of thieves and cutthroats.

Unlike Saltzman's later Bond films, episodes were, overall, deficient in production values allowed for only modest special technical effects. With their limited budgets, stories often used stock footage repeatedly, with the same fight scenes and shadowy desert scenes presented often throughout the show's entirety.

The scripts tended to be tired, and Crabbe and the other actors gave bleak performances that lacked the quality of other kiddy action series such as "Superman" or "Captain Midnight." Nevertheless, "Captain Gallant" was a lively adventure series that managed to mix traditional values with good old-fashioned battles between good and evil, and children everywhere loved it.

Like Johnny Weissmuller, Buster Crabbe was chosen for his early jungle features primarily because of his athletic abilities in swimming and high diving. Unlike Weissmuller, however, Crabbe eventually broadened his acting career by accepting more challenging roles better suited to his talents. In addition to portraying the immensely popular Flash Gordon, Crabbe also appeared as Billy the Kid for the low-budget PCR studios in the 1940s. He was also featured as the hero of such other popular movie serials as *Pirates of the High Seas* (1950) and *King of the Kongo* (1952). After his television series ended its original production in 1957, Crabbe was featured in a few more movies, up until 1965, most of them Westerns. He later became the owner of a company chain that manufactured swimming pools bearing his name and likeness.

The series was sponsored by Heinz ketchup and Chunky Chocolates and appeared in a variety of time slots. Debuting on NBC Sundays from 5:00 to 5:30 P.M. on February 13, 1955, it was moved to Sundays, 11:30 to noon, on March 10, 1957. Its run ended on December 7, 1957, with only 65 episodes having been produced. The show returned as network reruns on ABC on June 6, 1960, airing Mondays from 5:30 to 6:00 P.M. and lasting through January 2, 1961. On April 1, 1961, NBC began airing reruns on Saturdays, 5:00–5:30 P.M. The last aired on

December 21, 1963. Afterwards the show went into syndication as "Foreign Legionnaire."

Captain Midnight / Jet Jackson, Flying Commando

Captain Midnight was kid television's first hero of the so-called Cold War Brigade. Actor Richard Webb starred in the title role as the American flying ace who battled gangsters, spies, enemy agents, and saboteurs with "justice through strength and courage."

Produced by George Bilson through distributor Screen Gems, the television subsidiary of Columbia Pictures, it was the first in a long string of 30-minute action shows to be produced by the studio. "Captain Midnight" was based upon the popular radio series of the same name created by Robert Burtt and Wilfred Moore. Stories involved the exciting exploits of a semiretired World War II aviator, Captain Jim Albright, recruited to perform dangerous secret missions that would improve the world's security. Albright's code name was Captain Midnight.

The character was originally conceived for early radio listeners as a sort of heroic Red Baron type who dogfought his way through various suicide missions to save France during World War I. In the early 1950s, he appeared as host for a syndicated half hour of old Republic movie serials. The role had also been played by actor Dave O'Brien in a 1942 15-chapter movie serial for Columbia Pictures. Richard Webb, like Clayton Moore's Lone Ranger, was very influential in his television role of the scientific flying hero, having actually served in the armed forces during World War II as an aviator. Patriotic, with the aviator's jacket and boots, he was the perfect role model for children everywhere, even though the show's producer originally preferred a much younger man for the part.

Assisting Albright in his missions were the other two members of the Secret Squadron, Aristotle Jones ("Tut"), played by Olan Soule, the squad's science monitor, and Sid Melton, as Ichabod Mudd ("Icky"), Jim's buffoonish assistant and copilot of his plane, *The Silver Dart*. Melton would even become more familiar to audiences later as Danny Thomas's friend Charlie Halper on the long-running sitcom "Make Room for Daddy," also known as "The Danny Thomas Show" (ABC/CBS, 1953–64).

Like many action-adventure dramas made especially for children, "Captain Midnight" was produced strictly for entertainment, and it contained nothing remotely educational.

Even the youngest viewers found it amusing to catch some of the show's notorious inaccuracies, such as the various fight scenes in which Albright dodges a punch, which is nonetheless accompanied by a loud "smack."

Below the surface of its child-oriented veneer, however, "Captain Midnight" did manage to convey themes associated with real postwar insecurities such as the atomic bomb and Communist propaganda. In an episode entitled "Operation Failure," for instance, Albright is sent behind the iron curtain where he attempts to rescue a small band of resisters and their leader, Zabor, from political oppression. In another episode, the U.S. defense program depends upon Captain Midnight's race with the clock to restore the "secret weapon."

As it had previously on radio, "Captain Midnight" became one of those shows closely identified with its sponsor. The sponsor was Ovaltine, which encouraged viewers regularly to send in 25 cents and the Ovaltine label to become an active member of the Secret Squadron. New members received such items as membership cards, emblems, and decoder rings that allowed them to receive secret messages sent by Captain Midnight himself at the end of each presentation. Children who were not necessarily fond of the chocolate drink had their parents buying it strictly to retrieve the labels.

A 30 minute show for CBS, "Captain Midnight" aired for only two seasons on Saturday mornings between 1954 and 1956 — in the 11:00 A.M. slot from September 4, 1957, through June 11, 1955; in the 11:30 A.M. position from June 18 through September 24 of 1955 and at 11:00 A.M. from October 1, 1955, through May 12, 1956. Because of a copyright problem with Ovaltine, the series was then syndicated in reruns for several years under the new title of "Jet Jackson, Flying Commando," with all spoken references to Captain Midnight dubbed to Jet Jackson.

Richard Webb continued to appear in a number of lesser-known roles throughout the next two decades. Die-hard fans of the series may recall his role as the deputy inspector in the 1960 syndicated "Border Patrol." His most memorable film role, however, came more than ten years later when he played the brave but sardonic sheriff in the 1972 camp film *Beware! The Blob.*

Captain Midnight remains one of the best remembered of children's action-adventure shows from the 1950s.

Disneyland see *The "Walt Disney" Shows*

Flipper

Ivan Tors, the creative genius behind several animal shows, produced this series, which starred a dolphin in the title role. Flipper, the seagoing equivalent to Lassie, was the pet of Sandy and Bud Hicks (Luke Halpin and Tommy Norden). Their father, Porter Hicks (Brian Kelly), was the chief ranger of Coral Key Park, a marine refuge in Florida. Like most other television animal stars, Flipper, brave and heroic, was ever ready to swim to the aid of his human companions, Sandy and Bud, whenever necessary. In the series' first 22 episodes, Andy Devine was featured as a salty old seadog who enchanted the boys with his fantastic yarns of the sea.

Chosen from a group of dolphins from the Caribbean, Flipper was actually a female dolphin named Suzie and was trained by Ricou Browning on a Miami, Florida, wildlife reservation. There also was kept Tors's extensive menagerie of other animal stars, including Gentle Ben the bear, Judy the chimp, and Clarence, the cross-eyed lion.

Unlike most animal shows, "Flipper" required a certain amount of endurance from the viewer, since most of the plots were limited to aquatic settings and required repetitive situations. Flipper was frequently warning the boys of danger or towing objects away from danger which were three to four times his own weight. In one episode he even outswam a hungry shark, and then found the strength in the last scene to rescue a visiting scientist from being blown to bits by a floating water mine.

"Flipper" was based upon a 1963 movie of the same name which starred television's "Rifleman," Chuck Conners, in the role of Porter Hicks. Luke Halpin was the only one to revive his original television role from the film.

Ivan Tors, the Norman Lear of the aquatic world, had previously succeeded in producing such favorites as the syndicated "Sea Hunt" (1957–61), "Malibu Run" (CBS, 1960–61), and "The Aquanauts" (1960–61). Also one of the leading producers of animal shows since the 1960s, Tors went on to produce such other adventure favorites as "Daktari" (CBS, 1966–69), "Cowboy in Africa" (ABC, 1967–68), and "Gentle Ben" (CBS 1967–69).

"Flipper," one of the best children-oriented shows to be presented in the evening, was shown for three years (from September 19, 1964, through September 12, 1967) in original episodes on Saturdays for 30 minutes beginning at 7:30 P.M. on NBC. The episodes aired between January 14 and September 8 in 1968 were all reruns and were featured on Sundays at 6:30 P.M.

Foreign Legionnaire see *Captain
Gallant of the Foreign Legion*

Fury / Brave Stallion

With the continuing success of children's shows featuring such animal stars as Lassie and Rin Tin Tin, it was only a matter of time before television producers sought out other animal favorites. "Fury" was about the adventures of a beautiful black stallion and a boy who loved him named Joey, played by Bobby Diamond. Joey lived with his foster father, Jim Newton, played by Peter Graves, and their ranch hand, Pete (William Fawcett), in a rural area near the town of Capital City on the Broken Wheel Ranch. Joey's young friends Packy Lambert and Pee Wee Jenkins were portrayed, respectively, by Roger Mobley and Jimmy Baird. Nan Leslie appeared occasionally as Jim's sister, Harriet.

Although a bit more subdued than most other juvenile shows of the genre in terms of action and excitement, "Fury" became a favorite of millions of youngsters, as well as their parents, through the promotion of such important values as morality, good sportsmanship, safety, and family responsibility. Episodes often expressed the importance of bravery and common sense in the face of extreme danger. Such was the case when Joey's young friend Pee Wee accidentally encountered an escaped circus lion in one of the series' early episodes. His courage and clear thinking helped him to deal with a potentially dangerous situation. The series received numerous awards and was praised for its stories of basic values, animal compassion, and nonviolence.

Not only was "Fury" outstanding in its realistic stories, but it also offered a positive portrait of American family life, as Joey's love for his horse is motivated by the loyal, strong support of his caring foster father, a former policeman, who adopted the orphaned boy. Another distinction lies in the fact that Fury was the last of the children's live-action dramas to appear on Saturday mornings for nearly a decade — appearing on NBC (a 30-minute show) at 11:00 A.M. from October 15, 1955, through September 28, 1963. The show was then moved to 11:30 on October 5, 1963, where it remained through September 3, 1966.

Fury was played by Beauty, a handsome black stallion owned and trained by Ralph McCutcheon. The horse had previously appeared in the films *Johnny Guitar* (1953) and *Gypsy Colt* (1954) just prior to coming to television. Like Lassie, Fury's character embodied human qualities worthy of respect. He was courageous and resourceful when faced with danger and wise in an understanding of humanity. After the first season of "Fury" ended in 1956, Beauty appeared with Elizabeth Taylor in the film classic *Giant* (1956).

Produced by Irving Cumming, Jr., on a budget of $20,000 per episode, the series was filmed at the Irverson Farm Ranches near Hollywood. One hundred and fourteen black-and-white episodes were filmed in all between 1954 and 1960, after a mature Bobby Diamond had somewhat outgrown the role of "young Joey." The series was rerun in syndication under the new title "Brave Stallion" while surviving another six years of Saturday morning network repeats as "Fury."

Bobby Diamond remained somewhat active in the business after the "Fury" series, appearing in a variety of teenage roles, most notably in the part of Dobie Gillis's cousin Duncan on the popular sitcom "The Many Loves of Dobie Gillis" (CBS, 1959–63). He eventually retired from acting in the 1970s to practice law. Peter Graves, brother of actor James Arness, whose only real claim to fame prior to "Fury" had been his role as a war prisoner in the Billy Wilder film *Stalag 17* (1953), went on to even greener pastures as the star of the hit action-spy drama "Mission: Impossible" (CBS, 1966–72).

Jeff's Collie see *The "Lassie" Shows*

Jet Jackson, Flying Commando see *Captain Midnight*

Jungle Jim

Johnny Weissmuller, the former movie Tarzan, appeared as Jungle Jim in this show based on the 1929 Alex Raymond, King Features comic strip. Weissmuller had previously played the character in a 15-film movie series for Columbia Pictures, and Grant Withers had played Jungle Jim in a 1937 12-chapter movie serial for Universal Pictures. Screen Gems, the television subsidiary of Columbia, and the show's producer, Harold Greene, realized Weissmuller's built-in publicity value from the Tarzan films, and his new persona as a jungle man with clothes would fit perfectly with the viewers' image of him. The 30-minute syndicated series, "Jungle Jim," costarred Martin Huston as Jim's young son, Skipper, Norman Frederick as his Indian aide, Kasseem, and Tamba the chimp, who bore a striking resemblance to Cheeta from the old Tarzan days.

James Bradley, known by the natives as Jungle Jim, was an African guide and adventurer who took considerable risks in his various travels across the continent. This often meant intervening in human conflicts or subduing savage animals. With episodes ranging from the bleak to the

Johnny Weissmuller as "Jungle Jim," syndicated 1955–57.

sublime, "Jungle Jim" was one of the best of the juvenile live-action shows of the 1950s, although some of the action became a matter of concern to children's advocacy groups. In the premier episode, "Man-Killer," for instance, Jim fights a lion, wrestles a crocodile, and battles a raging forest fire. Subsequent episodes involved such climactic finales as Jim's arriving in the nick of time to save Skipper from man-killing apes or charging rhinos. As in many shows of the day, the studio made regular use of any available stock footage with jungle settings.

A champion swimmer, Johnny Weissmuller had previously won five gold medals at the 1924 and 1928 Olympics. Approached by Louis B. Meyer in the 1930s to play the lead in a series of Tarzan films, Johnny Weissmuller became typecast in jungle films for his entire acting career. Except for a brief cameo in the 1970 film *The Sphynx* and a few guest appearances on television, Weissmuller did little else in front of the camera after his television series ended production in 1957. After retiring from show business altogether, he headed a Chicago-based swimming pool franchise and endorsed various swimming-related products. He was also the head of the Swimming Hall of Fame in Fort Lauderdale, Florida, where he lived until he became seriously ill in the mid–1970s.

Although hardly the athlete he once was, and noticeably slower and overweight, Weissmuller chose nonetheless to perform most of his own stunts for the "Jungle Jim" series. In the opening sequence it is indeed

Weissmuller shown leaping fully clothed from a towering cliff. Although this dive may have lacked the drama of Tarzan's dive from the Brooklyn Bridge in *Tarzan's New York Adventure* (1942), it still had quite an impact on viewers.

The show debuted October 14, 1955, and ran into 1957.

Land of the Giants

"Land of the Giants," like "Lost in Space," was produced by Irwin Allen as a futuristic space adventure aimed primarily for children. Gary Conway led the cast as Captain Steve Burton, and he and Don Marshall, his copilot, Dan Erickson, were aviators of the rocketliner *Spindrift*. Set adrift on June 12, 1983, while on an American test flight from Los Angeles to London, England, the ship inadvertently landed on a planet not like their own which was inhabited by giants. Other regulars as crew and passengers included Deanna Lune as airline heiress Valerie Scott, Don Matheson as wealthy industrialist Mark Wilson, Heather Young as stewardess Betty Hamilton, Stefan Arngrim as 12-year-old orphaned stowaway Barry Lockridge, and Kurt Kasznar as Alexander Fitzhugh, a foreign agent masquerading as a British commander. Kevin Hagen also appeared in a recurring role as Inspector Kobrick, a giant obsessed with the idea of exploiting "the little people" for his own evil purposes.

In the September 22, 1968, premiere episode, the voyagers are forced to land their craft after passing through a strange dark mist. Before long they realize their odd dilemma, as regular objects appear a hundred times their usual size. In the first few minutes they are nearly run over by a huge automobile, threatened by a curious cat, and attacked by flying insects that appear as aerial dive bombers. Subsequent episodes followed their attempts to repair their ship to return to earth, while trying to avoid being captured by reward-seeking giants.

With its lavish special effects, achieved at a cost of about $250,000 per episode, "Land of the Giants" was the most expensive television series ever produced up to that time. Settings required the constant use of giant props and models to make the actors appear to be miniaturized, providing the series with a moody, surrealist feel. Special effects technicians Art Cruickshank and Emil Kosa were responsible for creating such gigantic devices as a ten-foot pair of scissors, a nine-foot revolver, a 15-foot birdcage, a nine-foot pencil made of papier-mâché and plywood, and a variety of large fruits and vegetables. One episode called for a giant-size slice of bread, made of a five-foot-by-five-foot piece of styrofoam.

"Land of the Giants" enjoyed two successful years of first-run 60-minute episodes at 7:00 on Sunday nights, replacing "Voyage to the Bottom of the Sea," also produced by Irwin Allen. It was aired on ABC until September 6, 1970. Its strongest competitor during the first half hour of the program was CBS's "Lassie," which drew over 50 percent of the audience share of the ratings.

Episodes of the series are still periodically presented today over the USA cable network.

Land of the Lost

Brothers Sid and Marty Krofft were the creative forces behind this innovative live-action NBC series for Saturday mornings which centered on the Marshall family. Spencer Milligan starred as Ranger Rich Marshall, Wesley Eure as his son, Will, and Kathy Coleman as his daughter, Holly. They find themselves trapped behind a one-way time barrier after surviving a near-fatal plunge over a waterfall.

Each week the Marshalls battled for survival against giant prehistoric monsters, and participated in the conflict between a group of apelike people called the Pakunis, whom they befriended, and their enemies, the Sleestacks, evil reptilian creatures bent on conquest.

After two seasons of contrived plots and counterplots, Ranger Rich was lost in a terrible earthquake (actually the actor was seeking more challenging roles). He was replaced by Ron Harper, as Rich's brother, Jack Marshall, who had spent the previous two seasons searching for his lost relatives.

"Land of the Lost" was one of several new shows of the 1970s to reappear in live-action form for Saturday mornings. Unfortunately, despite some fine scripts, most of the show's action appeared dull. The new programs of the 1970s had little in common with their predecessors of the 1950s in terms of excitement and drama. With the 1970s also came organizations such as A.C.T. (Action for Children's Television), which urged a reduction in violence during the hours in which children watch television, especially Saturday mornings, the period most associated with children's television. But the series satisfied the demands of a new generation of kids reared on a constant diet of cartoons, and it remained a favorite for four years on NBC. The show aired on Saturdays at 10:00 A.M. from September 7, 1974, through September 4, 1976. The half hour show moved to 12:00 noon on September 11, 1976. The final episode appeared September 2, 1978.

With the gradual reintroduction of live-action shows such as

"Shazam!" (CBS, 1974–77), "The Secrets of Isis" (CBS 1975–78), and "Space Academy" (CBS, 1977–79), "Land of the Lost" should at least be commended for filling the void created when children's dramatic television left the airwaves in the 1960s.

Nonetheless, many children still prefer cartoons to drama, and today animation on Saturday mornings is more prevalent than ever before.

The "Lassie" Shows
Lassie / Jeff's Collie / Timmy and Lassie

One of the most beloved family-oriented series of all time was "Lassie," the story of a resourceful collie based on the Eric Knight novel and on the 1943 MGM classic *Lassie Come Home,* in which a faithful collie makes a hazardous 200-mile journey to rejoin his young master.

Over the course of two decades the program survived various format and cast changes without ever seeming to age. Actually, Lassie was played at various times by at least six collies and by a variety of look-alikes for the difficult stunts. All, like Lassie, were owned and trained for the show by the late Rudd Weatherwax.

In the show's first 103 episodes (1954–57), Lassie lived on the Miller farm near the town of Calverton. The cast included 12-year-old Tommy Rettig as Jeff Miller, Jan Clayton as his widowed mother, Ellen, George Cleveland as Jeff's granddad, George ("Gramps"), and Donald Keeler as his best friend, Sylvester ("Porky") Brockway. Lassie was the greatest of the animal heroes. Episodes often involved scenes in which Lassie leaped through plate glass windows or barked frantically to get help for her beloved Jeff, struggling against adversaries, both human and animal.

At the end of three successful seasons, the producers felt that Tommy Rettig had outgrown the part of Jeff, and Rettig himself had begun to tire of the role. Consequently, another young actor, Jon Provost, was written into the series, in a three-part episode entitled "The Runaway," as a young orphan entrusted to the care of Lassie upon the Millers' sudden move to the big city. The new cast also included Cloris Leachman and Jon Sheppodd as Timmy's foster parents, Paul and Ruth Martin. George Chandler was also featured as Uncle Petrie (George Cleveland had passed away at the start of the new season). Because of a verbal contract dispute, Cloris Leachman and Jon Sheppodd lasted only one season as the Martins. They were replaced the following year (1958) by June Lockhart and Hugh Reilly.

As in the earlier episodes, Lassie continued to show great dedica-

The second cast of "Lassie." From back left: June Lockhart, Hugh Reilly, Lassie aka "Pal" and Jon Provost.

tion to her new master, Timmy, with several of the episodes presented as minidramas over three to five weekly installments. In a 1963 five-part episode, Timmy and Lassie are cast adrift in a runaway weather balloon. The episodes were assembled the following year and presented to matinee audiences as the film *Lassie's Great Adventure.* That same year the Wrather Corporation, producer of the series, and its long-time sponsor, the Campbell Soup Company, decided upon another change, believing that Provost had now also outgrown the role.

It was explained this time that the Martins had sold the farm to move to Australia for a better way of life but were unable to bring Lassie along because of that country's strict quarantine laws for pets. In a tearful two-part episode, Timmy departed, leaving Lassie in the care of Cully Wilson, an elderly friend of the Martins, seen in previous episodes and portrayed by veteran comedy actor Andy Clyde. When Wilson became too sick to look after Lassie, Robert Bray filled in as forest ranger Corey Smith, introduced several episodes earlier. After Bray's departure from the series in 1968, Lassie joined forces with two other forest rangers, Jed Allen and Jack DeMave, respectively, as Scott Turner and Bob Erichson. During the last two seasons of the series, there were no human regulars at all, allowing Lassie to wander about in each episode looking for new adventures. In the last few original episodes, Lassie met and fell in love with a male collie, which eventually led to a litter of puppies. (An exceptional feat even for Lassie, considering that the role had actually been played over the years by a variety of male collies!)

CBS chose the 7:00 P.M. Sunday slot for this 30-minute show. The premiere episode aired on September 12, 1954. The final episode aired on September 12, 1971. In the fall of 1971, "Lassie" was syndicated on more than 200 stations across the United States and Canada.

Like most popular animals shows, "Lassie" was derived from a movie and its sequels, beginning in 1944 with *The Son of Lassie*, and *Lassie Come Home*. Lassie (whose real name was Pal) became the principal dog for many of the films' most dramatic scenes and went on to become even more popular several years later when the ABC radio network announced its plans for a radio program starring the canine in a series of her own. For five years Pal, alias Lassie, supplied the needed growls, whimpers, and barks that helped make the radio series a huge success. With television producers then seeking inexpensive properties for a children's audience, the Lassie character appeared to be a sure-fire winner. In 1953, in a 10 percent residual agreement with trainer Rudd Weatherwax, Lassie was turned over to producer Robert Maxwell, known previously for his production of the first television season of "The Adventures of Superman." The first television Lassie was played by Pal II, the first offspring of the original Lassie star, who had retired from acting in 1951.

Throughout the show's many revisions, one thing has remained the same: its popularity with children has never diminished. The basic formula was always a simple one: an intelligent, brave collie and her triumphs over adversity.

Earlier versions of the series began syndication in the 1960s under the titles "Jeff's Collie" and "Timmy and Lassie" (the latter is frequently rerun today over cable's Nickelodeon station). In 1973 an animated version of the series, produced by Norm Prescott and Lou Scheimer, was presented on Saturday mornings as "Lassie's Rescue Rangers."

The Littlest Hobo

Following closely in the pawprints of "Lassie," this 30-minute Canadian-based series followed the weekly adventures of a lonely German shepherd called Hobo who roamed the countryside while helping humans solve problems. Episodes usually ended with Hobo boarding an empty freight car to journey toward further adventures.

Based loosely on the 1958 children's film of the same name, Hobo (actually a trained dog named London) lacked the comfort and companionship of a young boy, like his American cousins Lassie and Rin Tin Tin. Aside from Hobo himself, the show featured no other regular in a continuing role, human or otherwise. Several of the show's stories resembled the last few original episodes of "Lassie" (which were not filmed until the 1970s), when the dog, like Hobo, became free to roam looking for new adventures.

Rather than attempt to upstage other canine favorites, such as Lassie, Rin Tin Tin, Yukon King, and Bullet, Hobo often appeared as a bit of an underdog. In several of the episodes he associates with an assortment of unsavory characters, social outcasts. One episode has a group of would-be robbers trying to train the shepherd in the fine art of thievery. Hobo pretends to oblige just long enough to be fed, before foiling the robbers at their own game. In most episodes, Hobo managed to come across heroically.

Surprisingly, the syndicated adventures of "The Littlest Hobo," with its similarities to such world-weary human counterparts as David Janssen in "The Fugitive," received good reviews as well as excellent ratings, despite the fact that the show often ran opposite the first or second half hour of such top-rated network shows as "Daniel Boone" and "Perry Mason."

The show ran from January 1963 to September 1980. Produced and directed by Charles Rondeau, reruns of "The Littlest Hobo" were syndicated once again in the 1980s for a new generation of kids to enjoy.

Lost in Space

Based on the popular syndicated comic book, *The Space Family Robinson,* "Lost in Space" was a 60-minute space opera presented on Wednesday's prime time for the entire family on CBS from September 15, 1965, through September 11, 1968. It was not long, however, before most of the stories became generally geared toward a children's audience.

Produced by Irwin Allen, the show featured Guy Williams and June Lockhart as John and Maureen Robinson, crew leaders of a futuristic space expedition aboard the *Jupiter II,* a mission in the Alpha Centauri system initially intended to last five years. Along for the ride were their three children: 12-year-old Will (Billy Mumy), 11-year-old Penny (Angela

Cartwright), and Judy (Mart Kristen), a mature 19-year-old with a crush on the ship's pilot, Major Don West, played by Mark Goddart. Bob May provided the voice of the ship's robot, a friendly, ambulatory machine resembling Robby the Robot from the film *Forbidden Planet* (1956). In a role originally intended to be limited, Jonathan Harris also starred as Dr. Zachery Smith, a villainous, contemptible fellow featured in the pilot episode as a stowaway sent aboard to sabotage the ship. It was his tampering that sent the ship off course and set the premise for the next episode. Ironically, most of the later shows centered on the cowardly, cringing Smith, who unwillingly remained with the Robinsons and Major West while constantly plotting with unsavory alien forces to return to earth alone.

For three seasons the space voyagers encountered all sorts of incredible situations and weird-looking creatures in stories that ranged from the amusingly dramatic to the bizarre. In one episode they are menaced by a colony of vegetable-type aliens who resemble huge carrot stalks. In many of the episodes they are threatened by invisible life forces that seek to control the universe and its lesser-known planets. Episodes always ended with a cliffhanger, to be resolved the following week.

Critics disliked the show, labeling it as "pure science fiction hokum." June Lockhart herself once admitted in a 1967 interview that the show's plots eventually became so corny that at times it was all the cast and crew could do to keep a straight face while lines were being recited. In one episode during the show's last season, however, Professor Robinson mentions to a group of aliens that the first earth-to-moon flight occurred in July 1970 — missing the actual date by only one year.

Producer Irwin Allen always expressed a flair for the dramatic, but he provided it far better a few years later with such blockbuster films as *The Poseidon Adventure* (1972) and *The Towering Inferno* (1974).

Despite the expected criticisms, "Lost in Space" became a huge hit with young audiences, making television history as one of the most popular science fiction shows of the time. It remains today, like "Star Trek," a cult favorite and very prominent among syndicated reruns (mostly on the cable networks), constantly being rediscovered by new generations of children.

Off to See the Wizard

Short-lived but immensely enjoyable, this ABC show was a 60-minute anthology series of children's films, documentaries, and humorous made-for-television productions. It aired on Fridays in the 7:30 P.M. slot from September 8, 1967, through September 20, 1968.

Hosted by animated characters from *The Wizard of Oz*, the program featured edited versions of such recent matinee movie favorites as *Clarence the Cross-Eyed Lion* (1965), *The Adventures of Huckleberry Finn* (1960), and *Captain Sinbad* (1965), presenting them regularly in two-part installments. Also presented occasionally were films about animals living in the jungle, the Arctic, and Canada, provided by Time-Life Films.

For an occasional change of pace, shows sometimes devoted the entire 60 minutes to productions made specifically for the program. One such show used celebrities as favorite storybook characters. Entitled "Who's Afraid of Mother Goose?," the program featured Frankie Avalon and Nancy Sinatra as "Jack and Jill," Maureen O'Hara as "Mother Goose," Dan Rowan and Dick Martin as "Simple Simon and the Pieman" (just months before their television history–making series "Laugh-In"), Dick Shawn as "Old King Cole," Margaret Hamilton as "Old Mother Hubbard," and the Three Stooges as "Three Men in a Tub." In another program, Leslie Caron recreated her famous "Cinderella" character for a presentation entitled "Cinderella's Glass Slipper" (February 1968). Several of the shows for the program were exciting live-action productions such as "Island of the Lost," with Richard Greene (1967), and "The Hellcats," with George Hamilton and Barbara Eden (1967), both serving as potential pilots for their own series.

"Off to See the Wizard" lasted in prime time for only a year, competing against such favorites as "The Wild, Wild West" (CBS, 1965–69) and "Tarzan" (NBC, 1966–68) on other channels.

Although ABC originally considered continuing the show on Saturday mornings, it later rejected the idea, only to revive an updated concept a few years later, "The ABC Afternoon Specials." The rest, as they say, is history.

Ramar of the Jungle

Jon Hall, a former Universal Pictures contract player and the star of such films as *Ali Baba and the Forty Thieves* (1943) and *Invisible Agent* (1945), premiered in this syndicated juvenile action series as Dr. Tom Reynolds, physician and scientist, who knew and worked in Kenya, finding cures for exotic ailments. Dr. Reynolds, who had been raised in the jungle by his missionary parents, was known to the natives only as Ramar ("great white doctor"). Ray Montgomery costarred as his friend and colleague,

Professor Howard Ogden, and M'liss McClure as his Indian servant boy, Sahib.

Episodes, which first appeared on October 7, 1952, often found the jungle hero up to his professional neck in complicated situations, with human types ranging from superstitious natives to disagreeable white hunters in search of valuable mineral deposits.

Hall, one of Hollywood's most versatile actors, began his film career as Charles Locher in 1935. He became something of a screen idol in the 1940s playing the male lead in such classics as John Ford's *Hurricane* (1937). He eventually divided his talents between heroic and villainous roles. He is among several of the distinguished actors of the 1930s and 1940s to gain new fame in a lead role in a children's action series. Toward the end of his career, Hall became more interested in the art of photography, frequently leasing valuable camera equipment to various movie studios.

By today's standards, "Ramar of the Jungle" perpetrated a blatant form of racism. Like Hollywood's Westerns, with their stereotypes of the American Indian, "Ramar" offered stereotypes of the African native. As on most early television shows or in films involving similar themes, natives ususally appeared as illiterate, bungling assistants, violent ritual murderers, or killer cannibals with an insatiable craving for the American Caucasians. In most of the episodes native dialogue was limited to such broken English as "Ramar Bwana him make sickness go way-away." Educators and critics agreed that the show for the most part provided youngsters with false impressions that proved particularly demeaning to black Americans. Jon Hall, however, and the executive board of one of the show's sponsors, Bosko, a chocolate-flavored drink, defended themselves against the accusations, insisting that most of the show's images were genuine. Perhaps they were referring to one of the series' two redeeming qualities, used throughout its 52 programs: its outstanding collection of stock footage, shot by real-life explorers, showing wild animals in their natural habitat, as well as their deadly fights for survival with other animals. Among the most memorable of these battles was one between a leopard and a bone-crushing anaconda. The show's other redeeming feature was the occasional background music, originally composed by Hershel Gilbert and Darrell Calker for the movie serials *Commander Cody* and *Jungle Drums of Africa*. The score was also heard in such other juvenile series as "Annie Oakley," "Rin Tin Tin," "Captain Midnight," and the first television season of "The Adventures of Superman."

Perhaps the one thing most memorable to many fans of the series was its brilliant opening scene, the camera zooming in vividly to a shot of a crocodile-infested river, to a flurry of spider monkeys scurrying up the trees, to Jon Hall's breezy introduction, with safari hat and rifle, to the big bold letters, RAMAR OF THE JUNGLE.

The series was produced at the old Eagle-Lion's studio in Hollywood by Rothchild and Fromkess Productions.

Robin Hood see *The Adventures of Robin Hood*

Rocky Jones, Space Ranger

It is unlikely that many people today, even those over the age of 40, will recall this short-lived science fiction series set in the twenty-first century, which starred Richard Crane in the title role. Nor are they likely to remember Sally Mansfield as Verna Ray, Rocky's girlfriend; Scotty ("Our Gang") Beckett as his friend Winky, copilot of Rocky's ship, the *Orbit Jet*; Maurice Cass as Professor Newton; or Robert Lyndon as Bobby. But the few who do remember may also recall that the show was among the first of the space operas to be produced on film exclusively for television, succeeding the live kinescope versions of such old classics as "Tom Corbett, Space Cadet" (CBS, ABC, NBC, Dumont, 1950–55), "Captain Video" (Dumont, 1949–55), and the original "Buck Rogers" (ABC, 1950–51).

As chief of a group of galaxy patrolmen called the Space Rangers, Rocky led the fight against corruption by attempting to free the inner galaxy from lawbreakers, interplanetary misconduct, and economic warfare. Episodes were sometimes presented in two parts and used the usual good versus evil format, at times with contemporary political overtones. Debuting in the era of peak ideological rivalry between the United States and the Soviet Union, "Rocky Jones" in a sense portrayed the ongoing battle for democracy. One story, for instance, involved the space team's efforts at recovering a valuable piece of machinery, stolen by space pirates, containing the formula for world peace. Although many of television's earliest programs worked within meager budgets, "Rocky Jones" managed to offer realistic settings, good special effects, and interesting story lines.

For some years now film and television historians have disagreed upon the actual airing dates of the series. Gary Grossman states in his book *Saturday Morning Television* (Dell, 1978) that the show was initially under production as early as January 1952 and that the pilot episode was screened no later than October of that same year. Others have claimed that the show premiered on local Los Angeles station KNXT in December

1953 and that it was featured on the ABC network where it concluded its run by 1955. Still others insist that the program's actual premiere was not until February 27, 1954, over the NBC network prior to syndication. To date, film scholars have largely agreed that the series first aired on January 20, 1954, and was originally featured in syndication before being picked up for a brief period (February 27 to April 7 in 1954) by the NBC networks for Saturday mornings. In the fall of 1954, the show's 39 episodes were featured once again in syndication in reruns through the distributorship of MCA-TV.

"Rocky Jones" was filmed at the old Hal Roach Studios under the supervision of Roland Reed Productions, which was responsible for such other weekly favorites as "Waterfront" (syndicated, 1954–56), "Life with Father" (CBS, 1953–55), and the hit comedy "My Little Margie" (CBS/NBC, 1952–55).

Richard Crane, once a favorite second lead among the bobby-soxer crowd of the 1940s, had previously appeared in such films as *Captain Eddie* (1945) and *Johnny Comes Marching Home* (1946). He died suddenly of a heart attack in 1969 at the age of 51. His costar Scotty Beckett first began his acting career at the age of three in the "Our Gang" comedy short, "Hi Neighbor." A bit of a ruffian in real life, Beckett was found dead in 1968 at the age of 39, an apparent victim of a drug-related slaying.

The Secrets of Isis /
The Shazam! — Isis Hour

A successful heir to the live-action shows of the 1950s was "The Secrets of Isis." It starred JoAnna Cameron as Andrea Thomas, a mild-mannered high school science teacher, who, after learning the secrets of an ancient Egyptian goddess (Isis), could transform herself into a female equivalent of Superman. Brian Cutler costarred as schoolteacher Rick Mason, Ronald Douglas (the first season) as student Renee Carroll, Joanna Pang as Cindy Lee, and Albert Reed as Dr. Barnes, head of the science department.

The adventures centered on Andrea and her decision to put her heroic new powers to good use, catching lawbreakers and helping those in need.

Andrea first acquired her strange powers when, on a scientific expedition in Egypt, she stumbled upon an amulet handed down by the royal sorcerer to the ancient queen of Egypt. It gave powers to the female bearer bestowed by the goddess Isis: the ability to fly like a bird, and to take complete control of the land and sky by uttering the magic words, "O Mighty Isis." As the incarnated Isis, Andrea is transformed into a beautiful princess, complete with a costume, including a gold head-band, a cape, and the magic amulet with an emerald in the center, the symbol of Isis.

Because of new rules governing the amount of violence presented on children's television shows, the program's action quota was usually low, with each episode usually ending by offering a moral to the story. "Isis" became an instant hit with children, and because of its star, JoAnna Cameron, many men also watched the program. It eventually became one of the children's shows most widely watched by adults in recent years.

However limited the action might have appeared, "Isis," like "Sha-zam!" (CBS, 1974–77), was one of the first shows of its kind to fill the void of live-action shows on the network's Saturday morning lineup. Pro-duced by Louis Scheimer and Norm Prescott and created by Mark Rich-ards, "The Secrets of Isis" first premiered on CBS at 10:30 A.M. on September 6, 1975 as the second half of "The Shazam!—Isis Hour." The 30-minute show remained in this programming slot until September 3, 1977. On September 10, 1977, the program was moved to 12:00 noon where it stayed until January 7, 1978. From January 14, 1978, through September 2, 1978, it was aired at 11:30 A.M. Forty-eight episodes in all were distributed through Filmation Studios.

Sergeant Preston of the Yukon

Richard Simmons starred in the title role as the Royal Canadian Mounted Policeman who always got his man in this 30-minute adventure series set in the wilds of the freezing Klondike. Although accompanied at times by his horse Rex, Sergeant Preston spent most of his time with his canine companion, Yukon King, trudging through the snow, ap-prehending fugitives, or tracking gangsters threatening the security of the great Northwest.

The series was set in nineteenth-century Canada, where idealists, dreamers, and crooks were taking advantage of the so-called Gold Rush of the 1880s. Preston was a dedicated law enforcement professional who, like several other fictional heroes, took the job after a series of personal tragedies. In this instance, Preston's father, a former Mountie himself, had been killed in the line of duty by an escaped fugitive originally wanted for murder. Swearing to avenge his father's death, young Frank Preston, a graduate law student, enlisted in the Royal Canadian Mounted

Police. After capturing the murderer, Officer Preston continued his crusade for justice in the Northwest and was later promoted to sergeant.

Created on radio in 1947 by George W. Trendle, who had previously created "The Lone Ranger" and "The Green Hornet," the half hour show featured flashbacks that reminded viewers of Preston's origins as well as of his first encounter with his beloved malamute, Yukon King. Preston raised the dog after taking the orphaned puppy from an overly protective mother wolf. Under Preston's guidance, the dog grew up to become the strongest in the Yukon, acquiring the name Yukon King and a place as the leader of Preston's sled team. King was trained by Stuart Mace.

The adventures of Sergeant Preston were first seen at 7:30 P.M. on September 29, 1955, and for the next three years, over the CBS network on Thursday nights. The show's sponsor was the Quaker Oats Company. Sergeant Preston and Yukon King closed their last case together on September 25, 1958, before being rerun on Saturday mornings on NBC in 1963. It aired at noon from October 5, 1963, through April 11, 1964.

Richard Simmons had no prior television experience when he accepted the role of the able-bodied Mountie. A pilot during World War II, Simmons had appeared briefly in several films during the 1940s.

George Trendle Enterprises, producer of the series, sold its interest in the show to the Wrather Corporation in 1958. Of the 104 episodes, the last 26 were in color.

The series was rerun once again in syndication in the 1970s.

Shazam! / The Shazam! — Isis Hour

This was the first time in almost ten years that a live-action series appeared on Saturday mornings. Produced by the Filmation Studios and loosely based on the comic book hero Captain Marvel, "Shazam!" featured Michael Grey as Billy Batson, who is chosen by five immortal Greek gods to possess the amazing power to transform himself into Captain Marvel, the "mightiest mortal of them all," simply by uttering the magic word Shazam!

Produced by Lou Scheimer and Norm Prescott, the series also featured Les Tremayne as Billy's traveling companion and mentor, John Davey (1974–76), and Jackson Bostwick (1976–77) as his older alter ego, Captain Marvel.

Unlike many of its live-action predecessors from the 1950s, this series presented action on the children's level. Most adults were able to appreciate this, since competing shows, mostly cartoons, involved more violence.

The original Captain Marvel character was created by Ralph Daigh and Bill Parker in the late 1930s. For a time the character's popularity rivaled even that of Superman, as *Captain Marvel* became the number-two best-selling comic book action series of the 1940s. In 1941 Republic Pictures featured a 12-chapter serial on the character entitled *The Adventures of Captain Marvel,* starring Junior Coghlan in the role of Billy Batson. Similar to Superman's "Up, up and away!" "Shazam!" became one of the nation's leading catchphrases and it helped to lift the character to soaring heights.

The television version of "Captain Marvel" was less violent than its predecessors, and the series often contained moralistic overtones, frequently emphasized at the end of each program (usually quotes by Billy) and directed specifically to the young audience. Many of the young viewers were totally unacquainted with the original comic book character.

Appearing on Saturday morning at 10:30 on CBS from September 7, 1974, through August 30, 1975, as a 30-minute series of its own, "Shazam!" was presented during its second season as the first half hour of "The Shazam! — Isis Hour." The show aired at 10:00 A.M. from September 6, 1975 through September 3, 1977.

The Shazam! — Isis Hour see *The Secrets of Isis*

Sheena, Queen of the Jungle

Premiering October 6, 1955, within eight days of the popular "Jungle Jim" series, was the least successful of the juvenile jungle series, "Sheena, Queen of the Jungle." It starred Irish McCalla in the title role and as the second actress to play a lead character in a children's action series, "Annie Oakley's" Gail Davis having been the first. The show was based on a once-popular syndicated comic strip created in 1937 by S.M. Inger and Will Eisner. Sheena was the female counterpart to Tarzan who, like the Edgar Rice Burroughs character, was raised alone in the African jungle after surviving an airplane crash that took the lives of her parents. Despite the odds, Sheena managed to learn to communicate with the animals while growing up. The leopard-skin-clad heroine was featured regularly in her weekly adventures with her friends Bob (Christian Drake), a white African trader, and Chim the chimp.

Like "Ramar," "Sheena" was based in Kenya, where the jungle girl had more than her share of problems dealing with such greedy adversaries as ivory poachers, diamond thieves, and, in several episodes, American fortune hunters, who sought to capture her for exploitation purposes.

"Sheena" received consistently negative reviews from critics. Several attacked the show viciously, with statements like "The series would actually have to improve to become bad." Jack Gould from the *New York Times* wrote, "The dialogue is strictly Tarzan, while the acting an elementary Ramar." Some even complained about the show's cheap-looking sets, and indeed the show did have very low production budgets and constantly used stock footage. Often the footage provided the high point of the program.

All things considered, though, Sheena's qualities placed her among television's strongest heroes, and however absurd the plot might have been, Sheena managed to overcome any adversary, whether two-legged or four. Twenty-six episodes in all were filmed in Mexico at the Edward Nassour Studios.

A former model turned actress, Irish McCalla got the role of the beautiful jungle heroine after actress Anita Ekberg allegedly turned it down. McCalla is credited with creating television's first sexy heroine image, which had enormous appeal to adolescent males and their fathers. This quality would lead to success nearly two decades later for "Isis" (CBS, 1975–78), "Wonder Woman" (ABC/CBS, 1976–79), and "Charlie's Angels" (ABC, 1976–81). McCalla later became a successful artist and designer.

Space Patrol

"Space Patrol" was episodic children's television at its best. Ed Kemmer starred as Commander Buzz Corry, head of the Space Patrol, a thirtieth century world security force assigned the task of policing an organization called the United Planets. Lyn Osborn costarred as Buzz's friend and copilot of the *Terra IV*, Cadet Happy, who was known for exclaiming "Holy smokin' rockets!" whenever he became excited, which was quite often. Buzz's female interests were played by Nina Bara, as Tonga, and by Virginia Hewitt, as Carol. Tonga, once villainous, was eventually persuaded to put her skills to good use, and she became a big help to the Space Patrol by tracking down bad guys who had been her cohorts. Carol was the daughter of Secretary-General Karlyle (Norman Jolley) and was more or less Corry's real girlfriend. Ken Mayer was also featured as Major Robbie Robertson, security chief of the universe. Episodes were narrated by Jack Narz who later became a game show host.

Kinescoped and televised live at the old Vitagraph Hollywood

Studios, now used by Warner Brothers for live stage productions, the series was originally presented daily, Monday through Friday, for 15 minutes at 5:45 P.M. on ABC (September 11, 1950, through December 29, 1950).

Based on the same premise as such other early science fiction operas as "Buck Rogers" (ABC, 1950–51), "Captain Video" (Dumont, 1949–55), and "Rod Brown of the Rocket Rangers" (CBS, 1953–54), "Space Patrol," produced by Mike Moser, was the first series ever to present an episode in 3-D. This occurred during a 1953 segment entitled "The Theft of the Rocket Cockpit," presented at the peak of the era's craving for 3-D films. For weeks prior to the show, children were encouraged to check the premium labels on their boxtops of Ralston Purina cereals (the show's sponsor) to obtain a special pair of 3-D glasses for the upcoming episode.

Cited by various parents' organizations for its wholesome content, which included scientific gadgetry, imagination, and comic overtones, "Space Patrol" managed to remain long on action without excessive violence. Captured outlaws, for instance, were immediately subjected to a process of "suspended animation" and brainwashed of all their evil thoughts. Once reformed, they were released into the custody of the Space Patrol and given the opportunity to become solid citizens. Another key to the series' success was the comradeship among the ship's crewmembers, an element relied upon even by the villains. In one episode a space pirate kidnaps both Carol and Happy, knowing that Corry's search for them would allow time for the pirate to plunder the universe.

Among Buzz and Happy's most notorious adversaries were the space spider, the wild men of Procyon, and Captain Dagger (Glenn Strange) of the spaceship *Jolly Roger*. Bela Kovacs appeared most frequently, however, as the devious Black Falcon, also known as Prince Baccarratti, ruler of the planet X. Marvin ("The Millionarie") Miller also made appearances as Mr. Proteus, a master in the art of deception.

"Space Patrol," produced on a meager budget of about $2,500 per episode for props, costumes, and special effects, was presented daily during its first four months on the air. It eventually shifted to several weekend slots in which it changed from 15- to 30-minute installments: Sunday, 4:30 P.M., January 7, 1951, through June 3, 1951; Saturday, 6:00 P.M., June 9, 1951, through September 1, 1951; Sunday, 6:00 P.M., September 9, 1951, through June 2, 1952; Saturday, 11:00 A.M., June 8, 1952, through March 7, 1955.

In 1952, at the height of its popularity, "Space Patrol" was seen by more children and adults than any other action-adventure show on television. It was reported to have tallied as much as $35–$40 million in merchandise tie-ins, which included such things as "Space Patrol" ray guns, spacesuits, rocketships, helmets, comic books, record stories, and insignia uniforms.

"Space Patrol" blasted off from its final countdown on March 7, 1955 (although a few have claimed that the date was February 26, 1955). Ed Kemmer, who had been an actual pilot during World War II, continued to act, mostly appearing as the lead in such unforgettable "B" films of the 1950s as Bert Gordon's *The Spider* (1958). He also returned to television for several guest appearances on such popular adult programs as "Gunsmoke," "Rawhide," and "Perry Mason." Lyn Osborn, responsible for much of the show's comic relief, died in 1958 of a brain tumor at the age of 32.

Although reruns of "Space Patrol" have not been available to audiences for years, episodes have unexpectedly resurfaced recently as an occasional segment of the USA cable network's late night compilation program, "Night Flight." There has even been talk by die-hard fans, now 40 and over, of reviving the series with an updated version for today's more sophisticated audiences. As star Ed Kemmer himself put it, "It will be just another pleasant way of tapping a favorite childhood memory."

Superman / The Adventures of Superman

For over 35 years, children of all ages have enjoyed the seemingly endless "Adventures of Superman." Rerun time and time again, the series, like "I Love Lucy," never seems to grow wearisome.

Many adults who once enjoyed the series as children have always considered actor George Reeves to be the only "Superman," the prototype of all twentieth-century comic book heroes who flew, had a dual identity, or possessed powers and abilities far beyond those of mortals. Kirk Alyn, a former dancer turned actor, was the first to play the visitor from the planet Krypton on film in two action-packed serials from Columbia Pictures, *Superman* (1948) and *Atom Man vs. Superman* (1950). Actor Christopher Reeve played a more modern-day version of the man of steel in four lavishly produced Superman movies, beginning with *Superman: The Movie* (1978) and concluding with *Superman IV: The Quest for Peace* (1987).

However, it is without a doubt the 104 television episodes, produced between 1951 and 1957, and starring George Reeves under the superb direction of Tommy Carr, that people most fondly remember today. Although the series originally began production in 1951, broadcast was unavailable for television until February 9, 1953. "Superman" was syndicated nationally for four years and its final season (1957), the show was broadcast over the ABC network from 5:00 to 5:30 P.M. It was syndicated on October 6, 1958, for rebroadcast.

Six-foot, one-inch George Reeves (born George Besselo) could not have been a better choice for mild-mannered reporter Clark Kent's alter ego. A former Golden Gloves champion, Reeves was selected for the role over hundreds of other applicants because of his square jaw and his resemblance to the comic book character created by Jerry Siegel and Joe Shuster. And while the series as a whole had its share of ups and downs, no one could dispute the quality of his performance. A splendid actor, Reeves's first big break came in 1939 with his screen debut in the film classic *Gone with the Wind* as one of the Tarleton twins. During a 1952 hiatus from the "Superman" productions, Reeves appeared opposite Burt Lancaster, Montgomery Clift, and Frank Sinatra in the Academy Award–winning war drama *From Here to Eternity*. Equally impressive were his fellow cast members from the "Superman" series: Phyllis Coates (1951) and Noel Neill (1953–57) as Lois Lane; and Jack Larson as Jimmy Olsen and John Hamilton as editor Perry White, Clark Kent's friends at the *Daily Planet* newspaper. Robert Shayne was also featured as Metropolis police inspector William J. Henderson, who had a habit of rounding up the culprits after Superman had performed the difficult task. Philips Tead also had a recurring role as a kindly old eccentric named Professor J.J. Pepperwinkle. Pepperwinkle created such off-beat inventions as the topsy-turvey machine, which turned people upside down; antimemory vapor, which made people forget; and a gold-making machine, whose chief ingredient was platinum.

"The Adventures of Superman" eventually became a cult favorite with at least three generations of children. Of course the show also had more than its share of criticism. Some parents felt that many of the first season's shows were too violent, and at times they were. Most of these shows created an atmosphere so menacing that younger children needed careful explanations. In one episode entitled "The Birthday Letter," a little crippled girl is mistreated by a group of desperate gangsters. Several others, such as "The Desert Village," "The Ghost Wolf," and "Mystery in Wax," involved science fiction and the supernatural. Presumably these sorts of episodes were intended to lure adults into watching the show. Even the 40-second preview of the following episode (dropped after the first season) resembled the hard-hitting crime trailers of the 1940s which used extremely violent scenes.

Robert Maxwell was producer for the 1951 season, with Lee Sholem and Tommy Carr as the principal directors. It was Maxwell and Sholem

George Reeves as Superman and Robert Shayne as Inspector Henderson from the Superman series.

who initially introduced the Superman character to television audiences as a tough, invincible crimebuster who was low on tolerance and heavy on the fisticuffs, a champion of justice who defeated such diabolical adversaries as saboteurs, foreign agents, extortionists, blackmailers, runaway robots, and cold-blooded murderers. Here Clark Kent was more often an amateur detective than a reporter, responsible for resolving many of the show's most sinister plots. Most of the exciting Maxwell episodes were filmed at RKO's Pathé Studios in Culver City.

Although a huge commercial success, the first season of the series was not without its share of personal disasters. Early flying scenes for the character required a breastplate harness that lifted Reeves high into the air. The technique was abandoned after several wires broke from the harness during the filming of "The Ghost Wolf," sending Reeves plummeting to the ground. Later sequences used running boards, and Reeves vaulting over the camera into a soft mattress. The later color episodes used a series of repeated process shots that showed Superman repeatedly flying over the same Metropolis skyline. In another episode, "The Stolen Costume," Reeves was nearly rendered unconscious when he ran into a plywood breakaway door that did not break away during the first take.

During "Superman's" second season (1953-54), Whitney Ellsworth replaced Bob Maxwell as producer and remained in this position throughout the show's entirety. Most of these episodes were filmed at the old Charlie Chaplin and Frederic Ziv studios in Hollywood. Responding to pressure from National comics and the series' long-time sponsor, Kellogg's cereals, Ellsworth brought the show's violence level down. In a 1954 episode titled "The Unlucky Number," Superman explains to a boy, for the benefit of the children's audience, that "no one, but no one, can do the things that Superman can do, and that especially goes for flying."

Nothing ever quite topped Ellsworth's first year with the series. His initial 26 episodes were unquestionably the best. Although he managed to produce a few good ones later when the series was shot in color (1954–57), somehow episodes never again measured up to those of the 1953 season, when the series was at its peak. Later episodes fell short in quality of the standards set by such earlier programs as "Panic in the Sky," "A Ghost for Scotland Yard," "The Jungle Devil," "Superman in Exile," and "The Face and the Voice," in which Superman matched wits with a villainous look-alike, a dual role played by George Reeves.

Unfortunately, many of the later shows were overacted, and stories ranged from the melodramatic to the sentimental, with an absurd sense of humor in between. The crooks, for instance, once worthy opponents, were now generally laughable, incompetent bunglers, often tripping themselves up before Superman could even lay a hand on them. The show's level of fantasy and action eventually became limited to suit the taste of younger children.

At the close of the 1957-58 season, "Superman" officially ended production, after six successful years on the air. The final season was presented over several of the ABC affiliates across the country with a repeat of the first episode ("Superman on Earth"), in which Superman is rocketed to earth as a child, grows into an adult, and hides his powers, disguised as mild-mannered Clark Kent, reporter, in the city of Metropolis. The series has been rerun constantly ever since, and has now been released on videocassette, along with Reeves's introduction of the character in the 1951 feature film, *Superman and the Mole Men* (later edited into the series as "Unknown People"). In 1966, an animated version of the character appeared on Saturday mornings on CBS.

Typecast by his television persona, Reeves had difficulty finding other roles. He did appear, however, as a wagonmaster in a 1957 Walt Disney film, *Westward Ho the Wagons*, with actor Fess Parker. But he became a target for the critics, who described his performance simply as "Superman without the foam rubber costume." In June 1959, Reeves, allegedly despondent over a faltering career, evidently took his own life in the bedroom of his Hollywood home. He might possibly have appreciated knowing today that his work in the series was not in vain, for many children and adults continue to enjoy the show. Even the feeblest episodes were a pleasure to watch, holding their own against any other program of Hollywood's Golden Age of Television.

Terry and the Pirates

Based on the popular syndicated comic strip, this series starred John Baer as Terry Lee, an air force pilot on inactive duty searching for a lost gold mine in East Asia bequeathed to him by his father. William Tracy costarred as his comical sidekick, Hotshot Charlie, Gloria Saunders was his seductress enemy, Lai Choi San (better known as the "Dragon Lady"), and Jack Reitzen was Chopstick Joe, his Chinese servant.

The comic strip was created by Milton Caniff for the *Chicago Tribune* in 1934, and like the comic strip, episodes consisted of high-flying action and with narrow plots of international intrigue. Unlike the comics, however, which were usually more concerned with catastrophic postwar threats to the United States, the television adventures tended to follow Terry's air-charting explorations in the Far East during the war years. Exploits involved encounters with such adversaries as smugglers, hijackers, and foreign agents.

Among the best of the children's shows for creating an authentic feel for the period, "Terry and the Pirates" resembled the exciting Saturday matinee serials of the 1940s. In several episodes, Terry and Charlie put off seeking their fortunes long enough to aid their country or to become personally involved with others. In "The Boxer's Rebellion," they assisted a young Chinese fighter (Victor Sen Young) who was receiving nothing from his fights in the ring. Some stories even involved such advanced concepts as missile conflicts and the threat of a nuclear war. While action and adventure constituted the focus of the series, humor was also a part. Like most comical sidekicks, Hotshot Charlie engaged in plenty of bungling. In one episode he accidentally devoured a small case of dynamite disguised as hot dogs.

Ironically, William Tracy was actually the original Terry Lee in the 1940 Columbia movie serial, *Terry and the Pirates,* but he was considered a bit too old and much too chubby for the television role in 1952. According to several film sources, John Baer was a 29-year-old student of the arts when he was first discovered for the part by actor Douglas Fairbanks, Jr., who served as executive producer for the series.

The show was syndicated on November 25, 1952. The television series premiered on Saturday mornings where it usually competed against such network favorites as "Captain Video" (Dumont, 1949–55) and "Space Patrol" (ABC, 1950–55). As a result of such fierce competition, "Terry and the Pirates" was canceled after only 18 episodes. In 1958, "Steve Canyon," another of Milton Caniff's popular flying heroes, appeared over the air in prime time on NBC. "Terry and the Pirates" remains obscure, but it ranks among the best of the genre.

Timmy and Lassie see *The "Lassie" Shows*

The "Walt Disney" Shows
Disneyland / Walt Disney Presents / Walt Disney's Wonderful World of Color

When the ABC network first agreed in 1953 to invest $500,000 in the projected Disneyland Amusement Park, the Disney Studios responded with a series of one-hour programs, originally intended for experimental purposes. The first show, entitled "Disneyland," appeared on October 27, 1954, to become an early evening favorite, with a variety of different titles for the next three decades.

The series was originally divided into four types of shows, "Fantasyland," "Frontierland," "Tomorrowland," and "Adventureland," each hosted by Disney himself. Eventually aired on all three commercial networks, the program became one of the most successful and entertaining shows in television history.

Walt Disney had already become a household word years before his television series even began. He and his brother, Roy Disney, first introduced their artistic talents to Hollywood in the 1920s, creating their own production facility. Here Walt created his most famous character, Mickey Mouse, originally called Mortimer in the 1928 animated short entitled, "Plane Crazy." Disney himself supplied the voice of Mickey in many of the character's early black and white films, until he found a replacement in voice actor Jim McDonald in 1940. After many other successful sound cartoons, Disney introduced a squawking new character called Donald Duck in a 1934 featurette entitled "The Wise Little Hen." Conceited but lovable, Donald gained a popularity that rivaled even that of Mickey Mouse. In 1937 Walt Disney produced his first feature-length animated film in Technicolor, *Snow White and the Seven Dwarfs*. Other films followed, such as *Fantasia* (1940) and *Song of the South* (1946), both mixing live action with music and animation, making Disney one of the top ten money-making producers of the 1930s and 1940s.

The most highly rated television series of the 1954-55 season, "Disneyland" succeeded in captivating both children and adults. One of its most popular programs during the first season featured actor Fess Parker as the legendary frontiersman Davy Crockett. The program became such a hit that it led to several sequels, including two the following season. It also brought instant fame to Fess Parker, whom Disney had chosen for the lead role after seeing the actor's brief but impressive performance in the 1954 classic science fiction thriller, *Them*. Actor Buddy Ebsen costarred as Crockett's friend and fellow trailblazer, George Russell. Before long "Crockett-mania" took the nation by storm: merchandise associated with Crockett (especially the coonskin caps) began to sell like hotcakes. Disney himself said that the enormous popularity of the character came as a surprise to everyone at the studio, but especially to Fess Parker. Several of the Davy Crockett segments were later combined and presented theatrically as part of a Disney double feature.

The success of the Crockett features eventually inspired several other live-action dramas, included in subsequent seasons, that were also based on legendary characters. In 1958 in the now named, "Walt Disney Presents," Jerome Courtland appeared in the lead role in "The Saga of Andy Burnett." "The Nine Lives of Elfego Baca" starred Robert Loggia as a mild-mannered but strict law official of the town of Tombstone. During this period a young Leslie Nielson appeared on the series as a Revolutionary War hero in "The Swamp Fox." The 1959 season featured Tom Tryon in several installments of "Texas John Slaughter." This was the second most popular of the programs since Davy Crockett; the segments were based on actual incidents in the life of the legendary lawman and cattle baron who became known for capturing Geronimo. Of the many dramatic characters seen on the show over the years, perhaps none was quite as mysterious as Patrick McGoohan's portrayal of England's seventeenth century antihero in "The Scarecrow of Romney Marsh." Presented in the tradition of "Zorro," this segment began its series of episodes in February 1964.

While action and drama remained a highlight of many of the Disney shows, humor and fantasy were also provided on many of the programs. In addition to the delightful cartoons starring Mickey, Donald, Goofy, Chip 'n' Dale, and the other characters that had enchanted movie audiences since the 1930s, many stories, both documentary and live, involved animals and their sometimes humorous encounters with humans. Some of the most popular of these presentations are "The Living Desert,"

"Sammy, the Way-Out Seal," "Ida, the Off-Beat Eagle," "The Jungle Cat" (based on the 1960 feature film), "Solomon, the Sea Turtle," "The City Fox," "Nosey, the Sweetest Skunk in the World," "The Owl That Didn't Give a Hoot," "Chico, the Misunderstood Coyote," "The Tattooed Police Horse," "Pablo, the Dancing Chihuahua," "The Horse in the Grey Flannel Suit," and "The Hound That Thought He Was a Raccoon."

In 1961 Disney ended his association with the ABC network. Disheartened for several years over the cancellation of two more of his popular productions, "The Mickey Mouse Club" (ABC, 1955–59) and "Zorro" (ABC, 1957–59), Disney switched over to NBC and was presented for the first time in living color. The series was retitled "Walt Disney's Wonderful World of Color." The show evolved through several other title changes over the years, but basically it remained one continuous series, with the format unchanged until Disney's untimely death in 1966. Dick Wesson, who for years was the program's unseen announcer, replaced Disney as narrator for many of the opening segments during the next two decades.

The airing history of the Disney shows follows: Wednesday, 7:30–8:30 P.M., ABC, October 27, 1954, through September 17, 1958; Friday, 8:00–9:00 P.M., ABC, September 26, 1958, through September 17, 1961; Sunday, 7:30–8:30 P.M., NBC, September 24, 1961, through September 13, 1981; Saturday, 8:00–9:00 P.M., CBS, September 25, 1981, through January 8, 1983; Saturday, 8:00–9:00 P.M., CBS, September 24, 1983, through September 25, 1984; syndicated, October 1984.

By 1981 it seemed that the Disney fad had finally run its course. Younger views favored such teen-oriented shows as "Diff'rent Strokes" and "Silver Spoons," leading to a huge decline in the ratings and to a switch to the CBS network. As in the case of many long-running series, "novelty" replaced consistency, and the networks were ready as always to comply. Nevertheless, syndication and Disney's many generations of fans have managed to keep the show alive today, featuring many of the studio's popular film productions, both old and new.

2. Cartoon Shows

Cartoons are without a doubt the most durable, if not the most profitable, of the children's programs. Throughout the years animated shows of all types have survived while the competition has given up. The catchy tunes, violent action, and rapid-fire, brightly colored images have created a successful children's product for over four decades.

Typically in the very early years of television cartoons were hosted by live performers who interrupted with a variety of jokes and skits; the late 1950s, though, gave birth to the "whole cartoon series," where even the host (if any) appeared in animated form.

In the mid–1960s, while parents began complaining about all the animated violence, something else was happening: Toys began replacing cereal and candy as the biggest selling commodity in the children's television commercial. Soon after the introduction of Mattel's popular Barbie doll, such favorite action figurines and comic book heroes as GI Joe and Spiderman moved from department store shelves to the video screen of children's bedrooms, demonstrating that quality and popularity are not necessarily linked when it comes to children's television.

Many of today's best cartoons are still those that have stood the test of time. On any station today can be found the creations of such animators as Paul Terry (Terrytoon Productions), William Hanna and Joseph Barbera, Jay Ward and director Bill Scott, Fritz Freleng and David DePatie, as well as the multitalented artists and producers of the Warner Brothers Studios.

The Adventures of Jonny Quest see *Jonny Quest*

The Adventures of Tom Terrific see *The "Tom Terrific" Shows*

The All New Pink Panther Show see *The "Pink Panther" Shows*

The All New Popeye Hour see *The "Popeye" Shows*

The Alvin Show /
Alvin and the Chipmunks

In the mid–1950s, recording artist Ross Bagdasarian sold over 4 million record copies of such hits as "Witch Doctor" and "The Chipmunk Song" for Liberty Records. The gimmick was his use of three speeded-up vocal tracks by characters he called the "Chipmunks." Using the stage name Dave Seville, he and his Chipmunks, whom he first presented in puppet form, were featured as guests on various programs, including the "Ed Sullivan Show" (CBS, 1948–71). In the fall of 1961 the Chipmunks, as well as Dave Seville, were presented in animated form as the stars of their own weekly cartoon series, "The Alvin Show." The series, a credit to Bagdasarian's vocal abilities, was the second animated series to be broadcast over the CBS network during prime-time evening hours, preceded by the "CBS Cartoon Theater" in 1956.

Bagdasarian had complete control of the series, providing the voice of his own character and those of the Chipmunks: the burly Theodore, the bespectacled Simon, and Alvin, the group's lead singer and star, whose trademark was an oversized letter sweater with a giant *A* and a tilted baseball cap.

Early cartoons focused on the antics of the Chipmunk brothers and their human foster father and mentor, Dave Seville, both as a family and as a recording group. Featured in such ten-minute episodes as "Love Struck Alvin," "Stanley the Eagle," and "Club Thy Neighbor," the high-spirited Alvin was the leading force in unpredictable situations. The show's only incorporated segment was "The Adventures of Clyde Crashcup," the saga of a nutty inventor and his assistant, Leonardo. Former radio comedian Shepard Menken provided the voice of Crashcup. A closing episode featured the Chipmunks in a musical interlude, which often involved locations in other parts of the world.

"The Alvin Show" ran for one season in prime time (7:30–8:00 Wednesdays on CBS; October 4, 1961, through September 5, 1962) before being rerun for three more years on Saturday mornings (10:00–10:30; June 23, 1962, through September 18, 1965). In 1979 the series returned for another year of Saturday morning reruns on NBC (8:00–8:30; March 10, 1979, through September 1, 1979).

An updated version of the series entitled "Alvin and the Chipmunks" returned to the NBC Saturday morning schedule at the 10:30 slot in September 1983, with Ross Bagdasarian, Jr., doing the job his late father had pioneered in the earlier series. In accordance with current expectations for cartoon shows, the new series focused much more on real-life situations that demanded common sense and good judgment. It became one of the top-rated children's shows and reruns are still aired on some cable stations.

The "Archie" Shows
The Archie Show Presents / The Archie Show / The Archie Comedy Hour / Archie's Fun House / Archie's TV Funnies / Everything's Archie / The U.S. of Archie / The New Archie and Sabrina Hour

Teenager Archie Andrews and his friends and teachers from Riverdale High School have become favorites of every generation since the group's entry into the comics pages in the 1940s. Although the lead story man Bob Montana is usually credited with the strip's creation, the characters were actually conceived by cartoonist John Goldwater. This popular misconception that has gone uncorrected for many years. Among the most popular comics ever created, the *Archie* comic book characters have become more familiar to readers than any others, with the exception of Superman and Batman.

In 1968 the red-headed Archie and his friends, the hamburger-munching Jughead Jones, rival Reggie Mantle, and girlfriends Veronica Lodge and Betty Cooper, were finally brought to television in their own animated series, which lasted for nearly a decade. As in the comics, Archie was the typical American youth. Wearing a traditional letter sweater and black-and-white oxfords, Archie, like most teens, was forever at odds with the adult world.

Although it appeared at different times on Saturday, it was really one continuous CBS series. During the 1968-69 season, "The Archie Show" aired at 10:00 A.M. A half hour show, the format featured several six- to ten-minute segments of Archie and the gang which were used to enhance several song-and-dance numbers. In a segment entitled "Archie's Jukebox" the following year, the group performed the song "Sugar, Sugar," which sold over a million copies. That same year the show was expanded to an hour and was retitled "The Archie Comedy Hour." In this program the group shared the spotlight with another comic book favorite, Sabrina, the teenage witch. This variation of the "Archie" show aired at 10:00 A.M. from September 13, 1969, through September 5, 1970.

In 1970 the series switched back to 30 minutes, aired at 10:00 A.M. and was retitled "Archie's Fun House." Here, Archie and the group were featured using a variety of jokes and double entendres in the familiar tradition of "Rowan and Martin's Laugh-In" (NBC, 1968–73). Sabrina had left to star in her own spinoff series, "Sabrina and the Groovie Goolies," which made its Saturday morning debut that same year. The following year, the show was changed once again to "Archie's TV Funnies," featuring 30 minutes of Archie and the gang running a local television studio that televised such other long-running comic book favorites as *Smokey Stover, Moon Mullens, Dick Tracy, Nancy and Sluggo, Broom Hilda,* and *The Katzenjammer Kids.* This format lasted for several seasons, only to be replaced in 1974 by "Everything's Archie," which closely resembled the series' first format in 1968. Keeping in step with the bicentennial period, the 1976 Archie television season retold the exploits of great Americans in "The U.S. of Archie." Here, the Archie characters showed a somewhat serious side, as they played famous figures from American history. Unfortunately, children found this variation of the series to be the least interesting, and the show was nearly canceled in midseason.

Archie and the gang returned in September of 1977, this time on NBC at 10:00 A.M. in "The New Archie and Sabrina Hour," featuring Archie once again with Sabrina the teenage witch. This format, however, was dropped by the network in January of 1978 and was replaced by the "Bang-Shang Lalapalooza Show."

Many viewers, some as old as the comic strip itself, identified particularly with Archie and friends, having followed their exploits through the comics pages for many years. Unfortunately, most of the "Archie" programs are considered by today's standards too obscure and outdated, which explains why the shows are seldom shown today in syndication. The shows were a production of Filmation Industries.

The Beany and Cecil Show

This popular animated series, based on the equally popular 1950s Emmy Award–winning puppet series "Time for Beany," featured a youngster with an ever-present smile named Beany who joined forces with a loveable seasick sea serpent named Cecil. Both shows were produced and created by Bob Clampett, who directed many of the old "Bugs Bunny" cartoons for Warner Brothers Studios.

In both versions, little Beany sailed the seven seas on the *Leakin' Lena* with his uncle, the fearless Captain Horatio K. Huffenpuff, who always had plenty of excuses when faced with danger. Cecil, however, was always ready to answer Beany's call for help. Cecil was only shown from his long neck up.

Along their various travels upon the high seas, the trio encountered such unforgettable characters as Thunderbolt, the Wonder Colt; Billy the Squid; Careless, the Mexican Hairless; Pop Gunn, the Western Explorer; The Incredible Three-headed Threep; Tearalong, the Dotted Lion; and the villain everyone loved to hate, the dastardly Dishonest John.

Evolving over the years into something different from the usual kiddy fare, the show sprang from creator Bob Clampett's imagination, which included a passion for snappy puns and clichés. Although some children may have found Clampett's wit a bit hard to follow at times, the energy of the show's narration, combined with its bouncy musical score, made it a delight to everyone who watched.

Clampett first captured the attention of audiences in the 1930s as cocreator of the characters Daffy Duck, Porky Pig, and Bugs Bunny. He was also responsible for creating the character of Tweety Bird for the 1942 Warner Brothers cartoon "A Tale of Two Kitties," which featured the likenesses of comedians Bud Abbott and Lou Costello as alley cats.

"Beany and Cecil" first appeared in animated form as a segment of "Matty's Funday Funnies," sponsored by Mattel toys. After just a few short weeks, the Beany and Cecil cartoons took charge of the entire 30 minutes at 7:00 P.M. on ABC on January 6, 1962, and moved into several time periods over the next five years: Saturday, 11:30 A.M., January 5, 1963, through September 4, 1965; Sunday, 10:30 A.M., September 11, 1965, through December 25, 1965; Sunday, 10:00 A.M., January 2, 1966, through January 8, 1967; Sunday, 9:30 A.M., January 15, 1967, through September 3, 1967. Programs occasionally featured incorporated segments of "Harecules Hare," a variation on Aesop's fable, "The Tortoise and the Hare," but with a twist: here the hare always wins. While his father Ben Hare is into body-building, the brainy Harecules instead enjoys "nuclear fishing." Ben is embarrassed, until his son beats the ever-scheming tortoise at his own game, proving that brains, not brawn, wins the final race.

Voices for the earlier puppet version of the program were provided by Bob Clampett himself as Cecil, preceded by Stan Freberg as both

Beany and Cecil.

Cecil and Dishonest John. Daws Butler, a familiar voice actor who was heard frequently over the next three decades, supplied the voices for Beany and Uncle Captain. Voices for the later cartoon series included Erv Shoemaker, Jim McGeorge, and Walker Edmonston. Occasionally a guest voice would be heard from time to time. Lord Buckley and Scatman Crothers provided the voice at various times for Go Go Man Go, the Beatnik, Mickey Katz for Slopalong Catskill, and the distinguished John Carradine for William Shakespeare Wolf. Although the show's dialogue relied on constant wordplay, the final message to children was that crime never paved the way to fame and fortune.

An all-new version of the series appeared at 9:00 A.M. Saturday on ABC from September 17, 1988, through December 10, 1988.

The "Bugs Bunny" Shows
The Bugs Bunny Show /
The Bugs Bunny—Road Runner Show /
The Bugs Bunny—Tweety Show

For more than half a century, Warner Brothers cartoons have been entertaining audiences all across the world with their popular menagerie of animal characters.

After a long, successful career in animated films, Warner Brothers' most popular character, Bugs Bunny, became the first to star in his own animated series, as early as 1956, with the syndicated titles "Bugs Bunny and Co." and "Bugs Bunny and Friends." It was not until the fall of 1960, however, that the wise-cracking, carrot-munching rabbit and his friends—Daffy Duck, Sylvester and Tweety, Porky Pig, Speedy Gonzales, the Road Runner, Elmer Fudd, and Yosemite Sam—first appeared in prime time at 7:30 P.M. on ABC. The show, which lasted for two seasons (October 1960 to September 1962) during the evening hours, eventually led to a string of Saturday morning half hour formats that began in April 1962—Saturday 9:00, ABC, April 7, 1962, through September 2, 1967; Sunday, 11:00, ABC, January 8, 1968, through August 25, 1968; Saturday, 8:00, CBS, September 11, 1971, through September 1, 1973; Saturday, 11:00, ABC, September 8, 1973, through August 30, 1975. It has become the longest running cartoon show in the history of television.

The Bugs Bunny character had many fathers. Bob Clampett wrote the first Bugs Bunny story, "A Wild Hare," directed by Tex Avery, in 1940. Chuck Jones and Fritz Freleng created many of the later Bugs Bunny cartoons, as well as many of the other familiar Looney Tunes characters. The toothy hare's popularity outshone that of many of the characters previously created by the studio, and even rivaled that of Walt Disney's creation, Mickey Mouse.

One possible reason for such success is that Bugs Bunny, more than any other cartoon character, constantly uses his wit and ingenuity. In each of his adventures, he skillfully manipulates his adversaries by playing upon their own greed, conceit, and stubbornness. In nearly every episode, Bugs comes out a winner in the end.

Although many of the early Warner Brothers cartoons had been shown in syndication since the early years of television, the studio, along with the ABC network, profited greatly through the decision to combine many of the Bugs Bunny and Friends cartoons into a regular 30-minute weekly series. This proved to be a very smart move. While many cartoons were still being presented in movie theaters across the country "The Bugs Bunny Show" became one of the most successful television programs of all time.

Many writers and directors have worked on the cartoon series over the years, developing new adventures for Bugs and the gang just for television. Most notable of these was Bob McKimson, the originator of Foghorn Leghorn and the Tasmanian Devil. It was also his idea (along with Chuck Jones) to have Bugs share star billing with another up-and-rising Warner Brothers creation in the premiere of his eighth season on the air (his second on CBS). Although both Daffy Duck and Porky Pig seemed like the most suitable of candidates, the new show became "The Bugs Bunny—Road Runner Show." The Road Runner had previously been featured in his own series on CBS, while Bugs Bunny remained primarily with ABC. The combination of the two originated at CBS when ABC affiliates began to feel that the Road Runner cartoons were much too violent to be enjoyable. This version of "The Bugs Bunny Show" became a permanent fixture on Saturday mornings for over a decade. The programming history (all CBS) of "The Bugs Bunny—Road Runner Show": 8:30–9:30, September 14, 1968, through September 4, 1971; 8:30–9:30, September 6, 1975, through September 3, 1977; 9:00–10:00, September 10, 1977, through February 28, 1981; 8:30–10:00, March 7, 1981, through September 7, 1985.

In recent years, the long-running program became the target of such parent-involvement groups as the A.C.T. (Action for Children's Television) for its alledged acts of gratuitous violence—in the Road Runner cartoons, his crafty adversary, Wile E. Coyote, frequently sustains "extraordinary physical abuse." The CBS network responded to the allegations by editing most of the segments, and the show remained immensely popular with children and adults. Today's version of the "Bugs Bunny Show" is entitled "The Bugs Bunny—Tweety Show" and aired on ABC on Saturdays from 11:00 A.M. until noon beginning on September 14, 1985. It currently appears at various times on ABC station schedules.

The voice of Bugs, as well as that of many of the other characters, was supplied of course by the late, great Mel Blanc, whose vocal characterizations have become as much a part of children's television as Saturday mornings. June Foray provided the voice of Granny, as well as several other female regulars.

The Bullwinkle Show / Rocky and His Friends

A unique change from traditional cartoon shows, this half hour animated series featuring television's funniest moose was the brainchild of producer Jay Ward and writer-director Bill Scott. Ward had previously introduced his talent to television viewers as early as 1948 as the creator of the first successful made-for-television cartoon series, "Crusader Rabbit." Crusader, a Don Quixote–type hero, and his less intelligent pal, Rags the tiger, became the models for Rocket J. Squirrel and Bullwinkle Moose.

"The Bullwinkle Show" (actually a retitled version of "Rocky and His Friends," ABC, 1959–61) was presented on Sundays for two seasons on NBC in prime time (7:00 for the 1961-62 season and 5:30 for the 1962-63 season), before moving to Saturday and Sunday mornings, where it was rerun for over a decade — Saturday, 12:30 P.M., NBC, September 1963 to September 1964; Sunday, 11:00 A.M., ABC, September 1964 to September 1973; Saturday, 11:30 A.M., NBC, September 1981 to January 1982.

Rocky, the impish flying squirrel with the pilot's cap and goggles, and his devoted friend and comrade, Bullwinkle the Moose, who bore a resemblance to comedian Red Skelton's Clem Kadiddlehopper, were featured in two five-minute color segments. In the serial-style episodes, Rocky and Bullwinkle traveled away from their comfortable abode in Frostbite Falls, Minnesota, to combat such evil forces as Boris Badenov and Natasha Fatale. Episodes were narrated by actor William Conrad.

Other segments included the melodramatic adventures of Dudley Do-Right of the Mounties, a likable, square-jawed bungler who was not terribly bright. Dudley was in love with his chief inspector's daughter, Nell, who preferred instead Dudley's horse. "Fractured Fairy Tales" presented comic versions of familiar children's stories, narrated by Edward Everett Horton. In "Aesop and Son," Charlie Ruggles provided the voice of the worldly philosopher. "Peabody's Improbable History" told of the adventures of an incredibly smart, bespectacled canine named Peabody and his pet boy, Sherman, and their journeys into the Way-Back Machine.

Two of the show's additional sideline segments featured Bullwinkle on his own. As "Mr. Know-It-All," he frequently demonstrated the best way of doing everything wrong. In "Bullwinkle's Corner," the comical moose provided viewers with a distorted version of popular children's poems.

Bill Scott, who provided the voices for many of the characters, including Bullwinkle, was the one responsible for writing and coproducing many of the show's best scripts and story segments. June Foray provided that wonderful little-boy voice for Rocky, and was the voice as well for the accented Natasha and a host of other female characters. Other voice actors included Hans Conried, Skip Conway, Daws Butler, and Paul Frees as Boris, among others.

Although the series attracted many children over the years, most parents and critics agreed that the show, for the most part, aimed over the heads of children and was in some ways much better suited to an adult audience.

Jay Ward, who was fond of the wild and absurd, took all criticisms concerning the show as compliments, and felt personally responsible for creating a new wave in television by presenting his characters with a variety of eccentric human characteristics. One wonderful running gag concerned the "Kurwood Derby," actually referring to variety show host Garry Moore's second banana, Durwood Kerby. On a commercial announcement for the earlier series, "Rocky and His Friends," Boris Badenov interrupts William Conrad's narration to steal a letter from the show's opening title, changing it to "Rocky and His Fiends," promising to return the letter only if he receives "Top-villain" on the program.

Perhaps, however, the one thing that made the Bullwinkle and Rocky cartoons so popular was their ability to make people laugh at their most treasured ideals. In one episode, for instance, Bullwinkle is an unlikely candidate for a football college scholarship to "Whatsamatter U." In another, America's most enjoyable national pastime is threatened, as giant mechanical mice are found munching the television antennas off rooftops. The show's broad range of humor has left a lasting impression on many of today's adults, who once enjoyed the show as children. "The Bullwinkle Show" remains one of a kind.

Subsequent shows created by Jay Ward and Bill Scott with similar formats include *Hoppity Hooper* (ABC, 1964–67) and *George of the Jungle* (ABC, 1967–70).

CBS Storybreak

"StoryBreak" premiered in the spring of 1985 on Saturdays from 12:30 to 1:00 as a 30-minute variety show for CBS of animated adaptations of literature for young people. Hosted by Bob Keeshan, who decades earlier first captivated children as the beloved Captain Kangaroo (see chapter 6, "Informative Shows"), the program presented stories directed specifically to viewers ages 7 to 17. Selections are made based on popularity with readers and on informative qualities.

Produced and directed under the watchful eye of CBS Entertainment Productions, the series continues today as an innovative standout in a Saturday morning sea of unlimited animation. The show has proved to be a prime example of the type of cartoons parents have long wanted for their children.

The series has ranged from fantasy to real-life dramatizations, with the last few seaons providing a much broader spectrum for the younger child. One story, "Blood Brothers," based in medieval times, was about the relationship between two outcasts, a timid young knight and a shy baby dragon, who became the best of friends. "The Monster's Ring" was an amusing Halloween tale of an introverted adolescent who learns the true meaning of courage through the help of a magic ring that transforms him at will into a werewolf. In "Sarah's Unicorn," a little girl finds and makes a pet of the legendary animal. "Mommy Don't Allow" was about a boy possum and his love for the saxophone. "The Golden Fish" was an Asian tale about a magic fish who grants wishes to the poor. In "The Last Dinosaur," two boys find a dinosaur seeking refuge from civilization by disguising himself as a small mountain.

"StoryBreak" is credited with using some of television's most acclaimed animators of children's programs. These have included veteran cartoonists William Hanna, Joseph Barbera, Fritz Freleng, David DePatie, Lou Scheimer, and Norm Prescott.

The series continues to draw praise from parental organizations, such as Action for Children's Television (A.C.T.), as well as from various television critics, for its nonviolence, detailed animation, and creativity.

Captain Sailorbird / Captain Sailorbird and His Tales

"Captain SailorBird" was an animated parrot who told internationally flavored fairy tales on weekday afternoons for young people. Each program began with SailorBird perched on top of an old windjammer while introducing a chapter of the day's continuing story. SailorBird's vocal narrations were never heard in the actual story presentations; his opening segments were introductions only.

The cartoon stories were produced through Official Films and Kayo Productions, a distributor of foreign films. The show was syndicated in September 1960 and aired Monday through Friday in various morning hours. Based on literary films from all over the world, the cartoons became a favorite with many kids in the early 1960s on such locally hosted children's shows as "Garfield Goose" in Chicago, "Captain 11's Showboat" in St. Louis, and "Fun House" in New York, hosted by Officer Joe Bolton.

What really attracted viewers, however, was the stories themselves rather than who was the host. Segments were presented in a serialized fashion, with a question mark flashing across the final fade-out of the narrator's epilogue.

A true compilation of classic stories, the first was entitled, "The Shepherdess and the Chimney Sweep," a poignant 1956 Danish tale of a young mismatched couple in love, whose happiness is opposed by an evil king. The second, longest, and perhaps best remembered of all the stories was "Johnny Little and the Giant," a retitled dubbed version of the 1954 French fairy tale classic, "Johnny the Giant Killer." This story told the incredible adventures of Johnny, a little scout whose troop members are captured by a hideous evil giant. Johnny becomes involved in great peril: he is shrunk to the size of an insect by the giant's shrinking machine, battles a Komodo dragon, and assists a queen bee and her army in fighting the villainous black hornets. At the end, the grateful insects help Johnny return to normal size in the nick of time to rescue his friends from the giant. The most familiar tale, "The Enchanted Princess," was a retelling of the popular Brothers Grimm classic, "Snow White." Others less familiar but equally charming included "Turham and the Genie" and "The Princess and the Soldier," the latter a retitled version of Hans Christian Andersen's "The Tinder Box."

Produced in color but usually presented in black and white, the animation in each tale was complemented by a superb musical score. Story packages were syndicated through the mid–1960s under the "SailorBird" heading and were featured among several fairy tale incorporated programs for children.

Deputy Dawg

"Deputy Dawg" focused on the misadventures of an inept but likable canine law enforcer of the swamplands in the Deep South. Deputy Dawg was seldom bothered with the usual crooks and criminals; his biggest problem was keeping his friends Musky Muskrat, Vincent Van Gofer, and Ali Gator from raiding the henhouse.

In several episodes, the animal friends combined forces with Deputy Dawg to secure the swamplands against meddling outsiders. In one cartoon they are annoyed by a pest from outer space called little Whooper. In another, they come under fire from an old soldier who thinks he is still fighting the Civil War.

Other segments featured on the show included the theatrical reruns of the Terry Bears and Gandy Goose. Deputy Dawg's voice, which somewhat resembled Frank Fontaine's Crazy Guggenham character from "The Jackie Gleason Show," was provided by former "Howdy Doody Show" puppeteer Dayton Allen. Produced by the affiliates of Paul Terry and associates, "Deputy Dawg" became the Terrytoons Studio's first syndicated prime-time series. It was also their first to combine made-for-television cartoons with those from an earlier time.

Animator Paul Terry first began producing cartoons as early as 1915, and he shared in pioneering animation techniques when he created such one-dimensional characters as Farmer Alfalfa and Dinky Duck. In the 1920s, he became famous for the long-running silent cartoons, "Aesop's Fables." But it was not until the 1930s that he became well known as the producer and founder of the Terrytoons Studios, where he was associated with the creation of such familiar characters as Heckle and Jeckle, Mighty Mouse, the Terry Bears, Little Roquefort, and Gandy Goose. Retiring from the business in 1955, Terry had a stock of more than 1,000 animated shorts, which became the property of CBS.

"Deputy Dawg" was syndicated on September 24, 1960. Sponsored by Lays Potato Chips, "Deputy Dawg" was seen in its first year in more than 50 cities, usually as a late Saturday afternoon lead-in to the prime-time schedule. The show was presented on Saturday mornings at 9:00 for a period on NBC (September 11, 1971, through September 2, 1972).

Everything's Archie see *The "Archie" Shows*

The Famous Adventures of Mr. Magoo
see *The "Mr. Magoo" Shows*

Fat Albert and the Cosby Kids see
chapter 6, "Informative Shows"

"Felix the Cat" Shows
Felix the Cat / Felix the Cat and Friends / The New Felix the Cat

Felix the Cat's importance was not due to his inconsistency of appeal with viewers. His cartoons were not terribly funny, and they were crudely outdated even in the earliest years of television when they first appeared on the air. Furthermore, Felix lacked a strong characterization, unlike such successors as Krazy Kat, Top Cat, and Garfield. Nevertheless, Felix had more historical importance than any other cartoon character, previously or subsequently.

He was introduced to movie audiences as early as 1918 by cartoonist Otto Messmer through the Pat Sullivan Studios. The silent adventures of Felix, complete with subtitles and piano music, were presented on television in the 1940s (syndicated June 1947) in an attempt to capture children's attention. The cartoon's success paved the way for other early syndicated favorites, like Paul Terry's "Aesop's Film Fables," as well as sound cartoons "Betty Boop," "Scappy," and "Oswald Rabbit," and the Van Buren Studio collection of such obscure cartoon shorts as "The Little King," "Brownie Bear," and "Dick and Larry."

Felix the Cat actually began his career in television in the late 1920s. During this period the NBC network experimented in its first television broadcast by using a revolving statue of Felix as its test pattern. Also around this time Felix the Cat became one of the best-known international figures of his day: he was featured in more movie theaters than was any other character, animated or live, a record exceeded only by Walt Disney's Mickey Mouse a few years later.

In the early 1950s, when other cinematic cartoons began to appear on the home screen with a bit more regularity, Felix starred in several locally hosted syndicated shows (syndicated June 1954), which featured a variety of other cartoon characters as well. Kids watching the silent Felix the Cat cartoons for the first time never realized, nor did it matter, that they were enjoying cartoons produced nearly 40 years earlier. In the early black-and-white cartoons, Felix used his magic tail as a secret weapon, removing it to form objects when he was faced with danger. In perplexing situations, the tail would even take the form of a question or exclamation mark.

On January 4, 1960, the Trans-lux corporation syndicated 260 new episodes of "Felix the Cat" they had produced just for television, and this time of course the feline was provided with a voice for the first time in his long career. In his new format, Felix was forever at odds with his archenemy, The Professor, and his assistant, Rock Bottom, who was ever intent on stealing Felix's secret weapon, a magical bag of tricks. Final scenes closed with Felix having the last laugh on his scheming antagonist. The new cartoons, produced in color, were very popular with children when shown throughout the 1960s and 1970s.

The Flintstones
The Flintstones / The Pebbles and Bamm-Bamm Show / The Flintstones Comedy Hour / The Flintstones Show / The New Fred and Barney Show / The Flintstones Comedy Show

"The Flintstones" was television's first successful animated primetime series. Debuting on September 30, 1960, it lasted for six full seasons on ABC before being rerun on Saturday mornings on NBC. In the 1970s, it began a variety of spinoffs that led to a new decade of Saturday morning shows presented over both the NBC and CBS networks.

The series aired Fridays from 8:30 to 9:00 P.M. until September 13, 1963; the following week it moved to Thursdays at 7:30 P.M. and remained there through December 3, 1964. On December 11 it returned to the Friday lineup, this time at 7:30, and it remained in this slot through the first series' close on September 2, 1966. Reruns were picked up by NBC and shown Saturdays at 10 A.M. from January 1, 1967, through September 3, 1970.

Produced by television's leading producers of children's animated programs, William Hanna and Joseph Barbera, "The Flintstones" was designed with the intent of attracting as many adult viewers as possible, with its takeoff on the popular "Honeymooners" series, and parody of married life in the Stone Age, as portrayed by the Flintstones, Fred and Wilma, and their best friends and neighbors, Barney and Betty Rubble. While the show managed to attract viewers of all age groups, its funny but sophomoric humor eventually became better suited to a children's audience: talking prehistoric animals used as household appliances, and Stone Age vehicles being accelerated by running feet.

Episodes usually always involved the humorous escapades of Fred and Barney as they endured the never-ending trials and tribulations of work, marriage, and friendship while struggling to make ends meet. In several episodes, Fred and Barney, as members of the Royal Order of Water Buffalos lodge, were constantly seeking ways to exercise their alleged male superiority, usually by lying to their wives. Other episodes focused on their various "get-rich-quick" attempts, which neither worked nor deflated their egos.

During the show's third season, Wilma gave birth to a daughter, Pebbles. To promote the new arrival, Hanna and Barbera sponsored a contest several weeks prior to her arrival for viewers to select a name. The winner would receive a toy likeness created by Ideal Toys. The sex of the Flintstones' new baby was undetermined, by both Hanna-Barbera and the executive board of the Screen Gems company where the show was produced. The final decision depended upon an initial $40 million merger of complete merchandise commodity tie-ins among Ideal toys, Flintstones vitamins, and a concept from the General Food Corporation to name a cereal based on the infant character. This process also assured the producers of top ratings for at least another season.

Although Wilma's pregnancy was fully accepted, the idea of cartoon characters, even the married ones, having sex was at the time rarely considered. During the following season, the Rubbles became the adoptive parents of an incredibly strong boy, whom they named Bamm-Bamm.

"The Flintstones" eventually evolved into the children's Saturday morning slot where it remained a fixture for many years in both reruns and new shows with various related titles: In 1971, a teenage version of Pebbles and Bamm-Bamm appeared as a show of its own over the CBS network entitled "The Pebbles and Bamm-Bamm Show."

Beginning September 9, 1972, new episodes of the Flintstones expanded to an hour series entitled "The Flintstones Comedy Hour," which lasted until September 1, 1973. Then the show returned to its original 30-minute format where it remained for another ten years under such titles as "The Flintstones Show" (Saturday, 12:30–1:30 P.M., CBS, September 8, 1973, through January 26, 1974), "The New Fred and Barney Show" (Saturday, 10:00–10:30 A.M. [return], NBC, February 3, 1979, through November 15, 1980), and "The Flintstones Comedy Show" (Saturday, 10:00–10:30 A.M., NBC, November 22, 1980, through September 18, 1984). In the fall of 1981, from October 4 through October 18, several of the original *Flintstones* episodes reappeared briefly on Sundays from 7:00 to 7:30 P.M. as a last minute replacement for the halted production of NBC's "The Power of Matthew Star."

Alan Reed provided the voice of Fred Flintstone from 1960 until his death in 1977. Hardly a stranger to children's television, Reed had previously performed the role of Shortfellow the Poet on the 1950s "Smilin' Ed's Gang." Reed's voice replacement came in 1978, actor Henry Condon. Other voice actors for the series included Mel Blanc as Barney, Jean VanderPyl as Wilma, Bea Benaderet (1960–64) and Gerry Anderson (1964–) as Betty, Sally Struthers (1971–72) and Mickey Stevens (1972–) as Pebbles, and Jay North as Bamm-Bamm.

Although the series, in one form or another, has been affiliated with all commercial networks, it has also proved very popular with syndicated stations since the early 1970s.

Having been successful with such shows as "Ruff and Reddy," "Huckleberry Hound," and "Quick Draw McGraw," Hanna and Barbera originally called their first prime-time series "The Flagstones." Informed at the last minute that the title was inappropriate, they reluctantly changed the name to "The Flintstones," and the show has since become familiar to more than 300 million people in more than 70 countries around the world.

Grape Ape Show / The Great Grape Ape
see The "Tom and Jerry" Shows

He-Man and the Masters of the Universe

Licensed cartoon characters have been appearing on the market long before children's first television programs. But usually the characters appeared as toys only after having been introduced through some form of the media. The 1970s and 1980s changed all of that. Today there are over 100 new children's characters originated by toy companies prior to becoming successful animated programs. Some of the more successful have gone on to become extremely popular both on television and through commercial merchandise.

Two of the most familiar of these low-budget, toy-oriented animated creations were "He-Man and the Masters of the Universe" and its companion series, "She-Ra: Princess of Power" (see separate entry). Both shows, produced by the Filmation Industries, are 30 minutes in length, usually presented daily, and are based on a series of popular action figures created by Mattel toys. "He-Man" was syndicated in August of 1983.

"He-Man" relates the futuristic adventures of the good prince Adam of Eternia, who from birth was destined to defend the castle of Greyskull from the planet's evil ruler, Skeletor. Upon reaching manhood, Prince Adam was given the magic sword of power by his friend and guardian, the Sorceress. After saying the magic words "I am the power," Adam is transformed into the most powerful man in the universe, He-Man. He-Man is assisted in his various exploits by his faithful companion Battle Cat, as well as by his allies Orko the wizard, Man-at-Arms, the heroic master of weapons, and his brave daughter, Tee-La. Most of the storylines focus on the fight between good and evil. At the end of each episode, He-Man triumphs over the evil Skeletor, like the popular characters from Star Wars, Luke Skywalker and Darth Vader.

He-Man ended with a moral for the audience. In "House of Chicody," for instance, He-Man rescues a young warrior from the perils of a dark cave. He advises children in the epilogue of the real dangers involved in exploring such a place without the proper supervision.

Today, this show is still among the most popular with young viewers. Their success has led to a string of imitators, also underwritten by toy companies. Some of the most familiar are, "Challenge of the GoBots," "Jayce and the Wheeled Warriors," "Transformers," and the merchandising phenomenon, "Teenage Mutant Ninja Turtles."

The "Heckle and Jeckle" Shows
The Heckle and Jeckle Show / The New Adventures of Mighty Mouse and Heckle and Jeckle
(see also *The Mighty Mouse Playhouse*)

Television's twin magpies made their debut on the small screen in June 1956 on Wednesday nights as a segment of the "CBS Cartoon Theater," hosted by television newcomer Dick Van Dyke. The short-lived summer replacement series was the first to feature cartoons as part of the television prime-time schedule. Blackbirds Heckle and Jeckle first appeared on the "CBS Cartoon Theatre" in their premiere 1947 cartoon, "Flying South." Featured with such other Terrytoons favorites as Gandy Goose and Dinky Duck, Heckle and Jeckle provided the most laughs, which led to a Saturday morning series of their own eventually.

The mischievous pair were created by Paul Terry in the 1940s for a new series of theatrical shorts. Having previously created such characters as Mighty Mouse, Farmer Alfalfa, and Little Roquefort, Terry decided the new characters should be different from the others. After experimenting with various sorts of annoying animals, he came up with the concept of Heckle and Jeckle, two talkative blackbirds, with a frantic twin personality and a unique sense of surrealism.

Heckle, who spoke with a New York accent, and Jeckle, who had that of an English colonel ("By the by, old chap. . ."), were completely in charge of any situation in which they found themselves. Their cartoons usually involved them in a series of misadventures that put them at odds with authority figures. Like the Warner Brothers cartoons that featured Bugs Bunny or Daffy Duck, Heckle and Jeckle often played the antagonist to many an unsuspecting foil. As quick as a wink, the birds could outfox the foxiest fox, con the most cunning of wolves, and make mincemeat of anything that stood between them and having a good time.

As the "Mighty Mouse Playhouse" a year earlier, "The Heckle and Jeckle Show" consisted entirely of cinematic cartoons that were rerun without the aid of a live host.

The series appeared periodically on and off the CBS network for an entire decade (Sunday, 12:00–12:30 P.M., October 14, 1956, through

September 8, 1957; Saturday, 11:00–11:30 A.M., January 25, 1958, through September 24, 1960; Saturday, 11:30–12:00 noon, September 25, 1965, through September 3, 1966). After being absent for several seasons, it returned once again in the fall of 1969 to a one-hour format on NBC (Saturday, 8:00–9:00 A.M., September 6, 1969, through September 4, 1971). Here the show was featured along with a menagerie of such familiar Terrytoon favorites as Sidney the Elephant, the Terry Bears, Gandy Goose, and Little Roquefort.

The birds resurfaced once again in syndication beginning March 1979, taking second billing to another former Saturday morning superstar, in "The New Adventures of Mighty Mouse and Heckle and Jeckle." Presented by Filmation, the new version was developed just for television and was presented mostly on weekday afternoons.

Huckleberry Hound / The Huckleberry Hound Show

William Hanna and Joseph Barbera had only "The Ruff and Reddy Show" (NBC, 1957–60) to their television credits when this series premiered in 1958 about a dim-witted, good-natured hound dog with a Southern drawl and took television audiences by storm. Sponsored nationally by Kellogg's Cereals, the show was the first fully animated series made strictly for television, in contrast to those hosted by live performers or ones with a cinematic history.

With a limited budget of about $2,800 per television episode, Hanna and Barbera invented a technique called "limited animation." This process, used in their first series, greatly reduced the number of drawings needed to complete a single cartoon, and the technique would carry them to the top of the ratings chart for the next three decades.

Syndicated on October 2, 1958, and aired most frequently on Thursday afternoons, "Huckleberry Hound" was about an honest, hardworking dog who was trying out a variety of careers. In the premiere episode, "Wee Willie," Police Patrolman Huckleberry is assigned the difficult task of returning a playful escaped gorilla to the zoo. Subsequent episodes involved his pursuing such occupations as mailman, truant officer, veterinarian, lion tamer, explorer, mounted police officer, firefighter, and once even dogcatcher.

Huckleberry's relaxed Southern accent was provided by the late voice actor Daws Butler. A master of more than 100 vocal characterizations, Butler had previously worked with Hanna and Barbera at the MGM studios when the team was producing the extemely popular "Tom and Jerry" theatrical cartoons.

"Pixie and Dixie" and "Mr. Jinks" were the first additional segments on the 30-minute program. Pixie and Dixie were two little mice who were constantly menaced by their playful nemesis, Jinks the Cat, who "hates meeces to pieces." The theme was a low-budget version of Hanna and Barbera's old "Tom and Jerry" cartoons, with the addition of an extra mouse.

Perhaps nowhere in the annals of television cartoons has there been a character more popular than Yogi Bear, whose adventures made up the second featured segment. Calling himself "smarter than the average bear," Yogi was featured throughout the program in such episodes as "Brainy Bear," "Scooter Looter," "Nowhere Bear," and "The Stout Trout." An inhabitant of Jellystone National Park, the free-spirited bear was constantly trying to be as independent as a human being, when he was not busy pilfering picnic baskets, to the disapproval of his diminutive friend Boo Boo, as well as that of the generally good-natured Ranger Smith.

Like most cartoon characters, Yogi was based on a celebrity more familiar to adults than children. Voiced also by Daws Butler, Yogi resembled Art Carney's Ed Norton, from "The Honeymooners" series, from his vocal attributes to his pork pie hat with the tilted brim. Yogi's success on the program, which even rivaled that of its star, eventually led to his own series in the fall of 1961 (*see* separate entry). He was replaced by an even smarter animal, the conniving Hokey Wolf, whose gift for gab and deceit closely resembled comedian Phil Silvers's Sergeant Bilko.

Although children comprised the show's largest audience, "The Huckleberry Hound Show" also became a favorite with many adults. In 1959 it was awarded an Emmy for Best Children's Program. It was the only cartoon series ever to win such an honor, until the premiere six years later of Charles Schulz's "A Charlie Brown Christmas." The success of the series eventually led to a string of similarly animated types and brought in millions of dollars in sales revenue through products bearing the likenesses of the show's characters.

Through several revivals in the 1970s, with pal Yogi Bear, including repeats of the old shows, Huckleberry Hound remains one of television's most memorable cartoon characters.

Inspector Gadget

A recent foreign-made cartoon that became a hit with kids in the 1980s is the amazing 30-minute adventures of the world's most clever detective, Inspector Gadget.

Among the many gadgets he carried on his person at all times were a jet-propelled copter hat, a pair of mechanical extremities that could extend unlimited distances at the push of a button, and an instant radar screen and magnifying glass built into the crown of his hat. These items as well as others were used in the Inspector's continuous battle against the evil forces of MAD, headed by the sinister Dr. Claw. Assisting the well-meaning but bungling official was his little niece, Penny, and her dog, Brian, the real mastermind of the trio.

Inspector Gadget's vocal mannerisms are immediately identifiable by adult viewers as those of comedian Don Adams, as the bungling Maxwell Smart on the old series "Get Smart" (NBC, CBS, 1965–70). Adams also provided the voice for the lead character on the 1960s Saturday morning favorite, "Tennessee Tuxedo and His Tales" (*see* Total Television Productions).

"Inspector Gadget," syndicated in June of 1984 and still shown frequently on several cable stations today, is a Japanese-produced television series made for export to the United States. This kind of international television merger also created such action cartoons of the 1960s as "Astro Boy," "The Eight Man," "Johnny Socko and His Flying Robot," and "Speed Racer."

The Jetsons

"The Jetsons," the adventures of a modern space age family, was the series that launched the ABC network's prime-time debut into color programming. Producers William Hanna and Joseph Barbera had hoped adult audiences would respond to the series the same way they had to their previous hit prime-time series, "The Flintstones." But with the competition coming mostly from NBC's "Walt Disney's Wonderful World of Color," the show failed miserably in the night-time ratings. Ironically, "The Jetsons" became extremely popular with children when rerun on Saturday mornings almost continuously for nearly 20 years, at various times, over both the NBC and CBS networks.

Here is the programming history of "The Jetsons" which spanned three decades: Sunday, 7:30–8:00 P.M., ABC, September 23, 1962, through September 8, 1963; Saturday, 10:00–10:30 A.M., ABC, September 21, 1963, through April 18, 1964; Saturday, 9:00–9:30 A.M., CBS, September 26, 1964, through September 18, 1965; Saturday, 10:00–10:30 A.M., NBC, October 2, 1965, through September 2, 1967; Saturday, 10:30–11:00 A.M., CBS, September 13, 1969, through September 4, 1971; Saturday, 9:00–9:30 A.M., NBC, September 11, 1971, through September

4, 1976; Saturday, 10:30–11:00 A.M., NBC, February 13, 1979, through September 5, 1981; Saturday, 11:00–11:30 A.M., NBC, September 18, 1982, through April 2, 1983.

A spinoff from the show of their prehistoric cousins the Flintstones, the futuristic Jetsons were a plain but modern middle-class family who lived in the Skypad apartments with their robot maid, Rosie, and their big, lovable mutt, Astro, the family dog. Episodes, which closely resembled a twenty-first-century version of the *Blondie* movie series from the 1940s, focused mainly on the hectic life of the likable but bungling George Jetson, his more sensible wife, Jane, and their two children, Judy and Elroy. Stories typical of the series usually involved George and his futile attempts to please his overbearing boss at Spacely Sprockets by performing tasks that he hoped would overwhelm the company's largest competitor, Coswell's Cogs. In one episode, George is mistakenly credited for inventing a formula for flying, though in fact the device is a remote-controlled toy of Elroy's. In another, George is chosen as a guinea pig for testing an amazing indestructible suit. Other episodes concentrated more on the Jetsons' domestic life, as they faced such everyday twenty-first-century problems as selecting dinner from the automatic "food-a-vac" machine, sending the family space car in for its 2 billion mile check-up, and deciding between Las Venus and the moon for their summer vacation.

George O'Hanlon, known to moviegoers from the *Joe McDoak* short comedies, provided the voice for George Jetson. Actress Penny Singleton, who had played the role of Blondie in the movies, provided the voice of wife, Jane. Other vocals included Mel Blanc as Mr. Spacely, Janet Waldo as Judy, Daws Butler as Elroy, Don Messick as Astro, and Jean VanderPyl as Rosie.

In the mid–1980s audiences began to take a brand new interest in the Jetson family. The series became widely popular all over again, so much so in fact that 20 new episodes, using the original voices, were produced and syndicated in January of 1985. More recently a motion picture feature was made, starring the family for the first time on the giant screen. It is hard at times to evaluate today's sudden burst of interest in "The Jetsons," since the series has rarely been off the air following its premiere in 1962. It definitely remains one of the most highly rated syndicated cartoons of all time.

Jonny Quest / The Adventures of Jonny Quest

"Jonny Quest" was William Hanna and Joseph Barbera's first science fiction animated series. Initially appearing in prime time (Friday evening from 7:30 to 8:00 on ABC from September 18, 1964, through September 9, 1965), the series eventually became part of the Saturday morning schedule, where it was rerun successfully for more than ten years. Here is the programming for "Jonny Quest": Saturday, 12:30–1:00 P.M., CBS, September 9, 1967, through September 5, 1970; Sunday, 12:00–12:30 P.M., ABC, September 13, 1970, through September 5, 1971; Saturday, 10:00–10:30 A.M., ABC, September 11, 1971, through September 2, 1972; Saturday, 11:00–11:30 A.M., NBC, September 8, 1979, through November 3, 1979; Saturday, 11:00–11:30 A.M., NBC, April 12, 1980, through September 6, 1981.

Jonny Quest was the young son of Dr. Benton Quest, an eminent anthropologist and explorer, who constantly traveled in the pursuit of knowledge. Dr. Quest and Jonny were accompanied on their various journeys by Race Bannon, Dr. Quest's friend, bodyguard, and copilot; Jonny's little dog, Bandit, so called because of his masklike eye markings; and Hadji, Jonny's young Asian companion, with whom he first became acquainted in the premiere episode, "Mystery of the Lizard Men." In each episode, the team would overcome many different adversaries, both human and creatures thought to be extinct, as they sought to help the oppressed and the victims of crazed scientists, or tried to stop madmen bent on ruling the world.

Producers Hanna and Barbera had hoped adult audiences would take to the series, for most of the episodes had been carefully researched for scientific accuracy and the plot fixtures were based on live-action shows of the 1950s.

While the show's animation process remained within the usual standards, much of the action was presented across a series of realistic background settings that simulated the actual movements of limbs and mouths. With a budget of more than $2,800 per episode, "Jonny Quest" was Hanna and Barbera's most expensive animated series of that time.

Although it failed in the prime-time ratings, "Jonny Quest" inspired a succession of imitators, which led to the animated science fiction, superhero era that began on Saturday mornings in 1965: "Sinbad Jr. the Sailor" (syndicated, 1965), "Frankenstein Jr. and the Impossibles" (CBS, 1966), "Space Ghost and Dino Boy" (CBS, NBC, 1966), "The Herculoids" (CBS, 1967), "Sampson and Goliath" (NBC, 1967), and many others.

Voices for the "Jonny Quest" series were provided by a young Tim Matthieson as Jonny, John Stephenson (1964) and Don Messick (1964–65) as Dr. Quest, Mike Road as Race, and Danny Bravo as Hadji.

Rerun in syndication almost continuously throughout the 1980s, the series is frequently being discovered by each new generation of children.

King Leonardo and His Short Subjects /
The King and Odie Show

Established in 1960 as an outgrowth of Leonardo Productions (first formed in 1948), Total Television Productions became the first company of independent producers to collaborate in creating low-budget children's made-for-television cartoons.

With an animation process even more limited than that of the Hanna-Barbera cartoons, the productions usually had a somewhat amateur quality. This was a result of a cost-cutting measure that required fewer drawings and a greater variety of angles and camera movements to simulate character motion. The shows themselves, however, each sponsored nationally by General Mills, were enhanced by some of the best vocal characterizations ever heard in cartoons. Among the best known celebrities who lent their talents to the program were former radio personality Kenny Delmar, narrator Jackson Beck, game show host Sandy Becker, actor Wally Cox, and comedians Don Adams and Larry Storch. The corporation is credited with presenting to television one of the most endearing children's animated superheroes of all time: Underdog.

Although all the Total Television Productions were similar in format and incorporated segments, each remained distinct in terms of style and character development.

The first of these shows, "King Leonardo and His Short Subjects," appeared in October 1960 as a replacement for the "Ruff and Reddy" series. As "Ruff and Reddy" had been the first, "King Leonardo" was the second of the made-for-television cartoons to be presented on the network on Saturday mornings. It aired from 10:30 to 11:00 on NBC until September 28, 1963. King Leonardo was a kind-hearted but irresponsible lion who ruled the mythical kingdom of Bongo Congo, somewhere in Africa. Here the inhabitants manufactured, sold, and played the bongos. Inept at making even the simplest decisions on his own, King Leonardo was advised by his trusted aid and friend, Odie Cologne, a skunk. "Biggy" Rat constantly challenged Leonardo for the throne by plotting to replace him with the king's less than honorable brother, Itchy.

Other segments on the program included "The Hunter," a hapless canine sleuth with a Southern accent who was ever on the trail of that notorious criminal, The Fox. Another segment was "Tooter Turtle," a turtle who was magically transported into various fields of endeavors by his friend Mr. Wizard, the Lizard. Also presented on each program by the show's sponsor were the adventures of Twinkles the Elephant (and "the only cereal with the storybook package"). This segment featured a string of one-minute stories about Twinkles and his friends which could also be found on the back of the cereal boxes of the same name. "King Leonardo and His Short Subjects" ran for three seasons on NBC before going into syndication in January 1964 as "The King and Odie Show."

The Magilla Gorilla Show

Another in the line of popular Hanna and Barbera series featured the adventures of a gorilla named Magilla, who lived in a pet store window. The owner, Mr. Peebles, would go to great lengths in trying to unload the gorilla on the first available customer who happened to come along. No matter how often Magilla became the property of others, he somehow always managed an unwelcome, unexpected return to Mr. Peebles.

In different episodes Magilla is purchased by a variety of customers, such as an eccentric hunter in "Monkey-Businessman," a football coach in "Gridiron Gorilla," and a wealthy socialite in "Waltzing Magilla."

Other segments included in the show's 30 minutes were "Mush Mouse and Punkin' Puss," featuring a backwoods mouse and cat who constantly quarreled in such episodes as "Callin' All Kin" and "Chiveling Rivalry." Also included were the adventures of Sheriff ("bing-bing-bing") Ricochet Rabbit, fastest rabbit in the West. Ricochet was accompanied by his limping deputy sidekick, who always carried a pot of hot coffee. The gag was taken from the popular Western series "Gunsmoke" (CBS 1955–75). During the show's second season, the Ricochet Rabbit cartoons were replaced by a segment from another Hanna-Barbera series, "The Peter Potamus Show" (syndicated, 1964), featuring the adventures of Breezly and Sneezly, a polar bear and his friend, an ever-sneezing seal.

Vocals for the show were supplied by Allan Melvin, as Magilla and Punkin' Puss, Howard Morris, as Mr. Peebles and Mush Mouse, Don Messick, as Ricochet, Daws Butler, as Breezly, and Mel Blanc, as Droop-a-long Deputy and Sneezly Seal.

The series initially appeared in syndication on January 9, 1964, sponsored nationally by the Ideal Toy Company. It was picked up two years later by ABC for Saturday mornings airing at 11:30 from January 1, 1966, through December 17, 1967. "Magilla Gorilla," like several of the eternally popular Hanna-Barbera creations, was revived in the 1970s as part of the Yogi Bear crew in "Yogi's Gang" (ABC, 1973–75).

Matty's Funday Funnies

This 30-minute cartoon series was produced by Harvey Comics, in association with Paramount Pictures and the Mattel Toy Corporation. Hosted by Mattel's animated trademark figures Matty Mattel and his sister Belle, the program featured various cartoon segments taken from Paramount's animated film collection. Mostly associated with Harvey Comics, these included "Casper, the Friendly Ghost," "Herman and Katnip," "Little Audrey," "Tommy the Tortoise and Moe Hare," "Buzzy the Crow," and "Baby Huey," the oversized duckling.

Developed mostly as a promotional tool for marketing Mattel toys, the series helped to generate more interest in Mattel toys than in any other toys on the market. This publicity gimmick was unsurpassed until the 1962 debut of "The Funny Company," a five-minute series of educational excerpts designed to encourage children's creative abilities while introducing them to the latest in Mattel toys. It was through the "Funday Funnies" program that little girls across America were first introduced to the amazingly lifelike Barbie doll—a successful toy that even today shows no signs of decline in sales.

"Funday Funnies" was presented by ABC on Sunday evenings at 5:00 from October 11, 1959, through September 5, 1960. The show moved to Fridays at 7:30 on September 17, 1960, and remained in that slot through September 2, 1961, becoming the first animated series to appear on the ABC prime-time schedule. For a brief period in 1961 (October 1 through December 30), the show appeared on Saturday evenings at 7:00. In January 1962, when the show was moved to Saturdays, Matty Mattel introduced the Bob Clampett characters Beany and Cecil to the program. Within a few short weeks all the previous segments had been dropped, including Matty Mattel's introduction, as the entire half hour was turned into "The Beany and Cecil Show."

For reasons unclear, the Paramount–Harvey Comics cartoons have been absent for many years from the television screens. The studio along with cartoonist Max Fleischer was the first to develop the cartoon singalong, in which movie audiences would follow the bouncing ball to the words of a popular song. "Funday Funnies" repeated the process for home viewers.

The Mighty Mouse Playhouse / The New Adventures of Mighty Mouse and Heckle and Jeckle
(see also *The "Heckle and Jeckle" Shows*)

"The Mighty Mouse Playhouse" was network television's first Saturday morning cartoon series. Consisting entirely of theatrical reruns, the program premiered in 1955 in the midst of the live-action shows then presented on weekends for children.

One of the last original television productions of cartoon producer Paul Terry, the cinematic shorts, featuring Mighty Mouse as well as several other Paul Terry creations, were purchased for the CBS network in a $3 million merger between Terry and the network's film library department, a venture that would eventually make CBS the leading network in animated television shows.

Mighty Mouse, originally developed by artist Isidore Klein, was a combination of Superman, Mickey Mouse, and Caruso. From out of the sky he came to rescue his friends, usually from the clutches of scheming cats, while all the while singing operatically ("Here I come to save the daaaaay!").

Some segments were presented in the tradition of the serial melodramas of the 1920s and 1930s, as Mighty Mouse was pitted against his archrival, Oil Can Harry, for the love of his occasional girlfriend, Pearl Pureheart. Unlike most other superheroes, who had their strength from birth, Mighty Mouse was shown acquiring his physical abilities from various sources. In his 1942 premiere cartoon, "The Mouse of Tomorrow," the source is a huge bulk of cheese. In several episodes he gains vitality from such sources as vitamins, drinks, and rays from other planets of the solar system. While most of the Mighty Mouse cartoons emphasized the character's ability to fly in at just the right time to rescue his fellow rodents, others borrowed from such familiar fairy tales as "Hansel and Gretel," "Little Red Riding Hood," and "Little Boy Blue." Tom Morrison provided the voices for both the hero and the narrator of the series. Other segments at various times featured the Terry Bears, Gandy Goose, and Little Roquefort. The show remained on the air on CBS consistently for over ten seasons, to become one of the most durable Saturday morning cartoon shows of all time. Here is the programming history: Saturday, 11:00–11:30 A.M., December 10, 1955, through March 11, 1956; Saturday, 10:30–11:00 A.M., March 18, 1956, through September 2, 1960; Saturday, 11:30–12:00 noon, September 9, 1960, through September, 1, 1961; Saturday, 10:30–11:00 A.M., September 8, 1961, through September 4, 1965; Saturday, 10:00–10:30 A.M., September 11, 1965, through October 22, 1966.

In March 1979 "The New Adventures of Mighty Mouse and Heckle and Jeckle" premiered as a syndicated show, with new adventures of Mighty Mouse sharing the spotlight with two other former Saturday morning favorites, Heckle and Jeckle. The new series was produced by Filmation Industries, which decided this time around to relieve the mighty rodent of his operatic talents.

In the late 1980s another new version of "Mighty Mouse" appeared for a very brief period, again on CBS on Saturday mornings.

The "Mr. Magoo" Shows
Mr. Magoo / The Famous Adventures of Mr. Magoo / What's New, Mr. Magoo?

Quincy Magoo was one of television's strangest cartoon characters. First of all, he was human, which in itself was a contrast to an animated world of talking animals. Second, because of his nearsightedness, he was constantly bumping into all sorts of objects while mistaking them for something else — to the delight of millions of viewers, who were first taken by the little character's charm in a series of theatrical shorts in the early 1950s.

Produced and distributed through United Productions of America, the cartoons had a whimsical innocence all their own. Their greatest asset came from Magoo's inimitable voice, provided by the late Jim Backus, originally developed in his earlier career in radio.

Magoo's myopic condition led him into all sorts of off-beat situations, but his cartoons had little in common with most others of the same period, which relied heavily on violent situations for their humor. The best part of watching a Magoo cartoon was knowing that through it all he would remain invulnerable, never causing viewers to fear for his well-being despite his bumbling.

Created by Columbia Pictures animator John Hubley, Magoo was first seen in the 1949 short "Ragtime Bear." Although they became a popular television fixture in the 1960s, the shorts were actually the second of the acclaimed UPA series cartoons to be presented on television. The first, created and conceived by Theodor Geisel (Dr. Seuss), was entitled "Gerald McBoing-Boing," and it followed the adventures of a little boy who spoke with sounds instead of words. That series ran from December 1956 to October 1958 on Sundays on CBS. "Mr. Magoo" was syndicated in 1959.

In addition to becoming a children's favorite, Mr. Magoo also appealed to the adults, appearing as the spokesman in a series of humorous commercials for such products as Stag Beer and General Electric light bulbs.

In 1962, after being featured for several years in the syndicated market, Mr. Magoo played the role of Ebeneezer Scrooge in a 60-minute NBC special of the popular Charles Dickens classic, *A Christmas Carol.* Because of the show's surprisingly high ratings, Magoo later became the star of a 1964 30-minute series of further adaptations of classic tales; he was featured in a variety of roles that best suited his character. Entitled "The Famous Adventures of Mr. Magoo," the series lasted for one prime-time season on NBC, airing on Saturdays at 8:00 from September 19, 1964, through August 21, 1965.

In 1977, Mr. Magoo returned to network television in a new Saturday morning series entitled "What's New, Mr. Magoo?" airing at 9:00 on CBS from September 10, 1977, through September 9, 1979. Here he was featured with an equally nearsighted dog named McBaker, whose voice was also provided by Jim Backus.

Like "Bugs Bunny," "Rocky and Bullwinkle," and "Beany and Cecil," "Mr. Magoo" was one of the funniest cartoons ever on television.

The New Adventures of Mighty Mouse and Heckle and Jeckle see *The Mighty Mouse Playhouse*

The New Adventures of Tom Terrific see *The "Tom Terrific" Shows*

The New Archie and Sabrina Hour see *The "Archie" Shows*

The New Felix the Cat see *"Felix the Cat" Shows*

The New Fred and Barney Show see *The Flintstones*

The New Scooby and Scrappy Doo Show / The New Scooby-Doo Movies see *The "Scooby-Doo" Shows*

The New Tom and Jerry see *The "Tom and Jerry" Shows*

The New Woody Woodpecker Show
see *The "Woody Woodpecker" Shows*

The Pebbles and Bamm-Bamm Show see *The Flintstones*

The "Pink Panther" Shows
The Pink Panther Show / The Pink Panther Laugh and ½ Hour and ½ Show / The Think Pink Panther Show / The All New Pink Panther Show / The Pink Panther and Sons

"The Pink Panther" was one of Saturday morning's longest consistently running cartoon shows. The character was based on the one appearing in the animated opening credits of the 1964 Blake Edwards hit movie of the same name. The segment alone proved so popular that the following year the character was awarded a series of theatrical shorts all his own, produced by animators David H. DePatie and Fritz Freleng. In his 1965 premiere cartoon "Pink Phink," the Panther silently matches wits with a green letter that refuses to be painted pink. The success of these shorts eventually prompted the NBC network and the Mirisch film corporation to star the delightful but odd character in his own 30-minute series on Saturday mornings.

The cartoons were like no other previous cartoon show. Many of the laughs largely depended upon viewers' initial response to the Panther's double entendres in a variety of free-ranging situations, with visual sight gags and comical pratfalls. Also included was jazzy background music, provided by composer Henry Mancini, and an adult laugh track. Although the Pink Panther remained silent in most of his cartoons, he was featured in several speaking with a British accent. Like the theatrical shorts, which were rerun with those produced specifically for the television series, the cartoons all had the word *pink* in their titles ("Pink Lemonade," "Pink Ice," "Pink Paradise," and so forth). In the television opener, "Think Pink," the Panther rescues an ark full of animals held captive for profit by a greedy Captain Noah.

In his first season, the suave and silent feline was joined by the Inspector, an imitation of the bumbling Peter Sellers character Inspector Clouseau from the *Pink Panther* film. During its fourth season, the series was hosted by the Paul and Mary Ritts puppets. Here are the various programming slots (all NBC, 30 min., Saturday morning): 9:30, September

6, 1969, through September 5, 1970; 10:30, September 12, 1970, through September 11, 1971; 9:30, September 18, 1971, through September 8, 1973; 11:30, September 15, 1973, through December 29, 1973. In January 1974 the series expanded for the first time into a 90-minute format airing at 10:30 on NBC. The show remained in this time slot until September 14, 1974. From September 21, 1974, through September 6, 1975, a 30-minute show appeared on NBC at 11:00 on Saturday mornings. Producers returned to the expanded 90-minute format in September 1976 when the show was retitled "The Pink Panther Laugh and ½ Hour and ½ Show," the longest title ever given a children's television program and aired at 9:30 on NBC until September 3, 1977. On September 10, 1977, the show reverted to its original 30-minute format and was retitled "The Think Pink Panther Show." NBC presented "The Think Pink Panther" show at 9:30 on Saturday mornings until September 2, 1978. Its remaining eight seasons were featured on ABC as "The All New Pink Panther Show" and finally "The Pink Panther and Sons" (Saturday, 9:00–10:00, September 9, 1978, through September 13, 1986).

Throughout the various changes in format, other segments on the program have included "The Ant and the Aardvark," "Mister Jaws," and "The Texas Toads."

The Pink Panther cartoons still remain immensely popular in syndication and on cable stations today in more than 70 cities across the United States.

The "Popeye" Shows
Popeye the Sailor / The All New Popeye Hour

Popeye, the pipe-smoking sailor and the world's leading authority on spinach, was originally conceived as early as 1929 as a supporting character in the *New York Journal* comic strip *Thimble Theater*. Created by E.C. Segar, the character — a sawed-off, squinty-eyed sailor with muscular forearms — eventually became the strip's most popular creation, in stories that centered on his crusty mannerisms and Herculean strength.

Popeye, along with his skinny girlfriend, Olive Oyl, his friend, Wimpy, the moocher, the orphaned Swee'Pea, and archrival Bluto (later known as Brutus), had already become part of American culture when the Max Fleischer studios contracted with the King Features Syndicate, owners of the comic strip, to feature the characters in a series of theatrical cartoons with Popeye as the star. The final decision came as a result of audiences' response to the seaman's first appearance, in a "Betty Boop" cartoon entitled "Popeye the Sailor." Audiences took to the character right away, and before long the "Popeye the Sailor" shorts were under way.

Beginning with "I Yam What I Yam" in 1933, Popeye appeared in more than 200 Max Fleischer cartoons between 1933 and 1943, becoming the most exposed cartoon character on the screen. In 1943, when the production of the cartoons became less frequent, audiences' demand for more became overwhelming. The following year, the cartoons were given a new look, with a much younger, updated version of Popeye and Olive, this time produced through the original distributor, Paramount Pictures, in cooperation with Famous Studios.

On September 10, 1956, the cartoons were sold to Associated Artist Productions, along with many of the early Warner Brothers shorts, for syndicated television distribution. Usually presented with such titles as "The SS Popeye," "Popeye and Friends," and "Popeye Theater," the cartoons became an instant success, receiving higher ratings than any other syndicated children's show of that period.

Most of the 350 cartoons centered on the rivalry between Popeye and Bluto for the honor of courting Olive Oyl. These cartoons typically climaxed with Popeye eating his spinach and beating the bullying Bluto into a state of total submission. Several, however, with such titles as "Poop Deck Pappy," "Season's Greetnicks," and "Eat Your Spinach," did not involve the love triangle at all but instead focused on Popeye's good-natured ability inadvertently to cause trouble while helping others. Popeye had a keen sense of kindness and fair play which matched his ability for retribution when provoked. A few of the cartoons even focused on Popeye's domestic life, as he tried to be a father to his four nephews, Peep-eye, Pip-eye, Poop-eye, and Pup-eye.

The voice of the seafarer was provided by William Costello from 1933 to 1934. But it was his replacement, Jack Mercer, whose vocal characteristics and malapropisms became familiar to over four generations of viewers. Mae Questel did the voice of Olive Oyl. She originally began as the voice for Betty Boop, and later did similar voices for both Little Lulu (1937–47) and her replacement, Little Audrey (1947–53), all at the Paramount Pictures Studios.

By early 1960, "Popeye" was the most popular cartoon program in syndication and the second favorite syndicated film series behind the *Three Stooges* films. The cartoon's success led to the production of an additional 200 television episodes by the original syndicated distributor, the King Features Syndicate. With the familiar voices of both Popeye and Olive remaining intact, former radio narrator Jackson Beck replaced Pinto Colvig as Popeye's bearded antagonist, Bluto, now officially referred to by his comic strip name, Brutus. Although somewhat revised, the newer cartoons lacked the color and charm of the originals, which were usually combined to create a full 60-minute program.

In the fall of 1978, Popeye and company came to network television for the first time on Saturday mornings in "The All New Popeye Hour," with a series of brand new adventures produced through Hanna-Barbera Studios. Both Mercer and Questel reprised their vocals, with Bluto's voice now provided by actor Allan Melvin. Here are the various CBS program slots for "The All New Popeye Hour" (all Saturday morning): 8:00–9:00, September 9, 1978, through September 1, 1979; 10:30–11:30, September 8, 1979, through February 28, 1981; 11:00–12:00, March 7, 1981, through September 5, 1981; 10:00–11:00, September 12, 1981, through September 10, 1983.

Throughout its many revisions, the "Popeye" cartoons have entertained both children and adults for many years. Popeye is given credit by many parents for making spinach a wee bit easier for children to swallow. The cartoons remain a favorite on more than 50 syndicated and cable stations today.

A Pup Named Scooby-Doo see *The "Scooby-Doo" Shows*

The Puppy's Adventures Shows
Scooby and Scrappy Doo — The Puppy's New Adventures / The Puppy's Further Adventures
(see also *The "Scooby-Doo" Shows*)

This half-hour series, enriched by the popular "Lassie" series, involved the adventures of Petey the Pup, a loner who faced incredible odds in the search for his master. In an accident aboard a luxury liner, Petey was washed overboard and separated from his human family. Surviving the near-fatal plunge, the young pup was left behind, thought by his family to have drowned. Nevertheless, determined to be with his master once again, Petey began a near-impossible trek, requiring much strength and courage in the face of adversity.

In each episode Petey would travel on foot from one exciting place to another while encountering all sorts of people. In several episodes, he aided those along the way who, like himself, were victims of unfortunate mishaps, while others focused on his efforts at eluding shady lawmen and bounty hunters who are after him for crimes he has never committed.

"The Puppy's Adventures" made its weekly debut during the 1982-83 television season as a featured segment on the "Scooby and Scrappy

Doo" show as "The Puppy's New Adventures." "Scooby and Scrappy Doo—The Puppy's New Adventures" first aired on September 11, 1982, on ABC from 9 to 10 on Saturday morning. The show remained in that slot through September 3, 1983. Petey had been introduced to children's audiences a year earlier in a two-part presentation on the "ABC Weekend Special," where his saga first began. In a unique move for a cartoon series, the Puppy resolved his situation in the last few episodes of "The Puppy's Further Adventures," on the Saturday morning season of 1984-85. The 30-minute show ran from September 10, 1983, through September 7, 1985, appearing at 11:00 on ABC.

Joe Ruby and Ken Spears were the executive producers of the series. The team had worked in the late 1960s with the Hanna-Barbera crew on the shows "The Wacky Races" (CBS, 1968–70) and its spinoff, "The Perils of Penelope Pitstop" (CBS, 1969–71). They have since become better known for their action cartoon shows. Some of their most familiar shows are "The Plastic Man Comedy/Adventure Show" (ABC, 1979–81) and "Thundarr the Barbarian" (ABC, NBC, 1980–84).

One of the best in the new types of cartoon shows of the 1980s, "The Puppy's Further Adventures," is hardly if ever rerun today, but it remains an unforgettable, entertaining program.

Quick Draw McGraw

"Quick Draw McGraw" appeared on the air shortly after the success of the "Huckleberry Hound Show." It was the third series to be produced by William Hanna and Joseph Barbera in association with the Screen-Gems distributors and their second to be syndicated nationally by the Kellogg's Cereal Company.

Quick Draw was a bumbling horse marshall of a lawless Western town, somewhere deep in the heart of Texas. He was "the highfalutinest, fancy shootin'est cowboy you ever saw," and an equine Wyatt Earp who spoofed every Western cliché television has ever offered. Quick Draw was assisted in keeping the town free of wrongdoers by his friend and deputy Baba-Looey, a Spanish-accented burro who sounded a bit like Desi Arnaz's Ricky Ricardo, on "I Love Lucy." In episodes that ranged from amusing to absurd, Quick Draw always managed to make his way through situations that followed a formula of repetitive chases, rambunctious gunplay, and fickle-minded heroines. A few of the funniest cartoons featured Quick Draw, in a parody of "Zorro," as a swashbuckling masked avenger called El-Kabong, who used a guitar in place of a sword.

Incorporated segments included "Augie Doggy and Doggy Daddy," the domestic adventures of a cute little boy dog and his "dear old dad." Doggy Daddy, whose voice was provided by Doug Young, was a caricature of beloved comedian Jimmy Durante. Super Snooper and Blabber Mouse were an inept but funny pair of cat and mouse detectives. A satire of the private eye shows of the 1950s, these cartoons often involved characters from children's storybook tales. In "Fee Fi Fo Fumble," the sleuths are assigned the task of locating a missing bank building believed stolen by the giant from "Jack and the Beanstalk." And in "The Hansel and Gretel Case," they are the star witnesses in a court battle as the witch is accused of endangering the welfare of young people.

Daws Butler and Don Messick supplied the additional voices for the show's characters. "Quick Draw McGraw" was syndicated on September 29, 1959. A personal favorite of CBS program director Fred Silverman, "Quick Draw McGraw" appeared on that network on Saturday mornings in the mid–1960s. The 30-minute show appeared at 10:00 from September 28, 1963, through September 4, 1965. It moved to 11:30 on September 9, 1965, through its final appearance on September 3, 1966.

Quick Draw McGraw, like many of the old Hanna-Barbera favorites, was revived once again in the 1970s as a supporting character on several of the Yogi Bear spinoffs, such as "Yogi's Gang" (ABC, 1973–75). Reruns of "Quick Draw McGraw" cartoons are still shown most frequently today on the USA cable network.

The Richie Rich — Scooby-Doo Show
see The "Scooby-Doo" Shows

Road Runner Show see The "Bugs Bunny" Shows

Rocky and His Friends see The Bullwinkle Show

Ruff and Reddy

"Ruff and Reddy" was the first television series produced by William Hanna and Joseph Barbera. It was also the first made-for-television cartoon series presented for the network's Saturday morning schedule.

Ruff, a resourceful cat, and Reddy, a dim-witted dog, were pals who were featured weekly in a variety of serialized adventures ranging from outer space to the wilds of the Arctic. In the premiere episode the heroes are kidnapped while sleeping by a pair of metal monsters from the planet Munimula (*aluminum* spelled backward). They were then teamed with an eccentric scientist named Gizmo, who appeared in many of their later episodes. Throughout their many adventures, Ruff and Reddy were opposed by such comical foils as Cross-Bones Jones, the pirate Scarey Harry Safari, the explorer; Killer and Diller, the two terrible twins from Texas; and Captain Greedy and his giggling assistant, Salt Water Daffy.

When "Ruff and Reddy" premiered December 14, 1957, at 10:30 on NBC, its strongest competition was the theatrical reruns featuring Mighty Mouse and his friends on CBS. Both shows were presented at a time when live-action shows were still dominant on Saturday mornings.

For three whole seasons, "Ruff and Reddy" was hosted by singer Jimmie Blaine and his puppet friends Rhubarb the Parrot and José the Toucan. Blaine originally began each program by encouraging children at home to sing along, following the words on the screen, with the "Ruff and Reddy" theme song. The program ran in this format until October 8, 1960.

The cartoons were the first of the Hanna-Barbera productions to be distributed nationally by Columbia's television subsidiary, Screen-Gems Productions. The company had originally rejected the Hanna-Barbera competitors. It later reconsidered; an agreement worked out with Hanna and Barbera stated that the program would feature a number of old cartoons from the vaults of Columbia's short subject department. Included at various times between two "Ruff and Reddy" cartoons were "The Fox and the Crow," satirist Al Capp's "Li'l Abner," and "The Adventures of Willoughby," an all-but-forgotten cartoon about a little character with incredible strength gained from a magical cap woven from the hair of the mighty Sampson.

In the fall of 1962, the "Ruff and Reddy" cartoons were rerun for the first time in color. Since the team of Hanna and Barbera had now become a huge success, "Ruff and Reddy" was presented this time without the incorporated Columbia cartoons. Unfortunately, this version of the series focused more on the antics of the second host, Captain Bob Cottle and his puppet friends Jasper and Gramps, than it did on Ruff and Reddy. The program appeared at 8:30–9:00 A.M. on NBC from September 28, 1962, through September 26, 1964.

Don Messick and Daws Butler were heard as the voices of Ruff and Reddy, respectively. These two voice actors developed a long, successful association with Hanna-Barbera productions, providing the voices, together, for more than 600 television cartoon characters.

Ruff and Reddy made a rare come-back appearance on television in a 1972 Hanna-Barbera Saturday morning television movie entitled *Yogi's*

William Hanna (left) and Joseph Barbera.

Ark Lark (ABC). Oddly, Hanna and Barbera's first television stars stayed in the background with many of the team's other characters, where their roles were reduced to minimal, nonspeaking parts.

The "Scooby-Doo" Shows
Scooby-Doo, Where Are You? / The New Scooby-Doo Movies / Scooby-Doo—Dynomutt Hour / Scooby's All-Star Laff-A-Lympics / Scooby's All-Stars / Scooby and Scrappy Doo / The Richie Rich—Scooby-Doo Show / Scooby and Scrappy Doo—The Puppy's New Adventures / The New Scooby and Scrappy Doo Show / A Pup Named Scooby-Doo
(see also *The Puppy's Adventures Shows*)

As part of the trend toward mass-produced series for Saturday mornings, Hanna-Barbera's most popular Great Dane became a fixture for many years on both the CBS and ABC networks. At one time the series had the highest ratings of any Saturday morning program shown between the hours of 9:00 and 10:00 A.M.

More than any previous Hanna and Barbera series, the Scooby shows relied on viewers' willingness to accept the Great Dane in a variety of different concepts. The series originated in 1969 with its most familiar format, "Scooby-Doo, Where Are You?" The 30-minute Saturday show appeared at 10:30 A.M. on CBS from September 13, 1969, through September 2, 1972. Here Scooby was first introduced as a large, cowardly, but lovable mutt and traveling companion of four teenage amateur sleuths named Freddy, Daphne, Velma, and Scooby's best friend, Shaggy, who resembled Bob Denver's Maynard G. Krebs character on the old "Many Loves of Dobie Gillis" series (CBS, 1959–63). Each episode focused on the group's attempts to resolve various unexplained phenomena while driving around in their van, the Mystery Machine. Most of the stories had well-designed but somewhat predictable plots, and Scooby and Shaggy had more than their share of comical moments while the others carried out the routine of solving crimes. In several ways, the series was similar to the "Who Done It?" mystery dramas that first became popular with television audiences in the 1950s.

In the fall of 1972, the show expanded from 30 minutes to a full hour, in the first of its many format and title changes. Retitled "The New Scooby-Doo Movies," this version of the series featured many characters and the actual voices of such guest stars as Dick Van Dyke, Don Knotts, Sandy Duncan, Don Adams, the Harlem Globetrotters, Jonathan Winters, and Jerry Reed, to name a few. This hour long show aired at 10:30 A.M. on CBS on Saturdays from September 9, 1972, through August 31, 1974. In 1974, reruns of the original series were aired once again, for two more seasons on CBS. Under the program title "Scooby-Doo, Where Are You?" the show appeared from 9:00–9:30 A.M. on CBS on Saturdays from September 7, 1974, through August 7, 1976. The series moved over to the ABC network in 1976 and became "The Scooby-Doo—Dynomutt Hour," as a segment of the show that featured the adventures of Dynomutt, a bionic dog (9:00–10:00 A.M., September 11, 1976, through September 3, 1977). In the fall of 1977 it expanded to two hours under the title "Scooby's All-Star Laff-A-Lympics," as Scooby became involved in all sorts of athletic competitions with other characters (Saturday, 9:00–11:00 A.M., ABC, September 10, 1977, through September 2, 1978). The following year the show became "Scooby's All-Stars," as several familiar Hanna-Barbera characters from the past appeared on the program in supporting roles (Saturday, 9:00–10:30 A.M., ABC, September 9, 1978, through September 15, 1979). In 1979 Scooby returned to a 30-minute format in which he was reunited with his old pal Shaggy and joined a new character named Scrappy Doo, Scooby's feisty little nephew in "Scooby and Scrappy Doo" (Saturday, 9:00–9:30 A.M., ABC, September 22, 1979, through September 6, 1980). The following year Scooby took second billing for the first time, in "The Richie Rich – Scooby-Doo Show" (Saturday, 9:00–10:00 A.M., ABC, September 13, 1980, through September 4, 1982). Here he was featured sharing center stage with little Richie Rich, a popular comic book creation from the pages of Harvey Comics.

By now Scooby had become familiar to viewers for introducing new segments to the program, which was curious, considering that several shows were not the immediate property of Scooby creators William Hanna and Joseph Barbera. In one of the show's most popular formats, for instance, Scooby shares billing with "The Puppy's New Adventures," a program produced exclusively by Joe Ruby and Ken Spears (Saturday, 9:00–10:00 A.M., ABC, September 11, 1982, through September 3, 1983). It was assumed that new characters would be more favorably received by young viewers if introduced by a character with whom they had become familiar. The double-billing concept continued as a successful form of transition on many children's shows throughout the 1980s. Scooby was featured during the 1983–86 seasons in "The New Scooby and Scrappy Doo Show," which closely resembled the original show (Saturday, 9:00–10:30 A.M., ABC, September 10, 1983, through September 6, 1986). Featured once again were Shaggy, Fred, and Daphne in a somewhat revised version of their earlier roles. The show's final presentation aired in 1987 as "A Pup Named Scooby-Doo," with Scooby remembering his younger days as a pup (Saturday, 10:00–10:30 A.M. [return], ABC, September 12, 1987, through September 28, 1991. Unfortunately, most of these episodes were shelved to make way for such movie-oriented shows as "Bettlejuice" and "Slimer! and the Ghostbusters." The series was officially terminated in September 1991.

Don Messick has provided Scooby's voice over the years, in a characterization Messick claims is his best dog impression since that of Astro on "The Jetsons." Radio personality Casey Kasem provided his familiar voice for Shaggy.

Scooby-Doo has become one of Hanna and Barbera's most familiar and successful cartoon creations. Like his comrades Huckleberry Hound and Yogi Bear, the character continues to bring Hanna-Barbera Productions considerable revenue from merchandise items that bear his likeness, from stuffed toys to children's school supplies. The series is still being shown in various syndicated versions today.

She-Ra: Princess of Power

Aimed primarily at a female audience was He-Man's counterpart, "She-Ra:
Princess of Power," which premiered shortly after "He-Man" (see separate entry). "She-Ra" was syndicated in February of 1984. This series involved the saga of Princess Adora, born to King Randor and Queen
Marlena on the planet of Eternia. The peaceful planet soon came under
attack by the evil Horde commander, Hordak, who, as part of his plot
to steal the kingdom's treasure, broke into the nursery and kidnapped
the infant girl Adora. He also tried to take her twin brother, Adam, but
Man-at-Arms discovered him in time. Quickly retreating, Hordak managed to reach the one-dimensional gate with the girl child under his arms
and disappeared without a trace.

Little Adora grew up on the planet Whispering Woods under a spell
cast upon her by the demonic Shadow Weaver. She was deceived into
believing that the Hordes of Whispering Woods were good, but as she
came of age, her doubts grew. Through the help of her friend and guardian, the Sorceress, she eventually overpowered Shadow Weaver's mighty
spell. Now secretly She-Ra, Princess of Power, Adora struggles to restore
good on the planet by driving out the evil Hordes, aided by varied groups
that have superpowers of their own.

Smurfs

"Smurfs" at one time was one of the most popular of the new types of
animated shows presented on Saturday mornings in the 1980s. The series
involved the adventures of a lovable little group of blue humanoids who
lived in tranquility in an enchanted forest. The group was headed by
Papa Smurf, the bearded monarch whose knowledge and wisdom guided
the others safely into maturity. Their only real threat, which lay beneath
the forest, was their enemy, the evil Gargamel, who constantly tried to
capture them.

When "Smurfs" made its debut (September, 12, 1981; NBC, Saturday, 9:00–10:00 A.M.), children's cartoons had reached their peak in
terms of bright, energetic concepts. Refreshingly different, the program
began in a 60-minute format, and then expanded to 90 minutes extend-
ing the same programming slot until 10:30. The show aired in this format
until September 2, 1989.

The characters were adapted from the 1950s classic cartoon strips
of Belgian cartoonist Peyo Culliford. The Smurfs' newer adventures
were animated by the Hanna-Barbera Studios.

Despite the elegant animation and wonderful voice actors Don Messick, René Auberjonois, and ventriloquist Paul Winchell as Gargamel, the series lacked the usual cheer and humor that had become a trademark of most Hanna-Barbera shows. Instead, the show emphasized such imporant themes as sharing, safety, and responsibility, which made it all the more worth watching. Many episodes deliberately attempted to discourage young children from doing such foolish things as leaving home or school. Even the names of the Smurfs themselves—Brainy, Greedy, Grouchy, and so forth—represented certain emotions and attitudes familiar to children. Aside from the moralistic overtones, the show's most dramatic scenes involved the Smurfs' efforts to elude the persistent Gargamel, a frightening antagonist who took great pleasure in alarming the little people. In fact, this concept was possibly the most forceful part of the show: warning kids to stay away from those who might cause them harm.

The success of the series inspired several less successful imitators, like "The Littles," "Monchichis," and "Trollkins." There are also numerous dolls, toys, and various other "Smurfy" items distributed throughout the world.

Although well received by network television, the Smurfs left the Saturday morning slot in 1989 to become syndicated (August 1989) daily in an attempt to reach more viewers. The show has been rerun ever since in more than 100 cities across the United States.

Tennessee Tuxedo and His Tales

Following closely upon the success of "King Leonardo," Total Television Productions offered "Tennessee Tuxedo and His Tales," which made its Saturday morning debut on CBS airing from 9:30 to 10:00 on CBS from September 28, 1963, through September 3, 1966. (For further information about Total Television productions, see entry for "King Leonardo and His Short Subjects.") This series featured the adventures of a curious, wisecracking penguin (Tennessee) and his bumbling friend Chumbley, a walrus, who were always inventing schemes to improve their environment at the Stanley Livingstone Park Zoo. Several stories allowed Tennessee and Chumbley to venture outside the park gates to seek their fortune, with each undertaking resulting in a disastrous failure.

"Tennessee Tuxedo" was one of the earliest animated programs to feature live-action informative inserts. In each of the tales, Tennessee and Chumbley faithfully resorted to their friend "the Answer Man," Mr.

Whoopey, whenever a problem became too difficult for them to handle. With his three-dimensional blackboard, Mr. Whoopey explored such topics as highway construction, bridge building, how wells are dug, how windmills work, and so forth each time with an appropriate level of seriousness. The series was highly approved by parents and critics for this segment alone. Also featured at various other times were "The Hunter" and "Tooter Turtle," carryovers from the "King Leonardo" show. A new segment, "The World of Commander McBragg," told of the exaggerated, 60-second adventures of a stuffy English lord, who bored his staff with vivid tales from his imagination.

Don Adams, who provided the voice for Tennessee, also appeared during the year of the show's debut as a regular on "The Bill Dana Show" (NBC, 1963–64). He was only two years away, however, from a role in which he would be immortalized—that of Maxwell Smart, secret agent 86, on the spy spoof series "Get Smart" (NBC, CBS, 1965–70).

"Tennessee Tuxedo" remained on the CBS Saturday morning schedule for three seasons, before being presented for one brief period on ABC on Sunday afternoons (4:30–5:00 from September 11, through December 25 in 1966).

The Think Pink Panther Show see *The "Pink Panther" Shows*

The "Tom and Jerry" Shows
The Tom and Jerry Show / The New Tom and Jerry—Grape Ape Show / The Tom and Jerry—Grape Ape—Mumbley Show / The Great Grape Ape / The Tom and Jerry Comedy Show

William Hanna and Joseph Barbera first became known as the creative forces behind the popular "Tom and Jerry" cartoons for MGM Studios. Beginning in 1937, with producer Fred Quimby, they created and produced more than 100 cartoons in which seven—including "Yankee Doodle Mouse" (1943), "Quiet Please" (1945), "The Cat Concerto" (1947), and "The Two Mousketeers" (1951)—won Academy Awards for Best Animated Short Feature.

Twenty years later Hanna and Barbera left MGM to set up their own production company to make animated films distributed through the Screen Gems television corporation. At an average of one to two shows per season, Hanna and Barbera, with their low-budget animation technique, soon became the most familiar of children's made-for-television cartoon producers.

Unfortunately, when the "Tom and Jerry" cartoons first came to network television in 1965 as a regular Saturday morning series, MGM still remained the rightful owner of the characters. Here Hanna and Barbera for the most part were left in the background, with other producers receiving credit for most of the newer theatrical cartoons produced after 1957.

Tom and Jerry were originally conceived as cat and mouse enemies, and creating slapstick havoc was the basis for most of their cartoons. Except for occasional narration, most of the cartoons had no dialogue, with much of the tempo depending on hectic chase sequences that involved more than the usual amount of chaos.

Like most long-running theatrical cartoons, "Tom and Jerry" became an immediate television success, eventually moving into various Saturday morning time slots during the next two decades. Here is a rundown of the programming history of their schedule for CBS on Saturday mornings: 11:00–11:30 A.M., September 25, 1965, through September 10, 1966; 1:00–1:30 P.M., September 17, 1966, through September 8, 1967; 7:00–7:30 A.M., September 15, 1967, through September 17, 1972. In most of the newer cartoons made specifically for television, Tom and Jerry often had little in common with the characterizations of the 1940s and 1950s. Though audiences had become familiar with the pair's rivalry, the television cartoons focused far more on their situation antics as friends. Inspired by the formula of several of the 1960s' most popular situation comedies, Tom and Jerry appeared as bungling police patrolmen in "Calling All Scars," and "Afloat Without a Boat" paid homage to "Gilligan's Island" (CBS, 1964–67), with Tom and Jerry playing castaways in uncharted waters.

Beginning on September 6, 1975, after being with the CBS network for nearly ten seasons, Tom and Jerry reappeared on Saturday mornings after a three-year absence. This time the cartoons were presented on ABC, for the first time in a 60-minute format (8:00–9:00). In this version of the show the characters shared billing with a 60-foot purple ape, and the cartoons were produced at the studios of the original creators, William Hanna and Joseph Barbera, in association with MGM and Loews Productions. This program format aired for the last time on September 5, 1976. For three months during the following season (September 12, 1976, through December 26, 1976), Tom and Jerry and the Grape Ape were featured sharing star billing with Mumbley, the snickering hound, in "The Tom and Jerry/Grape Ape/Mumbley Show" airing in the 8:00–9:00 A.M. Saturday slot on ABC. In 1977 they were featured as an incorporated segment in reruns of "The Great Grape Ape Show." This series ran for one season on Sunday mornings (9:00–9:30 A.M., ABC, September 11, 1977, through September 3, 1978). In 1980 Tom and Jerry returned to their own series, as well as to Saturday mornings and to CBS, in "The Tom and Jerry Comedy Show," which ran for two seasons (8:30–9:00 A.M., September 6, 1980, through September 4, 1982). Here they were featured in a variety of new cartoons, with another incorporated MGM cartoon figure from the 1940s and 1950s, Droppy the Dog.

Like Bugs Bunny, Tom and Jerry are among the most familiar cartoon characters in television reruns. The "Tom and Jerry" adventures are second only to "The Pink Panther" as the last of the cinematic cartoons distributed for television. The characters remain as popular with young viewers today as they first were more than 50 years ago.

The "Tom Terrific" Shows
The Adventures of Tom Terrific / (Segment of Captain Kangaroo) / The New Adventures of Tom Terrific

The 1962 syndicated version of "Tom Terrific" was inspired by its huge success as a regular segment on the popular CBS "Captain Kangaroo" morning series which was televised on Monday through Friday throughout the 1950s. "Tom Terrific" appeared on the show at various times from 1955 to 1962 and then reappeared in 1964 until 1969.

Produced by Paul Terry and created by Gene Deitch as a CBS film incorporate, episodes featured the remarkable adventures of Tom Terrific, who possessed the amazing ability to transform himself into anything — animal, mineral, or vegetable — when he put on his funnel-shaped thinking cap. Naturally he chose to put his abilities to good use, helping humanity and fighting such despicable foes as Crabby Appleton, who was "rotten to the core"; Captain Kidney Bean, the Pirate; Silly Sam, the Sandman; the Flying Sorcerer; and Sweet-Tooth Sam, who was so mean he would even steal candy from a baby. Tom was assisted in every episode by his faithful canine companion, Mighty Manfred, the wonder dog, who would much rather curl up for a nap than fight villains.

Among the most popular of television cartoon creations of the 1950s, "Tom Terrific" stood out for a number of reasons. Breaking new ground as television's first juvenile hero, Tom acted out the ambivalence of children who envisioned themselves as triumphing over unsavory adults. Interestingly, the cartoons were immensely enjoyable even though they were presented in black and white in a series of line drawings with colorless backgrounds.

By the 1960s, Tom Terrific had gained such a following he was syndicated in September 1962 in his own 30-minute series called "The New Adventures of Tom Terrific." When originally presented on the "Captain Kangaroo" program, episodes began on Mondays and concluded on Fridays. The syndicated version was a compilation of the five five-minute episodes, which would make up an entire program. The newer version of the show was unfortunately short-lived, but episodes were repeated later when they returned to "Captain Kangaroo," where they alternated regularly with "Lariat Sam," another Gene Deitch creation.

"The Adventures of Tom Terrific" was Paul Terry's last original television production before he retired and sold his interest in Terrytoon Productions to the CBS network film library in 1956.

Underdog

"There's no need to fear — Underdog is here!" That was the familiar heroic cry of the canine caped defender, heard for ten full seasons at various times on both NBC and CBS. "Underdog" was the third and most popular Saturday morning cartoon series produced by Total Television Productions. (For further information about Total Television Productions, see the entry for "King Leonardo and His Short Subjects.") Like Mighty Mouse before him, Underdog was an amusing parody of the flying superheroes who possessed abilities far beyond those of other beings.

Based in Washington, D.C., Underdog, masquerading in the humble guise of a mild-mannered shoeshine boy, gained his super strength from a year's supply of energy pills he carried in a magic ring. Serial-like episodes often involved his continuing battle with evil figures who were obsessed with the idea of gaining control over the earth's resources.

Among them were the greedy Riff Raff, a seafaring wolf, and the sinister scientist Simon Bar Sinister, who created such inventions as the "Big Dipper Machine," which drained the world of its water supply, and the "Hypnotic Eye," which hypnotized anyone under its influence into doing what "Simon says."

Similar to Superman's Lois Lane was Underdog's occasional love interest, Sweet Polly Purebread, a television reporter who often fell into the hands of villains. Combining rhyme and reason, Underdog began each initial crusade with a bit of verse: "When the country's in trouble, I am not slow; it's up hip hip and away I go!" The lead voice was provided by a distinguished character actor, the late Wally Cox. Cox had previously become familiar to television's first generation of viewers as the mild-mannered Mr. Peepers on the show of the same name (NBC, 1952–55).

Various other segments included incorporated fillers from both the "King Leonardo" and the "Tennessee Tuxedo" shows. In 1966, when the series ended its run on NBC (Saturday mornings: 10:00–10:30, October 3, 1964, through September 4, 1965, and 10:30–11:00, September 11, 1965, through September 3, 1966), it moved to CBS for two more years of new episodes (Saturday mornings: 9:30–10:00 from September 10, 1966, through September 1, 1967; 7:30–8:00 from September 8, 1967, through September 7, 1968), with "The Go Go Gophers" appearing as the new incorporated segment. When "Underdog" was rerun by NBC in 1968 (Saturday, 11:30–12:00 noon, September 14, 1968, until August 6, 1969; Saturday, 12:30–1:00 P.M., September 13, 1969, through September 5, 1970), the Go Go Gophers, a pair of Indian rodents, remained on CBS for a brief period in a spinoff series of their own. The "Underdog" reruns lasted for two more seasons, then returned once again to the network in 1972 for a final season airing at 8:00 on Saturday mornings from September 2, 1972, through September 1, 1973.

"Underdog" was syndicated nationally in 1974 and by the end of the decade was rated among the top ten most popular syndicated children's shows on the air. The character's balloon likeness is still an annual feature of the Macy's Thanksgiving Day parade.

Tweety Show see *The "Bugs Bunny" Shows*

The U.S. of Archie see *The "Archie" Shows*

The "Woody Woodpecker" Shows
The Woody Woodpecker Show / The New Woody Woodpecker Show / Woody Woodpecker and Co.

Cartoonist Walter Lantz's world-famous Woody Woodpecker first came to television on October 3, 1957, after appearing previously as an immensely successful theatrical cartoon series for Universal Pictures. Hosted by Lantz himself, the television version made its debut on ABC originally as a Thursday evening replacement at 5:00 P.M. for the second half hour of "The Mickey Mouse Club." The program appeared in this slot until September 28, 1958. In addition to the featured antics of Woody and his friends Andy Panda, Chilly Willie, and costar Wally

Walrus, the show included a live segment, with Lantz explaining the various animation techniques. A former newspaper cartoonist, Lantz had begun his career as an animator for the New York Bray's Studios. He eventually became the lead story man for the Oswald Rabbit character, originally created by Walt Disney in 1927. When both he and Oswald were lent to Universal Studios several years later, Lantz was put under contract to create a new character similar to Tex Avery's Daffy Duck. According to a popular story, while Lantz was under pressure to come up with an idea, he was annoyed by the sound of a woodpecker outside his studio window. When he tried to frighten the bird away, it made a noise that resembled a hysterical laugh. Thus was born the concept of Woody Woodpecker.

Premiering in such shorts as "Knock Knock," "The Beach Nut," and "Who's Cooking Who?," Woody often appeared more antagonistic than lovable. He was a hyperactive bird with a childlike manner who would stop at absolutely nothing to have his own way, which more often than not inclined the viewer's sympathy more toward Woody's enemies than toward Woody himself. When the series returned to television in 1970 after a 12-year absence, Lantz responded to the new expectations regarding violence in children's television, toning Woody's nature down to make him appear a bit more tranquil.

Among the show's most familiar component features were the adventures of Chilly Willie, a little penguin who shyly strolled about the North Pole while dodging hungry animals or greedy poachers. "Andy Panda," another popular theatrical cartoon, involved the domestic adventures of Andy, a panda cub, and his "Pop." As in the sitcoms of the 1950s, Andy was always busy keeping his lovable, incompetent father from making a mess of things.

Several of the 1957 cartoon episodes were edited and repeated, along with 30 additional films, for the 1970 Saturday morning cartoon series on NBC. The newer series lasted for two whole seasons (8:30–9:00 A.M. from September 12, 1970, through January 9, 1971; 9:00–9:30 A.M. from January 16, 1971, through September 11, 1971; 8:30–9:00 A.M. from September 18, 1971, through September 2, 1972) and returned once again on Saturday mornings in 1976 (8:30–9:00 A.M. from September 11, 1976, through September 3, 1977). Since that time the Walter Lantz cartoons featuring Woody and his friends have been syndicated nationally on local stations, usually under the title "Woody Woodpecker and Co."

Vocal artist Mel Blanc was the first to do Woody's familiar whining voice. Walter Lantz's wife, Grace, followed Blanc, imitating every vocal sound, including Woody's victorious chuckle at the end of every cartoon.

The "Yogi Bear" Shows
The Yogi Bear Show / Yogi's Gang / Yogi's Space Race

"Yogi Bear" was the most popular television cartoon creation of the medium's first era. Created by William Hanna and Joseph Barbera, the "Yogi Bear" cartoons were first introduced as a component segment of the "Huckleberry Hound Show" in 1958. An inhabitant of Jellystone National Park, with his little bear buddy, Boo Boo, Yogi was for the most part a sarcastic, rule-breaking bear with a great yearning for picnic baskets who credited himself as being "smarter than the average bear." But Yogi was more than just an overweight pilfering pest. Whether demanding the same right as humans to ride the park train or traveling cross-country to assist the Chicago Bears in their battle against the Giants, Yogi interacted with life as he saw fit—he was wacky but also rebelliously sincere. Lacking the mass appeal of such cartoon superstars as Bugs Bunny and Mickey Mouse, Yogi Bear nonetheless projected a powerful image. The show was a golden parody of the human predicament as seen through the eyes of an animal who constantly agitated for equal consideration.

After three seasons of cartoons on "The Huckleberry Hound Show," Yogi appeared in his first spinoff series in January 1961. "The Yogi Bear Show" was the third Hanna-Barbera series to be syndicated (January 30, 1961) nationally on local stations, sponsored by Kellogg's Cereals. "Top Cat," the fourth Hanna-Barbera series to have Kellogg's as its sponsor, made its prime-time network debut later in the same year.

Featured along with Boo Boo and Yogi's friendly nemesis, Ranger Smith, several of the newer cartoons introduced such bright new characters as Cindy Bear, Yogi's love interest, and Park Ranger Tom Anderson, Ranger Smith's new assistant. Incorporated segments included "Snagglepuss," the happy-go-lucky mountain lion, who was first introduced on "The Quick Draw McGraw Show," and "Yakky Doodle," about a playful land-loving little duck, who also had previously appeared in some earlier Yogi Bear cartoons. While Snagglepuss resembled comedian Bert Lahr's cowardly lion from The Wizard of Oz, Yakky sounded as if he might have been related to Walt Disney's Donald Duck. Vocals for the series were provided by Daws Butler, Don Messick, Doug Young, Janet Waldo, and ventriloquist Jimmy Weldon, as Yakky Doodle.

During the early 1960s both Yogi and his pal Huckleberry Hound became national pitchmen for their sponsor, Kellogg's Corn Flakes. Their appeal to both children and adults created a merchandise phenomenon for the Hanna-Barbera Studios which has grossed over $100 million. Yogi's success also led to a 1961 comic strip that was syndicated in more than 100 newspapers nationwide, and in 1964 he became the first of the Hanna-Barbera characters to appear in a full-length theatrical production entitled *Hey There, It's Yogi Bear!*

During the 1970s Yogi even managed a few successful comebacks in a series of new cartoons that dealt with current issues. "Yogi's Gang" premiered on ABC in the fall of 1973, airing from 8:30 to 9:00 A.M., September 8, 1973, through August 31, 1974. The following season, the show returned to ABC in the 8:00 A.M. half hour slot and was aired from September 7, 1974, through August 30, 1975. It was Yogi's first in a series of Saturday morning spinoffs based on the "ABC Superstar Movie," *Yogi's Ark Lark,* presented on Saturday morning the previous season. Here Yogi battled such environmental enemies as Mr. Pollution, Mr. Litter, Mr. Waste, Mr. Prankster, and Mr. Bigot, along with several of the old Hanna-Barbera favorites who had been featured over the years in shows of their own. This series was followed closely by "Yogi's Space Race" in 1978 on NBC. Featured in a variety of different formats and time slots, this series gave the Yogi gang new adventures throughout the solar system. A weak attempt to recapture the flavor of the old series, "Space Race" was canceled in midseason. Here is the programming history of "Yogi's Space Race" which ran on NBC on Saturdays: 8:00–9:30 A.M., September 9, 1978, through October 28, 1978; 11:00–12:00 noon, November 4, 1978, through January 27, 1979; 8:00–8:30 A.M., February 3, 1979, through March 3, 1979. Today, after nearly ten years' absence, new episodes of "Yogi Bear" are shown in syndication, as are various cartoon episodes of the old shows. Yogi Bear's popularity has never diminished with viewers over the years.

3. Circus and Magic Shows

Magicians, clowns, and acrobats have unfortunately seen their day on weekly children's series. During the early years, however, network television competed for the right to entertain millions of youngsters with all types of programs involving three-ring circuses, lavishly dressed illusionists, trained animals, and miniskirted baton twirlers, all giving their best to entertain living rooms full of admiring young viewers and their mothers and fathers. Although these programs were similar to one another, each had some distinction that set it apart from the rest.

Many of these shows have been lost forever because they were one-time live performances. With television becoming more sophisticated, circus and magic shows were soon passed by, and fantasy took the place of variety as most children began to prefer animated talking animals to real ones.

The Big Top

This popular Saturday morning circus program for children highlighted the best of American and foreign novelty acts that had been featured throughout the world.

Hosted by ringmaster Jack Sterling, the program was broadcast weekly from Camden, New Jersey, through WCAU-TV, Philadelphia. It first aired for several months on a local CBS affiliate during the evening hours, before moving to the network's Saturday morning schedule airing from 12 to 1:00 P.M. beginning on July 10, 1950. A former carnival barker, Sterling had previously become a favorite with live audiences as a performer on the vaudeville circuit.

The series, unlike most other shows of its kind, allowed the viewer to see the circus in a way that most live audiences could not. A series of close-ups covered everything from tightrope performers to the inside of animal cages.

One of the show's most popular returning performers was a little clown known to audiences only as the Banana Man. He bore a resemblance to comedian Harpo Marx, and was identified with his whimsical obsession with a miniature train containing numerous crates of bananas.

Sealtest sponsored the series, which was produced by Charles Vanda. The regular performers included former Mr. America, Dan Luri, as Circus Dan, the strongman; New York state majorette champion Barbera Cubberly; and a young relatively unknown former radio personality named Ed McMahon as the head clown. Known to millions, of course, as Johnny Carson's announcer on the NBC "Tonight Show," McMahon had originally been hired for the job of head comedy writer for the show. His assuming the role of clown became Vanda's idea after MaMahon made a cameo appearance at the beginning of the program in which his nose lit up; this became a highlight of the series.

Artists for the programs were often booked several months in advance by George Hamid and his sons, the owners and proprietors of Hamidy's Steer Pier in Atlantic City.

Four years after the show's first live television appearance, the series moved its locale to North Philadelphia, with a weekly budget of only $12,000 per show — a small amount, considering the cost of production and of hiring different performing artists.

Being a live production, the series had more than its share of surprises. During several productions, animals became frightened, leading to uncontrolled behavior. Once, a small fire engulfed most of the clowns in front of thousands of television viewers across the country; they were assured that it was all part of the act.

"The Big Top" enjoyed seven successful years at the head of the CBS Saturday morning lineup of programs for children. During these years, the series managed to stay a step ahead of the competition, including both live dramatic and animated shows. On September 21, 1957, the show boarded the Sealtest circus train for one final time, leaving behind it an entire era in children's programming.

Circus Time

Hosted by ventriloquist Paul Winchell, this series featured a half hour of novelty acts from some of America's best-known circus shows. Embellished with great extravagance, the series became the first of such early efforts to feature on occasion big-name celebrities in unlikely daredevil performances. It was forerunner to today's prime-time "Circus of the Stars" specials. The show appeared on ABC on Thursday night from 8:00 to 8:30. First appearing on October 4, 1956, the last show aired June 27, 1957.

Although many of the acts had previously been performed on such shows as "Super Circus" (ABC, 1949–56) and "The Big Top" (CBS, 1950–57), each was presented with the flourish of an original performance.

The real star of the show, however, was Paul Winchell, who once again lent his fine talents to an otherwise ordinary parade of repetitive but enjoyable kiddy fare. His dialogue between acts with dummies Jerry Mahoney and Knucklehead Smiff helped provide the series with some lively characterizations. The series was only one of several prime-time shows to feature the multitalented performer (*see* chapter 8, "Puppets, Marionettes, and Dummies").

"Circus Time" was a production of Bill Hyer, sponsored by Hartz Mountain pet foods.

Hollywood Junior Circus

This 60-minute series of circus novelty acts was originally produced for CBS as a Sunday morning companion series to Saturday morning's "The Big Top." Sponsored by the Hollywood Candy Company ("The great big bars with the great big stars"), the show had previously been scheduled to begin in January 1951 on CBS. But the network's last-minute decision to cancel the project resulted in a $1 million lawsuit by Hollywood Candy, which left more than a bitter taste in the mouths of CBS executives.

Hosted by ringmaster Art Jacobson, the series moved to the NBC network in March 1951. Carl Marx costarred as Jacobson's assistant, Carl the Clown. Midget Max Bronstein was featured enticing kids each week by eating the show's sponsor's product. The show was presented on Sunday afternoons opposite ABC's top-rated "Super Circus," appearing at 4:00 from March 25, 1951, through July 1, 1951.

In its second season, "Hollywood Junior Circus" ended up on ABC in the 10:30–11:30 Saturday morning slot, first appearing September 8, 1951, and shown last on January 19, 1952. Only Max Bronstein returned for the revised series. Art Jacobson and Carl Marx were replaced by Paul Barnes as ringmaster and Buffo, the Master Clown. Lacking the lavish settings and musical choreography previously presented by the best in the business, the show still featured a fine variety of winning acts and performances.

Both versions of the series were actually broadcast live from Chicago (not Hollywood, which referred only to the sponsor), a production of Bill Hyer and George Byrne.

International Showtime

Actor Don Ameche hosted this hour-long Friday night series that showcased performing acts, from the European traveling circuses to the best in circus acts from all around the world. While it never really captured the thrill and excitement of a live circus, the show was especially interesting to those who had never had the opportunity to visit one in person. It also provided viewers with the chance to see interviews with the directors and stars of some of the most popular circus acts.

Although this circus emphasized the European style, as opposed to the "thrills and chills" of American circuses, the acts were entertaining and managed to get good ratings for NBC, opposite such top-notch shows as "Rawhide" (CBS, 1959–66) and "The Gallant Men" (ABC, 1962–63). "International Showtime" aired at 7:30, first appearing on September 15, 1961. Unfortunately for the casual viewer, however, live circus acts are seldom presented effectively in an edited made-for-television format.

The program originally intended to feature a different celebrity host each week. But this changed, and Don Ameche, an unlikely candidate, wound up serving as master of ceremonies throughout the show's entirety. A distinguished actor since the 1930s, Don Ameche became known in films for his portrayals of the debonair man-about-town. His typecasting in light comedy came about in 1943 after he played the lead in Ernst Lubitsch's critically acclaimed *Heaven Can Wait*. He later made several successful comebacks in both television and movies. His roles in such hit films of the 1980s as *Trading Places* (1983) and *Cocoon* (1985) received praise from the critics.

Initially intended for a limited run, "International Showtime" lasted for four years on NBC's prime-time schedule until September 10, 1965, before being replaced by the situation comedies "Camp Runamuck" and "Hank."

The Magic Clown

Presented on Sunday mornings at 8:30, this early 15-minute series was produced in front of a live children's audience, which participated in a variety of magic and games. Produced for NBC, the series was hosted by Zovella, the Magic Clown, an illusionist and prestidigitator, who amazed children between games with his artful tricks and deceptions. Sponsored by the Bonomo Candy Company, "The Magic Clown" became one of the first programs to be sponsored nationally for children on Sunday mornings, first airing on September 11, 1949. Written and directed by Al Garry, the series was a very early attempt to capture the imagination of young viewers without alarming them, as certain illusions might be quite frightening. With only 15 minutes to air, each show usually consisted of two tricks between children competing for prizes of Bonomo's Turkish Taffy.

After five seasons on NBC, Zovella performed his greatest vanishing act as he disappeared from television altogether. The final show aired on June 27, 1954. Al Garry continued during the decade as coproducer of several children's shows even less familiar than "The Magic Clown."

The Magic Land of Alakazam

Illusionist Mark Wilson and his wife, Nani Darnell, were the host and hostess of this popular Saturday morning kid's show that blended magic tricks with a delightful mixture of music and fantasy.

Alakazam was an enchanted land, home to puppets Basil and Bernie Bunny, Doris the darling dove, and Charles, the charming chicken, who constantly needed Mark's help in overcoming Evilo, the malicious wizard of Alakazam. Inserted weekly as a continuing segment, each story contained just enough humor and suspense to keep audiences happily returning for more. Others featured throughout the series were Mike Wilson, Mark's young son; Bev Bergerson, as Rebo the Clown; and Bob Towner, as the king of Alakazam. During the show's first year, while being sponsored by Kellogg's cereals, Hanna-Barbera cartoon characters Huckleberry Hound, Yogi Bear, and Pixie, Dixie, and Mr. Jinks were featured periodically as incorporated segments of the program.

Wilson first brought his magic to television in 1954 in a show called "Time for Magic," which was broadcast over a local Dallas station. The show eventually led to "The Magic Circus" in 1959, as Wilson first began to appear with his wife and assistant, Nani Darnell. The show soared so high in the local ratings that the following year it was picked up by CBS, revised, and given a live audience and a new title, "The Magic Land of Alakazam."

For two seasons (October 1, 1960, through September 22, 1962) appearing from 11:00 to 11:30 A.M., Wilson delighted youngsters with his magical land of fun, excitement, and puppets. Another segment of the show entitled "Kookies" consisted entirely of sight gags that emphasized on the type of humor that kids really enjoyed.

In a futile attempt to lure children away from the land of Alakazam, ABC launched a magic series of its own entitled "The Magic Ranch," hosted by magician Don Alan. But it was unable to compete with Wilson's show, so ABC coaxed Wilson over to its side with a handsome salary that even CBS found difficult to match. In the fall of 1962, the series was presented on Saturday mornings over the ABC network one hour earlier than previously scheduled by CBS, and it lasted on the air for another two seasons. The programming slot was 10:00–10:30 A.M., appearing from September 29, 1962, through December 28, 1963, and from April 25, 1964, through December 12, 1964.

Both the CBS and ABC versions of "The Magic Land of Alakazam" were produced by Dan Whitman. Mark Wilson served as executive producer.

Magic Midway

One of television and radio's most familiar vocal personalities, Claude Kirchner, appeared as ringmaster and host of this short-lived but likable Saturday morning circus show for children. Kirchner had previously been the host for "Super Circus" in the 1950s; he later became recognizable as spokesman for the Marx toy company, a position he accepted in 1958.

Accompanying Kirchner were baton-twirling majorette Bonnie Lee and circus performers Phil Kiley, Bill Bailey, and Douglas ("Mr. Pocus") Anderson, a magician. Jack Miller, coproducer and creator of "Captain Kangaroo," served as the show's producer.

Although most of the acts were adequate, the show was mostly a thinly disguised promotional tool for Marx toys, the show's sponsor. The series is best remembered as being among the last of the original Saturday morning circus programs for kids. The show appeared from 11:30 P.M. to 12:00, beginning on September 22, 1962. Although Kirchner tried hard to recreate some of the fun and excitement generated by his earlier series, "Magic Midway" presented itself more as a long advertisement for the Ringling Brothers Circus. In fairness to the series, a few programs were enhanced with bright performances and high-quality special effects.

Younger children who remembered neither "Super Circus" or "The Big Top" found the show all the more appealing. Unfortunately, however, NBC canceled the series after just six months, last appearing on March 16, 1963.

Super Circus

This long-running Sunday afternoon circus program was hosted by former radio personality Claude Kirchner as ringmaster and by the beautiful Mary Hartline as hostess. Produced by Jack Gibney, the series was broadcast live during its first six years from Chicago over the ABC network, where it ruled its time slot (4:00–5:00) for over six seasons (January 16, 1949, through June 3, 1956). The show is probably remembered far better than many for its outstanding variety of music, comedy, animal acts, and audience participation, all held in front of an imaginative but realistic circus background. Other cast members included regulars Cliffy Sobier, Sandy ("Scampy") Dobitch, and Nicky Francis as the show's clowns. The 60-minute series was sponsored during most of its run by Quaker Puff cereals—"The only cereal shot from guns," which was proved at the end of every show by actually shooting the cereal from a cannon.

Like all good circuses, this series offered something for everyone: there were clowns, trapeze artists, tightrope walkers, jugglers, magicians, and every type of trained animal, from chimpanzees to elephants. Having previously been broadcast over radio in the 1940s, "Super Circus" went on to become the highest-rated new children's television program of its time and the only daytime show to rank among the network's top 20 shows.

According to Kirchner, although the radio show centered around a variety of acts and stunts, it failed to create a true image of the circus and its surroundings. When the opportunity for television arrived in 1949, the productions became a live series of shows that featured a different circus format every week. One program, for instance, was devoted entirely to the clown profession, which included the work of mimes and other artists who perform in makeup. Some shows consisted of aerial acrobatics, cyclists, trampolinists, and animal trainers, who amazed viewers both at home and in the audience with their thrilling feats of daring. As on CBS's "The Big Top" (which this show closely resembled), there were several unexpected incidents that placed cast and crew under great stress. But everyone became adept at dealing with such incidents, making them appear to the home viewers as quite normal.

Many times headliners were shown promoting the program's commercial products. It was "Super Circus" that first proved to children everywhere that M&M's "melts in your mouth, not in your hand," a slogan that has made this product into the nation's largest "seller of bagged candy" today.

Because it was presented via kinescope, many local ABC affiliates were forced to delay broadcast until the following week, where the show was featured on Saturday mornings between the hours of 9:00 and 10:00 A.M.

A contributing factor in the show's huge success was the appeal of Mary Hartline. A former cheerleader, majorette, and beauty contestant, she had good looks and a charming personality that instantly transformed her from the girl next door into an international sex symbol who sent both adolescent males and idolizing females scurrying to television screens in droves.

During its sixth season, "Super Circus" moved to New York. Both Claude Kirchner and Mary Hartline remained in Chicago to pursue a series of related interest. They were replaced by comedian Jerry Colonna and Sandy Worth in the show's remaining season on the air.

Six foot, five inch Claude Kirchner later became one of television and radio's most recognizable voices, for advertising kids' products. He first became acquainted with the circus world in 1936 as a young man when he became one of the finest carnival barkers in the business. A few years later he accepted a job as a commercial announcer for a local radio station in Dallas. His deep baritone voice attracted the attention of local ABC affiliates that were planning to air a national circus program for children. The success of the radio version of "Super Circus" brought Kirchner worldwide television exposure and then a position as spokesman for Marx toys when he left the series in 1955. In 1962 he hosted the short-lived Saturday morning series "Magic Midway."

Mary Hartline continued to promote her fairy godmother image as the star of a local Chicago children's program entitled "Princess Mary's Castle." Earlier, she had lent her talents to a 15-minute daily series, as talk show hostess of "The Mary Hartline Show."

With the onrush of competing shows, mainly Westerns and other live-action dramas, it is surprising that "Super Circus" lasted as long as it did. The series, though barely recalled today, once stood out as a superior entry in the then familiar genre of circus programs.

4. Comedy Shows

During television's infancy, producers found children's comedy the most suitable choice to fill any programming gaps. Knowing that kids would laugh at almost anything funny, they scheduled theatrical shorts and situation comedy reruns. Although shows such as "Gilligan's Island," "Leave It to Beaver," and "The Munsters" were not originally meant for the children's hour, each has remained extremely popular in syndication with generations of new audiences. It was decided in the 1970s that perhaps a new set of situation comedies—this time tailor-made for a Saturday morning children's audience—could enjoy the success of original sitcoms. The results, however, proved that this was a mistake. While kids continued to watch shows like "The Brady Bunch" on weekdays, newer ones such as "The Ghost Busters" and "Far Out Space Nuts" were no match for their competition—the Saturday morning cartoons.

The Abbott and Costello Show

Bud Abbott and Lou Costello were one of America's most popular comedy teams in the 1940s and 1950s. Abbott, the tall, irascible straight man, and Costello, the burly fall guy, made a total of 52 half-hour shows for television during the 1950s which highlighted many of their old routines from burlesque, radio, and feature films. They had originally made their television debut as guest hosts on the NBC "Colgate Comedy Hour" before beginning production in 1951 on their own weekly series.

Although there were several stories about how the two comics actually came to form a team, most film historians agree that their status as an established comedy duo resulted from a single guest appearance on "The Kate Smith Hour" radio show in 1938, where they disregarded

Bud Abbott (right) and Lou Costello.

their written material and performed their own rendition of "Who's on First" for the first time to a national audience. The success of their performance led to other radio appearances and eventually to their own program, as well as a contract with Universal Pictures, where they remained on the list of top ten money-making film stars for nearly ten years.

The television series was directed by Jean Yasbrough, while Lou's brother Pat Costello served as executive producer for the final 26 episodes.

In each show, Abbott and Costello played themselves, as two unemployed actors down on their luck, often working a variety of jobs in an effort to pay their back rent. In the premiere episode, "The Drug Store," Lou becomes a frustrated soda jerk. In another, they attempt to sell pots and pans door to door, and in one of their funniest, they become salesmen for a discount roller skate company, with business cards that read ABBOTT AND COSTELLO — CHEAP SKATES.

"The Abbott and Costello Show" was aided by an impressive stock company of supporting players, all of whom had previously worked with the comedians. Sidney Fields was featured regularly as the overbearing landlord; he was also seen in a variety of other roles, often as his own relatives. In an episode entitled "Jail," he appeared as Bud and Lou's lawyer and as a jail inmate who became frantic whenever Lou mentioned the term *Niagara Falls*. In "Peace and Quiet," he played a doctor attempting to cure Lou of insomnia, and "Getting a Job" had him playing the head of the Fields Employment Agency. Fields also doubled as one of the show's head writers. Other cast members included Lou's brother-in-law Joe Kirk, as Mr. Bacciagalype, an Italian street vendor; Gordon Jones, as Mike the Cop; Joe Besser, as Lou's childlike pal Stinky Davis; and Hillary Brook, the first season, and Joan Shawlee, the second, as the female regulars.

The half hour show was originally presented in syndication, and it aired on Friday nights at 10:00 during its premiere presentations under the sponsorship of the Chevrolet Company, from 1952 to 1954. In the fall of 1954, the series was syndicated once again but this time for rebroadcast on Saturday mornings by the Campbell Soup Company. This was considered an odd time slot for the comedians, but a large portion of their audience was composed of admiring children, and Saturday mornings seemed like an ideal time to highlight the team's comic shenanigans.

During the first 26 episodes, each show opened with Abbott and Costello emerging from behind a curtain (like Burns and Allen), where their conversation with an imaginary audience set the premise for the show. Many of these episodes were composed of the team's most memorable routines, including their famous baseball sketch, "Who's on First." Many of the skits after a time became so predictable and so very, very silly that it seemed as if they were being performed for the first time. In the episode "Getting a Job," for instance, Bud explained to a perplexed Lou that he had found a loafing job in a bakery shop and learned his trade from a long line of loafers. In the same episode, Bud and Lou recreated their "Floogle Street" routine from burlesque, in which they encounter several loonies on the street who go crazy whenever Lou asks for directions to the Susquehanna Hat Company on Floogle Street.

The show's second season, however, appeared a bit more limited and was not quite as funny. Because of poor health, both Abbott and Costello were no longer up to the physical demands that their type of comedy required, and it often showed. To make matters worse, these episodes suffered from a much too noisy laugh track.

In February 1959, in conjunction with the resurgence of the Three Stooges films (which "Abbott and Costello" closely resembled), "The Abbott and Costello Show" was resyndicated on weekdays, where it alternated in several markets with sitcom reruns of "My Little Margie," "Amos 'n' Andy," and "I Married Joan."

Today, 40 years after the premiere of the first episode, "The Abbott and Costello Show" is still one of the most widely syndicated series in the United States, proving that their timeless appeal has remained unchanged.

In 1966 Hanna and Barbera produced a series of cartoons based on the comedians which featured the voice of Bud Abbott as himself.

The Brady Bunch

Actor Robert Reed starred as Mike Brady, a successful architect and widower with three sons: Greg (Barry Williams), the oldest, Peter (Christopher Knight), and Bobby (Michael Lookinland). In the premiere episode, Mike is engaged to Carol Martin, played by Florence Henderson. Carol has been left a widow and is the mother of three daughters: Marcia (Maureen McCormick), the oldest, Jan (Eve Plumb), and Cindy (Susan Olsen). After a somewhat rocky beginning, the two families eventually become one (with the girls even adopting the Brady name), and the premise for each succeeding episode was set. Ann B. Davis was also featured as Alice Nelson, the Brady's dutiful, wisecracking housekeeper, who had more one-liners than Henny Youngman.

Produced and written by Sherwood Schwartz, the series was loosely based on the 1968 film *Yours, Mine and Ours,* which starred Henry Fonda and Lucille Ball.

Like most situation comedy shows of the 1960s, "The Brady Bunch" told the usual stories of families in unpredictable situations. But unlike the shows of the previous era, which usually linked a wholesome atmosphere and the hectic lives of scatterbrained adults, "The Brady Bunch" was geared primarily toward the juvenile audience, as most of the stories revolved around the Brady children. For some viewers, the show represented the depths to which television families sank in the years between "Ozzie and Harriet" and "All in the Family." Nevertheless, the corny but lovable clan has become a television mainstay in reruns ever since it left the network in 1974.

Here is the programming history of the ABC Friday night show: 8:00–8:30, September 26, 1969, through September 18, 1970; 7:30–8:00, September 25, 1970, through September 15, 1972; 8:00–8:30, September 22, 1972, through August 30, 1974.

Over the years, fans have become familiar with such plots as these: little Bobby defending little Cindy against the bully at school; Peter juggling two dates on the same night with a look-alike classmate; and the boys sabotaging the girls' pajama party. Each episode ended with a moral provided by Dad Brady, in his best Ward Cleaver impersonation. Several stories revolved around the sibling rivalry of Marcia, the rosy-cheeked teen idol, and Jan, the smart but introverted wallflower, each of whom secretly envied the other.

Barry Williams in particular became popular with teenage girls. In the 1970s, he became the lead vocalist when the Brady kids formed their own singing group, The Brady Six. In a 1973 episode they performed their first hit single, "Time to Change." It was also during this period that an animated version of the group entitled "The Brady Kids" appeared on Saturday mornings featuring the vocals of the young actors.

When "The Brady Bunch" ended its original prime-time run on ABC, it was released immediately into syndication where it became a daytime hit among youngsters of all ages. Reruns of the series became so popular that there were demands for a revival. In 1977 most of the original cast returned to their roles for a musical variety hour in which the Bradys entertained at home. Four years later the Brady cast returned once gain, this time for a two-hour television movie sequel to the original series entitled *The Brady Girls Get Married*, in which Marcia and Jan make plans for a double wedding. As a result, a short-lived spinoff series entitled "The Brady Brides" ran for two months on NBC.

Dennis the Menace

Based on the popular Hank Ketchum comic strip, this show featured Jay North as the mischievous little rascal Dennis Mitchell for four years on Sunday nights. In an attempt to attract as many youngsters to the program as possible, it was sponsored for most of its run by Kellogg's cereals—which by now had changed its slogan from "The Greatest Name in Cereal" to "The Best to You Each Morning."

Like the comic strip character, Dennis was forever at odds with adults, who often found him annoying, unlike his friends, who considered him something of a hero.

Herbert Anderson costarred as Dennis's easygoing father, Henry, who resembled his comic strip counterpart even more closely than North did Dennis. Gloria Henry portrayed his mother, Alice, and Joseph Kearns played his long-suffering neighbor and main antagonist, "good old" George Wilson. After Kearns's unexpected death midway through the third season, familiar character actor Gale Gordon joined the cast, as John Wilson, George's brother. Other cast members included Sylvia Field, as the kindly Martha Wilson (George's wife), Billy Booth and Gil Smith, respectively, as Dennis's friends Tommy and Joey, and Jeannie Russell, as his female nemesis, the snooty Margaret Wade (also called, in several episodes, Margaret Moore).

Typical episodes usually involved Dennis and his well-meaning but capricious attempts to help his parents and grown-up neighbors with problems he considers "too big" for them to handle alone. Dennis usually lives up to his reputation as a menace by presenting himself to others as an overly precocious six-year-old with an inadvertent penchant for causing trouble. In the premiere episode, for instance, Dennis eludes his baby-sitter and rides his tricycle into a movie theater in search of his parents.

"Dennis the Menace" appeared on Sunday nights from 7:00 to 8:00, beginning on October 4, 1959. The final episode aired on September 22, 1963. After four seasons and a total of 146 episodes, Jay North outgrew his role. Following a pattern set by the show's closest rival, "Leave It to Beaver," "Dennis the Menace" was rerun for a time in syndication, but it failed to capture a large audience.

Jay North continued to act throughout the 1960s in both film and television. In 1967 he costarred in the hour-long adventure series, "Maya," about the friendship of two boys who lived in India with their pet elephant Maya. He was also featured during this period in the Ivan Tors film *Zebra in the Kitchen,* with costars Marshall Thompson and Andy Devine. In the 1970s, he provided the voice characterization for the teenage Bamm-Bamm in the Hanna-Barbera cartoon series "The Pebbles and Bamm-Bamm Show."

Although reruns of "Dennis the Menace" have been hard to find, the show can be seen today on the cable Nickelodeon network. Harry Ackerman served as executive producer for the series. A cartoon version of the Hank Ketchum characters also appears in syndication today.

Far Out Space Nuts

In the mid–1970s, a new wave of situation comedies for Saturday mornings was conceived, to begin what network executives and producers hoped would become the creative choice of children. If successful, these new shows and others like them would become the best alternatives to the violent cartoon shows that had dominated the networks for nearly two decades. Ironically, most of these new programs lasted for only a single season, and some are rarely remembered today.

"Far Out Space Nuts" is one of the best-remembered of these shows. Created by producers Sid and Marty Krofft, the 30-minute series featured Bob Denver and Chuck McCann as two maintenance workers for NASA who accidentally launch themselves into space after being locked overnight in a rocket ship. The show appeared on Saturday morning at 9:30 on CBS from September 6, 1975, through September 4, 1976.

Each week Barney (McCann) and Junior (Denver) would travel

through the galaxy, encountering new friends such as Honk (Patty Moloney), an alien pet with a long, horned nose, and space pals Lantana (Eve Bruce) and Crakor (Stan Jensor) the robot, while trying to find their way back to earth.

Filmed at the old Samuel Goldwyn Studios, episodes were a concoction of adventure and slapstick in its purest form. Stories often involved Barney and Junior's entanglements with various space monsters, created of papier-mâché costumes that appeared laughable even to the youngest viewers. Several episodes attempted to parody the old Flash Gordon serials of the 1930s, with, for instance, Junior humorously battling the ferocious Malak, the Gladiator of Death, and the wicked Kayla, the would-be ruler of the universe.

Bob Denver, a name that has become synonymous with "far out" comedy, had previously made a name for himself in such hit comedy shows as "The Many Loves of Dobie Gillis" (CBS, 1959–63) and the cult favorite, "Gilligan's Island" (CBS, 1964–67). A natural for children's television, Denver proved that his appeal, like that of former Dead End Kid Huntz Hall, was better suited to a children audience than to an adult, which he demonstrated far better in "Space Nuts" than any previous series.

Chuck McCann had previously provided his vocal talents as the voice of Oliver Hardy in a series of cartoons based on the characters Stan Laurel and Oliver Hardy, produced by Larry Harmon. He had also been the star of his own local television series, "The Chuck McCann Show," in 1963. But he is perhaps best remembered as the jovial jester who shares a medicine cabinet with his next-door neighbor in the Right Guard deodorant commercials of the late 1960s.

"Far Out Space Nuts" was one of the first shows of its kind to feature live action with comedy adventure on Saturday mornings. Unfortunately, it lasted for only a year, as it proved no match for its strongest competitor, the profitable cartoon series.

The Funny Manns

Silent comedy shorts from Hollywood's golden era was the basic concept of this compilation film series hosted by Cliff Norton. A change of pace from the type of assembly line shows usually presented to children, "The Funny Manns" was presented in most cases to audiences by a local television host, who featured them regularly with such other favorites as "Popeye," "Little Lulu," "The Little Rascals," and "The Three Stooges." When presented separately (as in several independent markets), two

15-minute episodes were run back to back, with Norton appearing in the commercials as Tootsie Roll Mann. "The Funny Manns" was syndicated in September 1960.

The series included some outstanding silent comedy films that starred such comedians of the silver screen as Ben Turpin, Chester Conklin, Andy Clyde, Harry Langdon, Bobby Vernon, the comedy team Tons of Fun, and seven-year-old Mickey Rooney, as a Little Rascal–type character who was called Mickey "Himself" McGuire. Several films even featured a young Stan Laurel, years before he teamed up with Oliver Hardy.

To introduce children to this series of vintage films, veteran character actor Cliff Norton was chosen because of his slow-moving but unique method of getting the attention of his audience. It was Norton's own idea to portray a different character in each segment who would blend into the film's story. So, Norton dressed accordingly, each time differently, while crediting his experience to the "Funny Mann" in the preceding film. Bobby Nicholson was featured in several introductory segments as Norton's foil.

"The Funny Manns" was featured for a brief period throughout the mid–1960s. Regrettably, it is one of the better children's comedy compilations which rarely (if ever) resurfaces.

The Ghost Busters

This 30-minute situation comedy series featured the former stars of "F-Troop" (ABC, 1965–67): Larry Storch, as Eddie Spenser, and Forrest Tucker, as Kong. Together they fought the spirits of historical villains with their pet gorilla, Tracy (Bob Burns), which completed the trio of ghost busters — Spenser, Tracy, and Kong.

Unlike today's animated version of the movie *Ghostbusters*, this group handled their problems with methods more deceptive than inventive, and even the villains were presented strictly for laughs. The show's attempt to parody some of the Hollywood's most popular horror clichés helped it succeed in an old formula, the scare comedy. In one episode, for instance, the trio investigated a deserted roadside motel, haunted by the memories of its former owners, a reclusive young man and his invalid mother. The show first appeared on September 6, 1975, in the 9:00 program slot where it remained through September 4, 1976.

While much of the fun in the series came from the reteaming of Larry Storch and Forrest Tucker, it was Storch who created most of the comedy. He first appeared in children's television as early as 1960 when he provided the voices for a number of animated characters for Total Television Productions.

Created by Mark Richards and produced by Norm Prescott, the series preceded "Far Out Space Nuts" on Saturday mornings, a show that made its debut on the same day and network. Both series, filmed as children's situation comedies, were to serve as alternatives to the usual type of children's programs, a venture that cost the network a lot of money. Situation comedies, old or new, have proved to be less successful on Saturdays when up against the durable cartoon show, a factor that has remained constant for over four decades.

Gilligan's Island

Created and produced by Sherwood Schwartz, this off-beat comedy, starring Bob Denver in the title role, surprisingly became one of the top-rated new shows of the 1964 television season. Considered unanimously by critics to be one of the "worst TV shows ever," the series concerned itself with the misadventures of seven stranded castaways on an uncharted island somewhere in the Pacific. Bob Denver played Gilligan, the inept first mate of the shipwrecked excursion boat, the SS *Minnow*; Alan Hale, Jr., costarred as the Skipper, Jonas Grumby; Jim Backus and Natalie Schafer, as the wealthy Mr. and Mrs. Thurston Howell III, from Wall Street; Tina Louise, as sultry movie star Ginger Grant; Russell Johnson, as a professor of science, Roy Hinkley; and Dawn Wells as Kansas farm girl Mary Ann Summers. Here is the programming history of this CBS half hour primetime comedy: Saturday, 8:30, September 26, 1964, through September 4, 1965; Thursday, 8:00, September 16, 1965, through September 8, 1966; Monday, 7:30, September 19, 1966, through September 4, 1967.

Although fans of the series may find it difficult to imagine anyone but Denver in the role of the bungling crewman, Schwartz had originally considered several other actors for the part, including comedian Jerry Van Dyke. He feared that Denver's previous role as the bearded beatnik buddy of Dobie Gillis had become permanently embedded in the minds of most viewers. As it turned out, it was the role of Gilligan (whose first name was never revealed) that Denver would find hard to erase.

In 1973 Denver appeared in a new and thinly disguised version of "Gilligan's Island" with a new set of costars and a different setting. Titled "Dusty's Trail," this series concerned seven stranded homesteaders on their way West; it was also created and produced by Sherwood Schwartz.

While critics had a field day lambasting the series for its absurd plots, inane situations, and inferior dialogue, "Gilligan's Island" nevertheless became extremely popular with young viewers, especially when shown in syndicated reruns beginning in 1968.

Perhaps what irritated critics most was the way in which outsiders were allowed complete feedom to leave the island, while the castaways remained, ever helpless. This problem was remedied some ten years later, when most of the cast returned for a series of sequels based on the original programs. Tina Louise was replaced in these sequels by Judith Baldwin. In the first, "Rescue from Gilligan's Island" (NBC, 1978), the castaways are finally returned home after a hurricane sweeps them to the shores of civilization. The show proved so successful that more sequels appeared the following year: "The Castaways on Gilligan's Island" and "The Harlem Globetrotters on Gilligan's Island," both over the NBC network. In the 1970s and 1980s, two animated versions of "Gilligan's Island" appeared on Saturday mornings, with most members of the original cast providing their own voices.

Presuming that much of the show's success came from Bob Denver's childlike appeal to youngsters, Schwartz, a former writer for "The Red Skelton Show" (NBC, CBS, 1951–71), helped create the show's broad slapstick humor. It was his first successful series as a producer and a forerunner to such other children's favorites as "The Brady Bunch," where he served as executive producer.

The Krofft Super Show / The Krofft Superstar Hour

This 60-minute comedy variety series first appeared on ABC, hosted by a rock group called Kaptain Kool and the Kongs. The group included actors Michael Lembeck, as Kaptain Kool, Debbie Clinger, as Superchick, Mickey McMell, as Turkey, and Louise Duart, as Nashville; they introduced the several live components that formed the basis of the series. The show was televised at 11:00 on Saturday mornings from September 11, 1976, through September 2, 1978.

Segments featured at various times included the filmed comedy adventures of Wonderbug, an amazing magical Volkswagen owned by teenagers John Anthony Bailey, David Levy, and Carol Anne Seffinger; "Electra Woman and Dyna Girl," starring Deidre Hall and Judy Strangis as two female reporters turned superheroines; "Dr. Shrinker," with midget Billy Barty, Ted Eccles, Jeff Mckay, and Susan Lawrence as a group of kids miniaturized by a mad scientist, Dr. Cyclops, played by actor Jay Robinson; and "The Lost Saucer," a segment originally considered a series of its own, which featured the combined talents of comedian and singer Jim Nabors and former "Laugh-In" regular Ruth Buzzi as two visitors from an advanced planet who are set adrift to study the inhabitants of earth.

The show, produced by brothers Sid and Marty Krofft, was another in a series of innovative programs designed to attract the attentions of cartoon-watching youngsters. Although kids were generally enthusiastic about the show's variety, it became all too obvious after a time that the complicated story lines contained little humor and used a formula that could not compete with the onrush of action-oriented cartoon shows.

In the fall of 1978, "The Krofft Super Show" switched over from ABC to NBC in a retitled version of the series, "The Krofft Superstar Hour." In this version, the series was hosted by the popular rock group the Bay City Rollers, with the basic premise remaining unchanged. It lasted for a total of seven weeks (Saturday, 11:30–12:30 P.M., September 9, 1978, through October 28, 1978).

Laurel and Hardy

Hal Roach was one of the first of the former movie producers to find new opportunities in reviving his old film properties for early television. His popular "Laurel and Hardy" comedy shorts, produced by the Roach Studios in the 1930s, became among the first of these acts to benefit from the new medium as early as 1948.

The characters, played by Stan Laurel as a skinny, lovable, but dim-witted chap, and a jovial Oliver Hardy, who was just as dim-witted but unwilling to acknowledge it, generated more laughter than any others of their era. Characterized in each film by endless buffoonery and pratfalls, the comedians became naturals for television and a huge hit with children who had never seen them perform. Their screen appeal stemmed from their likable personalities, which differentiated them from most other screen comics. Abbott and Costello, for instance, relied heavily on witty verbal exchanges, and the Marx Brothers on pandemonium, but Laurel and Hardy always played themselves as the unfortunate victims of life's simplest problems, having only themselves to blame for the inevitable catastrophes that occurred in all of their films. The basis of each film was always the same: to place Laurel and Hardy in the most simple of situations and sit back and watch the fun and mayhem begin.

Originally appearing as single artists in the silent films of comedy

Stan Laurel and Oliver Hardy from the Hal Roach Laurel and Hardy television shorts.

producer Mack Sennett, Laurel and Hardy appeared in their first film together in 1917, titled *Lucky Dog*. In it, Oliver portrayed a burglar who held a frightened Stan at gunpoint. A few years later, Laurel and Hardy were persuaded by Roach director Leo McCarey to join forces and become a team. The decision proved to be a wise one, and the comics eventually came to be known as the "most successful, beloved comedy team of all time."

The comedies were syndicated in August 1948. By the end of the 1950s and into early 1960s, the "Laurel and Hardy" comedies were featured on a regular syndicated basis, usually presented by a local host with whom children were familiar in their hometowns. Many episodes were released individually by such early television syndicators as the Interstate Television Corporation and the Official Film Company. The latter was responsible for bringing to television such obscure theatrical cartoons as "The Little King," "Brownie Bear," and "Dick and Larry" (two characters who rarely spoke a word but bore some similarity to Laurel and Hardy).

Regrettably, the Hal Roach shorts, along with many edited versions of the team's feature films, were presented on television without the comics receiving a cent in residuals. Stan Laurel, the British mastermind behind many of their greatest comedies, became bitter over a situation that many other great artists would also face in the new era of television. But Laurel agreed in the early 1960s to producer Larry Harmon's request to revive the likenesses of him and the late Oliver Hardy (who died in 1957) in a new series of animated shorts. Unfortunately the project did not get under way until 1966, a year after Laurel's death. The new show was filmed through the Hanna-Barbera Studios; Harmon himself provided the voice of Stan Laurel and Chuck McCann that of Oliver Hardy.

Leave It to Beaver

This situation comedy about the Cleaver family of Mayfield, USA, was one of the most popular family series of all time. In most of the show's 234 episodes the stories revolved around the well-meaning efforts of the Cleaver's youngest child, Theodore, better known as "Beaver," and played by Jerry Mathers. Hugh Beaumont starred as his patient, understanding father, Ward; Barbara Billingsley was his well-dressed mother, June; and Tony Dow was his all–American brother, Wally. Also featured were Ken Osmond, as Wally's contemptible friend Eddie Haskell; Frank Banks, as the dim-witted Clarence ("Lumpy") Rutherford; Richard Deacon, as Lumpy's father, Fred; Rusty Stevens, as Beaver's chubby friend Larry Mondello; Stephen Talbot, as another friend, Gilbert Bates; and Sue Randell, as the elementary school teacher Miss Landers. Ken Osmond's Eddie Haskell was probably the show's most memorable supporting character. While appearing respectable to adults, Eddie was a master at conniving.

Created and produced by Joe Connelly and Bob Mosher, the series became one of several of the 1950s era to gain cult status, mostly among today's adults who were children when the show first aired. Despite the show's critical success, CBS dropped it after its first season, believing that kids were not really watching. It was picked up by the ABC network the following year, where it remained in a variety of different time slots over the next five seasons. Here is the programming history of this half hour show: Friday, 7:30 P.M., CBS, October 4, 1957, through March 5, 1958; Wednesday, 8:00–8:30 P.M., CBS, March 12, 1958, through September 17, 1958; Thursday, 7:30–8:00 P.M. (return), ABC, October 2, 1958, through June 25, 1959; Thursday, 9:00–9:30 P.M., ABC, July 2, 1959, through September 24, 1959; Saturday, 8:30–9:00 P.M., ABC, October 2, 1959, through September 15, 1962; Thursday, 8:30–9:00 P.M., ABC, September 22, 1962, through September 12, 1963.

The show's major virtue lay in the Beaver himself, who, like so many kids his age, hated "mushy stuff" and brussels sprouts and would rather kiss a frog than a member of the opposite sex. Beaver was the first true representative of the average child and possibly the most original character since Spanky McFarland. Although stories involved him in one unpredictable situation after another, children of all ages and backgrounds readily identified with him as he confronted such issues as friendship, rivalry, and adult relationships.

Several episodes focused on Beaver's integrity, in contrast to his less than honorable friends, who delighted in playing upon his trust and gullibility. In several stories peer pressure took the place of common sense and good judgment: Beaver being persuaded to make a funny face in the school picture; Beaver driving the go-cart without his father's permission; Beaver being convinced that a sweater would be appropriate attire at an awards banquet, rather than a suit and tie. In each case Beaver relied on solutions from his wise and sensible father, whose ability to steer his boys in the right direction was a factor in nearly every episode.

By the end of the series' second season, both Jerry Mathers and Tony Dow were on their way to becoming television's most popular child stars. During the show's six-year run, fans watched the boys grow up. A child actor since the age of six, Jerry Mathers had been previously featured with comedian Bob Hope and Eva Marie Saint in the 1956 feature film, *That Certain Feeling*. Upon completion of the "Beaver" series in 1963, he joined the U.S. Marine Corps, leading to false rumors of his death in the Vietnam War. Tony Dow, whose virtuous portrayal of Wally Cleaver turned him into something of a heartthrob to teenage girls, continued to act briefly as a youth, most notably in the teen-oriented daytime serial, "Never Too Young" (ABC, 1965–66).

Throughout the years, "Leave It to Beaver's" popularity with young viewers has remained strong. Even today young children have become very familiar with the Cleavers as the series continues to rerun in syndication.

In 1983 a grown-up Jerry Mathers returned to the role in a two-hour reunion, made-for-television movie entitled *Still the Beaver* (CBS). Today, he and several of the original cast members, Tony Dow, Barbara Billingsley, and Ken Osmond, are featured in an updated syndicated version of the series entitled "The New Leave It to Beaver."

The Little Rascals

The profitable "Our Gang"/"Little Rascals" comedies were produced in the 1930s by the Hal Roach Studios. The popular series of "kid comedies"

Hal Roach's "Our Gang"/"The Little Rascals." From left: George "Spanky" McFarland, Billy "Buckwheat" Thomas, Eugene "Porky" Lee, Carl "Alfalfa" Switzer, and Darla Hood.

first appeared on the air in 1954, through Interstate Television Corporation, a division of Allied Artists and syndicator for the Hal Roach Studios. Local stations across a small portion of the country were so impressed by the high ratings that the shorts were featured the following year in more than 60 cities nationwide.

Of the 221 "Our Gang" comedies filmed between 1922 and 1943, the first 88 were silent. A dozen or more of these were featured during the gang's first year on television, while a choice variety of the remaining silents appeared on such programs as "The Uncle Johnny Coons Show" (NBC, CBS, 1955–56) and its own syndicated series "The Mischief Makers." The talking "Our Gang" comedies produced between 1929 and 1938 were retitled "The Little Rascals" after being sold to television by Hal Roach, because MGM still owned the distribution rights to the remaining 52 shorts produced by the studio from 1938 to 1943.

The idea of basing a comedy series on a group of children came from Hal Roach himself, as he became amused one day watching the antics of a bunch of kids playing on the back lot. Having previously done two-reel comedies featuring such stars as Charlie Chase, Lloyd Corrigan,

Thelma Todd, Patsy Kelly, and the aforementioned Laurel and Hardy, Roach originally wanted to feature black child actor Ernie ("Sunshine") Morrison as the main star of the series and surround him with kids of various physical types. After previewing the first short, Roach decided to call the group the Our Gang Kids.

Although each version of the group was hugely successful with audiences over the years, the final 81 shorts, filmed on the Roach lot, were Roach's best work and are the ones most people recall fondly today. During this period the group began to form its most memorable cast of characters, names that would become familiar to over five generations of viewers. Jackie Cooper, for instance, gave several outstanding performances in such classic two-reelers as "Teacher's Pet," "Love Business," and "School's Out." In 1932, a two-year-old toddler in an oversized Buster Brown hat named George ("Spanky") McFarland made his film debut, in "Free Eats." And three years later, a crackly voiced crooner named Carl Switzer made his first appearance, in "Beginner's Luck"; the seven-year-old actor with a cowlick was referred to in his remaining films with the gang as Alfalfa. The list at various times included such familiar names as Allen ("Farina") Hoskins, Bobby ("Wheezer") Hutchins; Mary Ann Jackson; Norman ("Chubby") Chaney; Dickie Moore, Dorothy De Bora; Matthew ("Stymie") Beard, Scotty Beckett, Billy ("Buckwheat") Thomas, Tommy ("Butch") Bond, Darla Hood, and Eugene ("Porky") Lee, just to name a few. The series also included the gang's dog, Pete, a friendly bull terrier with a black circle around his eye. Nine-year-old Robert ("Mickey") Blake joined the cast when rights to the group were sold to its distributors, MGM, in 1938. He was joined by another newcomer to the series, Billy Laughlin, called "Froggy" because of his deep voice.

While the Roach shorts were distinguished for their humor, dialogue, and lively score by Marvin Hatley, the MGM shorts suffered from excessive pathos, linked mostly to stories involving the war effort. Patriotism came to dominate the story lines, and thus the "Our Gang" comedies finished their long theatrical run in 1944.

Today, nearly 40 years after their television debut, edited versions of "The Little Rascals" are still shown occasionally through King World Productions. Unfortunately, much of the subject matter now seems outdated and obscure by today's standards, and contains humor occasionally based on stereotypes, an element that may require family discussion.

In 1979 a prime-time animated version of "The Little Rascals" was aired during the Christmas season, featuring the voices of former "Our Gang" regulars Darla Hood and Matthew ("Stymie") Beard. An updated cartoon series appeared on Saturday mornings in 1982 produced through the Hanna-Barbera Studios.

The "Mr. Sweeney" Shows
The Kate Smith Hour (Segment) /
The World of Mr. Sweeney

Set in the imaginary town of Mapleton, USA, this 15-minute weekday series featured actor Charles Ruggles as Cicero P. Sweeney. As proprietor of the town's general store, Sweeney lived for the moments he shared with his young grandson Kippie, played by Glenn Walken. Between chores, Mr. Sweeney spent most of his time with Kippie, sitting for hours spinning tall tales from his vast experience and knowledge and spouting homespun cracker-barrel philosophy. Helen Wagner was also featured as Kippie's mother, Marge.

The series originally began as a featured segment on the "Kate Smith Hour," where it was presented at various times with such other segments as "America Sings" and "The Houses in the Garden." "The Kate Smith Hour" aired Monday through Friday, 6:00–7:00 P.M. on NBC from September 25, 1950, through June 18, 1954. An early favorite among mothers and preschool children, the series debuted on its own in the summer of 1954 on NBC as a lead-in to "The Pinky Lee Show" (NBC, 1950–56). The title of the show was "The World of Mr. Sweeney." The programming slot was 4:45–5:00 P.M. on Monday through Friday. The show aired in this slot from June 30, 1954, through December 31, 1955.

Although the show was provided with a studio laugh track, its live presentation gave it a look much closer to that of a serial. Media experts have long debated its actual place in the children's television genre.

Ruggles's kind-hearted elderly persona was first created in the late 1940s after a long screen career of playing middle-aged wistful types, often opposite comedienne Mary Boland. His Cicero P. Sweeney established a type for similar characters to follow, in particular, television actor Cliff Arquette, whose lovable bumpkin alter ego Charlie Weaver was seen on a variety of shows throughout the mid–1950s and 1960s. Ruggles became much more familiar to children's audiences during television's second generation, as the voice of the worldly philosopher Aesop on the ground-breaking cartoon series "Rocky and His Friends."

The Munsters

The year 1964 was a big one for situation comedy shows based on supernatural themes. In the past television producers depended on such familiar names as Lucille Ball, Danny Thomas, and Andy Griffith to draw a good audience; this year's top-rated new series, however, involved the domestic adventures of a witch named Samantha. Also on ABC Charles Addams's bizarre characters from the *New Yorker* magazine, "The Addams Family," came to life on the television screen for the first time.

Meanwhile CBS premiered its own unusual new series, "The Munsters." The Munsters resembled popular creatures from Universal's horror era. The cast included Fred Gwynne, as Herman, a 150-year-old, green, eight-foot moron who shared an amazing likeness with the Frankenstein monster; Yvonne DeCarlo, as Lily, a Vampira type, who married Herman at the ripe old age of 203; Al Lewis, as Grandpa, an aging Count Dracula and part-time mad scientist; Butch Patrick, as Herman and Lily's nine-year-old son, Eddie Wolfgang Munster, who seemed to be a cross between a boy and a preteen werewolf; and Beverly Owen (1964) and Pat Priest (1965–66), as the lovely but "normal looking" Marilyn, Lily's niece. Veteran character actor John Carradine also made several guest appearances as Herman's ghoulish boss, Mr. Gateman, of Gateman, Goodbury, and Graves Mortuaries, where Herman worked as a parlor boy. In the show's original unaired pilot, Joan Marshall played Herman's wife, Phoebe, and Happy Derman, a midget actor, was initially cast in the role of Eddie. Included in the Munster household were pets Spot, a fire-breathing dragon, who lived beneath the hall staircase; a raven, who occasionally pops out of a clock to recite Edgar Allan Poe; Igor, the bat; and Eddie's snake, Elmer, who is never seen but is referred to in several episodes as "the little one who crawls about the house."

Created and produced by Joe Connelly and Bob Mosher, "The Munsters" ran for two seasons on CBS, where it often placed no higher than 22nd in the overall ratings. The half hour show appeared at 7:30 from September 24, 1964, through September 1, 1966. Like several shows produced both before and after, "The Munsters" became much more successful when rerun in syndication than it had been during its original run.

Although the series would hardly be considered classic television comedy, the show did provide its share of humorous moments as the Munsters tried to adapt to the life-styles of their surrounding community. In the premiere episode, for instance, "Munster Masquerade," Herman and Lily accept an invitation to a swanky masquerade ball in an attempt to land a husband for Marilyn. Herman inadvertently wins first prize for best costume after accidentally removing his mask and revealing his real face.

During the summer reruns of their final season on CBS, the show's cast was presented in the feature film *Munster Go Home*. Produced by Universal Pictures (the copyright owners of the Frankenstein and Dracula characters), the movie involved the creepy clan's inheritance of an English castle. British comedian Terry Thomas costarred. In keeping with the then current trend of television revivals, most of the original cast reassembled once again in 1981 to produce the made-for-television movie *The Munsters' Revenge*. Although it was somewhat lacking in the charm and humor of the original series, fans finally got a chance to see what the Munsters looked like in ghoulishly living color.

While reruns of the original series are still being shown today in more than 60 cities, a new syndicated version appeared, entitled "The Munsters Today," starring John Schuck and Lee Meriwether in the roles of Herman and Lily.

The Three Stooges / The New Three Stooges

Although the Three Stooges comedy team actually made its television debut performing on several live programs during the early years, its slapstick comedy shorts did not become the phenomenon that they are considered today until 1959. It was then that all of their 194 movie shorts for Columbia Pictures were released to television in one complete package for the first time. Youngsters who had never seen them before loved them, despite parents' consistent complaints about the violence.

The Stooges were composed of former vaudevillians Moe Howard, as the leader, Larry Fine, as the semistraight man, and at various other times Curly Howard, Shemp Howard, and Joe Besser, as the funny third Stooge. The team members had previously become well known with movie audiences of an earlier generation from their film shorts produced between 1934 and 1957. When television revived these shorts in 1959, the Stooges achieved new heights in popularity. It was during this time of comeback appearances, live engagements, and command performances that Joe DeRita, another former burlesque comic, joined the group as the third Stooge. He was called Curly-Joe because of his resemblance to the original "Curly" Stooge (which has often caused confusion among new fans).

The "Three Stooges" films eventually became one of the hottest new properties in the history of television. Even today, the Stooges' syndicated shorts continue to flourish, enjoyed by millions of children

The original Three Stooges: Curly, Moe and Larry with guest star Lola Jensen in a posed scene from "Flat Foot Stooges," Columbia, 1938.

as well as by their parents, who grew up watching them on television.

It is easy to understand why the team's appeal never seems to diminish with each new generation of children. The grand masters of slapstick never pretended to convey any image other than that of the hard-working artist striving for prominence in their field while achieving the least distinction. Although some found their humor a bit too cruel to be funny, it mattered little to others, who had come to expect the usual knockabout farce that became their trademark.

Learning their trade during the vaudeville years of the 1920s, the Stooges were originally part of a team called the Racketeers, also known as Three Southern Gentlemen, led by a straight man named Ted Healy. In 1930 Ted Healy and His Stooges, Moe, Larry, and Shemp (Moe's older brother), were presented in their first feature film, *Soup to Nuts,* released by Twentieth Century–Fox. Because of a personal difference with Ted Healy, Shemp left the act two years later to pursue a solo career in films. He was replaced by his younger brother Jerome, better known as Curly, who would eventually become the best loved of the Stooges.

After a brief stint at the MGM Studios, the Stooges, minus Ted Healy, signed a contract with Columbia Pictures in 1934 to appear in a series of two-reel comedies under the guidance of such directors as Charlie Chase, Del Lord, and Jules White. That same year one of their first shorts, "Men in Black," a zany spoof on the medical profession, won an Academy Award nomination. In 1946 Curly was forced to leave the act after suffering a severe stroke while halfway through the production of "Halfwits Holiday." Shemp then rejoined the team, where he remained for another nine years before his untimely death in 1955. He in turn was replaced by comedian Joe Besser, who remained with the group until their contract expired in 1958. "The Three Stooges" was the last of the live comedy shorts to be produced at Columbia and the longest running.

Grateful to television for its role in their remarkable comeback, the Three Stooges made many public appearances at local stations that featured their shorts. Officer Joe Bolton, one of the most recognized of the syndicated children's show hosts, from the New York–based series "Fun House," was one of the first to feature the Stooges' films on a regular basis. For the benefit of very young children and sensitive adults, Moe, Larry, and Curly-Joe advised children of the real dangers in inflicting bodily harm on others. Many a concerned parent also observed a big change in their new feature films of this period, which contained little or no violence at all. In *The Three Stooges Go Around the World in a Daze* (1963), Moe tells a Japanese group of Stooge impersonators, who are knocking each other about, that their violence is definitely out of vogue: "We don't do that anymore."

In September 1965, the Three Stooges were featured in a new series of animated shorts that also included them in a live introductory segment. Titled "The New Three Stooges," the programs were produced by Moe's son-in-law, Norman Mauer.

In recent years, the comedians have been recognized for their comic genius, through biographies, tapes, and a place on Hollywood's distinquished Walk of Fame.

5. Fun and Games

Programs of a spirited nature have not always been limited to the adult world. At one time children danced, named that tune, ran around huge game boards, and did just as many silly things as adults still do today for money and prizes. As a matter of fact, several of today's best-known game show hosts started out in juvenile versions of such once popular adult games as "Beat the Clock" and "Video Village." At one time the networks were jammed with young contestants of all types trying desperately to reach the finish, ring the buzzer, or give the correct name of a capital city before their eager opponents did. Meanwhile, in the mid–1950s, another type of activity show developed which provided teenagers with the latest in songs, dances, and fashions, interests that remain constant even today. Presently, only a few cable stations have made the attempt to recapture some of the fun and frolics often involved in shows of this kind. It is to be hoped that we have not seen the last of them.

American Bandstand

"American Bandstand" was one of the first network shows aimed primarily at the teenage audience. Originally broadcast daily from Philadelphia, the dance series became one of the longest running, most successful television shows in the history of the medium.

Originally hosted by former radio disc jockey Bob Horn, the series premiered in 1952 as "Bandstand," a local sensation telecast over Philadelphia station WFIL. When Horn left the series in 1956, he was replaced by a handsome 21-year-old newcomer to television named Dick Clark, whose cheery, well-rounded charm would make him a part of the American rock scene for nearly four decades.

The show, featuring records, local music celebrities, and dancing teenagers, eventually attracted nationwide attention as it became the highest-rated daily program in the Philadelphia area.

In 1957 the series was distributed coast to coast in both 60- and 90-minute formats over 67 ABC affiliated stations. It was not long before the show became the highest-rated afternoon show across the United States. This great success led to an additional prime-time version that ran for several months beginning in October 1957. Both programs gave performers both old and new the opportunity to sing their hit recordings. And in a move similar to one by "The Ed Sullivan Show" (CBS, 1948–71) (considered unusual at the time), black records, performers, and teenagers were integrated on the program, in the midst of the historic struggle for civil rights.

Here is the programming history for this ABC show: Monday–Friday, 4:00–5:00 P.M., September 5, 1957, through August 30, 1963; Monday, 7:30–8:30 P.M., October 7, 1957, through January 6, 1958; Saturday, 12:00–1:00 P.M., August 31, 1963, through September 9, 1967; Saturday, 12:30–2:00 P.M., September 16, 1967, through October 1, 1977; Saturday, 1:00–2:30 P.M., October 8, 1977, through September 12, 1981; Saturday, 12:30–1:30 P.M., September 19, 1981, until September 1990.

Throughout the show's many years, almost every star in the music industry has appeared on the program at one time or another, some more frequently than others. Near the close of the show's first year on the network, Clark introduced two teenagers from New York City who called themselves Tom and Jerry. Less than ten years later the duo reappeared on the program singing their newest hit single, "Sounds of Silence," this time using their real names, Paul Simon and Art Garfunkel. In 1961 Philadelphian Chubby Checker created a national dance craze on the program after performing his new hit record "The Twist." And in July 1963, Clark introduced to the world a blind 12-year-old singer from Detroit, Michigan, called Little Stevie Wonder, performing the song "Fingertips," a tune that became a major hit in the very early years of the Motown record company.

One popular continuing segment of the program was the rating of new records by a boy and girl who were chosen from the dance floor to give their opinion of a new recording artist. In January 1964, during a Saturday morning telecast, two teenagers rated a new single titled "I Want to Hold Your Hand," by a British group from Liverpool called the Beatles. "I gave it a 90," one replied, "because it had a good beat and was easy to dance to."

Despite the various guest performers, it was the young audiences themselves who were the real stars. They were responsible for teaching

American young people dance steps, from the pony and the swim, to the jerk and the hustle.

In the fall of 1963 "American Bandstand" was shown on Saturday afternoons, surviving with little change in format today through a series of slot changes and occasional preemptions to allow for the airing of sporting events and children's educational programs. In 1964 "American Bandstand" was broadcast from the Los Angeles area, where programs were often taped several weeks in advance.

Dick Clark, once labeled by *New York Times* critic Jack Gould "The Pied Piper of Bedlam," eventually became one of television's wealthiest entrepreneurs, working as host and producer for a number of television specials and game shows. Under the Dick Clark banner came such youth-oriented musical presentations as "Dick Clark's World of Talent" (ABC, 1959) "The Dick Clark Show" (ABC, 1958–60), "Where the Action Is" (ABC 1965–67), "Happening '68" (ABC, 1968–69), and the ABC special, "Dick Clark's Live Wednesday" (1978). He subsequently produced a number of movie and television films, such as *The Young Doctors* (1961), where he made his dramatic film debut as an actor.

In 1974 Clark was featured, with his own production company, hosting the CBS daytime version of the popular prime-time game series "$25,000 Pyramid." He still appears today in a syndicated version of the program entitled "The $20,000 Pyramid," and is the occasional host of the irregularly scheduled series TV's "Bloopers and Practical Jokes," on NBC. He became one of the most conscientious television celebrities of all time, often working on all three networks at once. But his popularity also has a downside. In the spring of 1960, Clark became the target of a congressional committee in its investigation of a payola scandal within the music industry (with money or favors being given in exchange for the broadcasting of a record). Clark denied the charges, but admitted to investing in the record companies whose songs he played; this was not illegal but to some represented a conflict of interest. Although it found him innocent of any wrongdoing, the committee suggested that he sell his holdings, which resulted into a loss of over $3 million.

As the founder and director of the Unistar Radio Network, Clark remains today ever the financial investor and the host of various beauty pageants and award shows, and the promoter for a series of traveling rock concerts, nightclub acts, and celebrity benefit appearances. His production company has even been responsible for several of the award-winning ABC "After School Specials" for children.

In 1977 ABC celebrated "American Bandstand"'s 25th anniversary with a prime-time special. CBS followed suit in 1988 with "Live! Dick Clark Presents," an homage to the show's best presentation. Both specials featured many of the stars who helped make "American Bandstand" a huge success and an institution of American broadcasting.

Choose-Up Sides

Produced by Mark Goodson and Bill Todman, "Choose-Up Sides" was hosted by former "Tonight Show" announcer Gene Rayburn. The series featured two children's teams that competed in an assortment of stunts and games for prizes. A somewhat juvenile version of the popular adult favorite "Beat the Clock," "Choose-Up Sides" was originally a local program in New York City hosted by Dean Miller (who later starred as Matt Henshaw in the popular sitcom series "December Bride" on CBS, 1954–59). As with most game shows, the prizes were the main attraction, as kids competed feverishly for the privilege of riding off the stage on a Schwinn bike or wearing a new Speidel watch. Although the concept of a Saturday morning children's game series appeared to be a good one, NBC reluctantly canceled the series after just three short months on the air (January 7, 1956, through March 31, 1956, airing 12:00–12:30). It had become all too obvious that games were no competition for the Saturday morning lineup of Westerns that then dominated the networks.

The show's producers, Mark Goodson and Bill Todman, however, went on to become the leaders in producing game shows, with such adult favorites as "I've Got a Secret" (CBS/syndicated, 1952–76), "Beat the Clock" (CBS/ABC/syndicated, 1950–80), "What's My Line?" (CBS/syndicated, 1950–75), "The Price Is Right" (NBC/CBS/syndicated/CBS, 1956–), and "Family Feud" (ABC/syndicated/CBS, 1976–), each with a long-running broadcast history. Gene Rayburn went on to become host of "The Match Game" (NBC/CBS/syndicated 1962–82), still another in the long line of favorites from Goodson and Todman Productions.

Harlem Globetrotters' Popcorn Machine

This 30-minute children's variety game show featured several members of the famed Harlem Globetrotters basketball team in a series of comedy sketches, games, and songs with members of the studio audience. Appearing in various presentations with child actor Rodney Allen Rippy, Globetrotters Meadowlark Lemon, Curley Neal, and Geese Ausbie presented viewers with a medley of activities that generally emphasized themes of fair play and good sportsmanship, reminders that are valuable for adults as well as children.

Comedian Avery Schreiber, popular for his Doritos chips commercials, was also featured in a running segment of the program as "Mr. Evil." In this skit, Evil repeatedly gets himself involved in all sorts of misfortunes because of his greed and selfishness. Each ending provides viewers with a valuable lesson. Another of the show's most popular segments was "One on One." Here, several youngsters from the studio audience were invited to compete on the court with the Globetrotters, with prizes for the most points scored.

Rodney Allen Rippy, an influential figure for young people at the time, had previously appeared on television in several of the "ABC After School Specials." In the fall of 1976, he was also featured in an episode of "The Six Million Dollar Man" series. Unfortunately, his efforts to retool his acting career in the 1980s failed. Standing over six feet tall today, he is best remembered for his early commercials for Jack in the Box, an image that has solidified his reputation as one of television's most natural child actors.

The Globetrotters had previously appeared in animated form on CBS from 1970 to 1972 in a Hanna-Barbera cartoon series that bore their name as its title.

"The Harlem Globetrotters' Popcorn Machine" was featured for two seasons on CBS. The program slots were as follows: Saturday, 11:00–11:30 A.M., September 7, 1974, through August 30, 1975; Sunday, 10:30–11:00 A.M., September 7, 1975, through September 5, 1976. The show was a production of Norman Baer's Funhouse Production Company.

Juvenile Jury

Producers Dan Enright and Jack Barry were among the earliest creators of children's popular game shows. Barry and Enright were responsible for more kids competing against one another than any other production team of the same era. Their pioneering work in the children's genre set the mold for a series of successful prime-time game shows that have become familiar names today, such as "Tic Tac Dough" and "The Joker's Wild."

Their first series, "Juvenile Jury," featured a panel of youngsters who issued unrehearsed answers to questions sent in by viewers and by members of the studio audience. The game series became a favorite and was presented for nearly a decade on both NBC and CBS in the following program slots: Thursday, 8:00–8:30 P.M., NBC, April 3, 1947, through September 28, 1953; Thursday, 8:00–8:30 P.M., CBS, October 11, 1953, through September 14, 1954; Sunday, 4:00–4:30 P.M., NBC, January 2,

Dan Enright (left) and Jack Barry.

1955, through March 27, 1955. An updated version was developed and syndicated in 1970. Barry and Enright brought the series to television from radio in 1947, initially on a irregular basis. Its appeal to youngsters created a fad, encouraging children at home to participate in guessing the correct answers.

Furthermore, Barry and Enright's behind-the-scenes involvement with the quiz show scandals of the 1950s was just as interesting as the shows they produced for the television. In 1954 the "big money" game shows first appeared on the air with the premiere of the "64,000 Dollar Question" (CBS, 1954–58). The appeal of seeing ordinary citizens answering difficult questions in their specialized area for big money prizes became tremendous, eventually spawning a series of imitators, including Barry and Enright's "Twenty-one" the following season. One of their first series created for adult audiences, "Twenty-one" became one of several to be taken off the air after two seasons when allegations were made charging the show with providing answers to several of its contestants in advance. Originally denying all charges of fraud, Enright later admitted that several contestants were indeed prompted, in an attempt to generate enthusiasm from the audience. One such contestant was Charles Van Doren, whose defeat of Herbert Stempel after 14 weeks turned him into an international celebrity. Stempel later revealed to news sources that he was persuaded to throw the contest in favor of Van

Doren, who was considered a much more appealing contestant. The scandal brought a quick end to the era of big money quiz shows; it also kept Jack Barry from appearing on the air as a game show host for the next ten years.

In 1983 a new version of "Juvenile Jury," produced by Black Entertainment Television, debuted on the cable channel, with comedian Nipsey Russell as its host.

Kids and Company

Long before Saturday mornings became a haven for all types of imaginative programs, Johnny Olsen and cartoonist Ham Fisher produced and served as cohosts of this 30-minute kid's talent series featured on the old Dumont network. The half hour program aired on Saturday mornings at 11:00 from September 1, 1951, through May 2, 1953. The program consisted of having a variety of talented youngsters perform before a live audience. In several instances there were guest appearances by famous celebrities in the entertainment field. Each program colorfully presented children in a singing and dancing format in which they felt comfortable. As on "Arthur Godfrey's Talent Scouts" (CBS, 1948–58), several of the winners went on to become national celebrities themselves. In 1952 12-year-old Leslie Uggams made her television debut on the program with her rendition of a popular folk ballad. On a later program a young Rob Cassotto performed an old Bing Crosby tune; five years later he became better known to audiences as Bobby Darin when he topped the music charts with the hit single "Splish Splash."

One of the show's regular segments was "Johnny Olsen's Hall of Fame." Here, a different child was profiled each week for his or her acts of strength and courage in the face of adversity. Many children who suffered from polio at the time were honored by the "National Junior Chamber of Commerce." The late Johnny Olsen was destined to become much more familiar to adult audiences later as the exuberant announcer for "The Price Is Right" game show (NBC/ABC/syndicated/CBS, 1956–). Ham Fisher is remembered better for his comic strip creation of Joe Palooka, a dim-witted but honest pugilist.

"Kids and Company" was sponsored nationally by the St. Louis International Shoe Company, the makers of Red Goose Shoes for children.

Picture This

For three months during the summer of 1963 (June 25, 1963, through September 17, 1963), comedian Jerry Van Dyke hosted this 30-minute replacement series geared toward young viewers. The CBS show aired at 9:30 on Tuesday nights. "Picture This" featured two competing teams made up of both celebrities and young contestants from the studio audience. One member from each team would try to have an opponent identify a given phrase by his or her teammates. At the end of a match, cash prizes were awarded to the team with the most points. In each program the celebrity players were usually young actors with whom children had grown familiar over the years.

Though its run was limited, "Picture This" proved very popular with viewers. When the series left the air in September 1963 to make way for the returning "Jack Benny Program," producers Ben Joelson and Art Baer considered reviving the program for a Saturday morning crowd the following season. Unfortunately, nothing ever came of the idea. Perhaps if presented on the networks, or even syndication, for a longer period, the show could have served as a fine launching pad for the underrated talents of host Jerry Van Dyke, whose career had gone from one disaster to the next. His most memorable role was that of the son of a 1928 porter in what the critics called the "worst situation comedy of all time," "My Mother, the Car" (NBC, 1965–66).

Runaround

Ventriloquist Paul Winchell hosted this Saturday morning game show designed to attract the attention of hyperactive children. Programs consisted of several young contestants racing around on stage to reach the proper squares that represented a correct answer. By the end of the game, contestants were narrowed down to two remaining players, who competed for the day's big prize. Consolation prizes were awarded to all the players.

"Runaround" was produced in conjunction with the NBC network, as well as a variety of consultants who were responsible for educational programs. Like similar shows, "Runaround" was presented as a game of fair competition under the rules of discipline and self-control.

But the show's main strength was veteran children's emcee Paul Winchell, who had by now become known to three generations of viewers. He was a great star, who, besides acting as host, could sing, act, clown about, and of course provide magical chemistry with his beloved dummies Jerry Mahoney and Knucklehead Smiff (for more about Winchell, see chapter 8, "Puppets, Marionettes, and Dummies").

"Runaround" was presented on Saturday mornings for one season: 11:30, NBC, September 9, 1972, through September 1, 1973.

Shenanigans

This 30-minute lively game show series was hosted by veteran character actor Stubby Kaye. It featured two different children in each show who competed on a huge three-dimensional game board that was marked out into squares. Each square represented a different task to be performed by the competing youngster who landed there on his or her way to the "finish." Prizes were then awarded to the first contestant to reach square one, the home square. Both critics and educators agreed that the show's practical drills helped teach kids the techniques of strategy.

Stubby Kaye, popular for his supporting roles in such films as *Guys and Dolls* (1955) and *Li'l Abner* (1959), provided mostly conversation for both the home and studio audience, while relying on the support of studio assistants for demonstrating the game's procedures.

This program appeared on ABC Saturday mornings at 10:00 from September 26, 1964, through December 18, 1965. Among the faster-paced games for children, "Shenanigans" became popular enough to be marketed as a home game by the Milton Bradley Company.

Soul Train

Following closely in the steps of "American Bandstand," "Soul Train" was another series designed particularly for the teenage audience. Created, hosted, and produced by former disc jockey Don Cornelius, the show was designed primarily as a forum for black recording artists and sponsors who catered to the needs of African-American young people. Thus, programs provided national exposure for many artists, especially those who were rarely given the opportunity to perform before a nationwide television audience. Gladys Knight and the Pips, for instance, were one of the first to appear on the program with their song "Midnight Train to Georgia." Other first appearances have included the Isley Brothers (1972), Isaac Hayes (1974), Barry White (1974), the Miracles (1976), and Luther Vandross (1984). Great care was also taken in each program for the stars to give the audience a list of their artistic accomplishments and to encourage pride and awareness of goals in audience members.

"Soul Train" began as a local dance program in Chicago in 1970. It became syndicated nationally the following year, and by 1972 it was seen in more than 60 cities across the United States. Over the years the show has undergone changes in format and style, but its most appealing feature has been the Soul Train Dancers. Their visual appeal popularized a dance style well before disco became the national craze of the 1970s. One of the show's most popular segments, the Soul Train Line, features the dancers brilliantly demonstrating their prowess individually. Another segment was entitled the Scramble Game. Here two contestants were selected from the audience to unscramble the name of a well-known celebrity to win prizes from the sponsor, Johnson and Johnson.

Although the show has managed to maintain good ratings throughout its long syndicated run, little of its success has been credited to host Don Cornelius. Somewhat mechanical, his announcing style has been parodied by stand-up comics, both on the show and off. Nevertheless, he is a good-natured, hard-working promoter, and his cool, collected manner and signature catchphrase "Peace, love, and soul" have helped make him a television mainstay who has lasted for over 20 years, with a show that audiences continue to love today.

In the 1980s, two developments made "Soul Train" a favorite with people of all groups. First, the show's theme song became a hit on the national music charts. Second, the series began to invite white performers whose songs also appealed to minority audiences.

"Soul Train" remains today one of the most popular continuing shows in syndication.

Video Village Junior

This 30-minute Saturday morning version of the popular adult game show was hosted by Monty Hall. As on the daily weekday series, contestants rolled a giant pair of dice to advance from one square to another, on a larger-than-life Monopoly-style gameboard. The first to finish would receive the week's big toy prize, usually provided by one of the biggest toy manufacturers, well-known brand with which children had become familiar. Hall was assisted in hosting each show by pretty Eileen Barton and announcer Kenny Williams, who appeared in costume as the Video Village Town Crier.

Like others before and after, the series was conceived with the good intention of providing children with a choice for something new on Saturday mornings. Produced by Merrill Heatter and Bob Quigley, the show was intended to encourage children's imaginations, good sportsmanship, and fair play. The program appeared on CBS Saturday mornings at 11:30 from September 30, 1961, through June 16, 1962.

Monty Hall later became one of the most memorable game show hosts of the 1960s and 1970s. More than anything else, he is best remembered for hosting the classic game show "Let's Make a Deal" (NBC, ABC, 1963–84), where he gave away prizes to adults dressed in silly costumes.

Way Out Games

One of the later Barry and Enright productions that managed to attract the attentions of older children to some degree was "Way Out Games." The series featured 30 minutes of physical education in the form of competition among teenagers from all across the United States. Hosted by Sonny Fox, "Way Out Games" was often shot on location in one of the weekly competing towns. As on the syndicated "All-Star Anything Goes," prizes were rarely awarded, but participants were given instead the satisfaction of competing on nationwide television. "Way Out Games" was broadcast by CBS on Saturday at 12:00 for a half hour from September 11, 1976, through September 4, 1977.

Comedian Soupy Sales hosted a similar series on ABC that same year titled "Junior Almost Anything Goes." Both shows were in keeping with the spirit of the Olympic games, which were broadcast in Montreal, Canada, the year of the shows' debut, 1976.

"Way Out Games" was yet another effort at competing against the Saturday morning cartoons. Like the others, "Way Out Games" finished behind in the final competition and lasted for only one season.

Winky Dink and You

A new sort of children's instructional game series, "Winky Dink and You," became one of the most popular children's shows of the 1950s. For four consecutive years (before his ten-year banishment from television), Jack Barry became one of the most familiar Saturday morning faces. As cocreator of the series, Barry conversed with cartoon characters Winky Dink and his little dog, Woofer, while viewers who chose to do so participated at home in helping the characters along their illustrated course by drawing on a transparent screen attached to their television sets. This could only be accomplished by purchasing the "Winky Dink Kit," which viewers were encouraged to do at the end of every program. Networks, always looking for a good merchandise tie-in, discovered this item to be a very profitable one indeed.

After receiving instructions from Barry, participating viewers would use the crayon provided in their kits to trace letters, discover secret messages, play word games, and assist Winky and Woofer in their various journeys. When the show was over, viewers erased the drawings with a cloth also provided with the kit. The Winky Dink Kit became a hit with children everywhere. It was one of the first in a long line of promotional tools aimed at children.

As expected, some children who lacked the kit followed Barry's instructions by drawing on the screen. Many irate adults then purchased the kits to avoid damage to television screens by preschoolers who disobeyed Barry's warning about using the proper equipment. Kits consisted simply of a roll of clear acetate paper, crayons, and a cloth; they could be purchased by mail for a mere 50 cents, a fair price even at that time.

In addition, Barry served as a foil to an assembly of other characters, both live and animated. Dayton Allen, for one, costarred in several of the segments as Barry's bumbling assistant, Mr. Bungle; his incompetence served as a reminder to children that they should follow directions. Hardly a stranger to children's television, Allen had previously provided his talents as puppeteer and writer on several of the early "Howdy Doody" programs. He became much more familiar to adult audiences later as one of the "crazies" on the "Steve Allen Show" (NBC, 1956–60).

"Winky Dink and You" was presented for four Saturday-morning seasons on NBC (Saturday, 11:30–12:00 noon, October 10, 1953, through May 27, 1957), a grand feat for a show of this type considering its competition.

6. *Informative Shows*

PBS has without a doubt done the finest job of educating while entertaining young children. But shows of an informative nature have been in existence in one form or another ever since television began. Although many of the early shows meant well, most failed in their efforts to attract attention, because of their straightforward manner.

Informative shows have appeared in all forms, from hosts and news to puppets and instructional cartoons. Because of these different styles, children have been able to maintain a balance between shows they like to watch and those they should watch. Over the years children have learned through television about arts, science, religion, and general information about the world. For those who grew up watching them, many of these shows became a primary source of information about a better life.

Captain Kangaroo

Before Bob Keeshan first donned that now familiar uniform with the big trademark pockets in 1955, most children's shows offered little to the creative imagination. "Captain Kangaroo" thrived almost entirely through the gentle whimsy of its beloved host, the Captain, whose Treasure House of stories, conversations, puppet friends, and animated features (such as "Tom Terrific," "Lariat Sam" and "Pow Wow, the Indian Boy") have entertained and helped children learn for over a quarter of a century. During its many years on the air, the show has been regarded as the first important influence on preschool children's programming, and it has received numerous awards and citations from parents and educators from all across the United States. Here is the programming history for "Captain Kangaroo": Monday–Friday, 8:00–9:00 A.M., CBS, October 3, 1955, through January 6, 1956; Monday–Saturday, 8:00–9:00 A.M.,

135

CBS, January 9, 1956, through September 19, 1964; Monday–Friday, 8:00–9:00 A.M., CBS, September 21, 1964, through September 3, 1984; Monday–Friday, 10:00–10:30 A.M., PBS, September 15, 1986, until September 1991.

Keeshan, a veteran of more than 40 years of broadcasting, first began his career as a page for the NBC radio network, before joining the Marines at the onset of World War II. Following his discharge, he returned to the NBC studios but this time as a page for its television network. There he met Bob Smith, a former radio children's host, who took him on as an assistant for a new show he had designed for NBC's "Puppet Playhouse Theater," based on a puppet character he created called Howdy Doody. There, Keeshan appeared in the role of Clarabell, the speechless clown. After five seasons on the program, Keeshan signed with the network to do a program all his own called "Time for Fun," in which he appeared on the air briefly as Corny the Clown. A year later Keeshan teamed with Hugh ("Lumpy") Brannum and created as well as starred in a short-lived local children's program entitled "Tinker's Workshop." Although the show failed to gain much attention, it did create a friendship between the two actors that would help turn their next venture into a children's institution. In October 1955, at the ripe old age of 28, Keeshan shrugged on the coat with the big pockets for the first time as a kindly old grandfather whom he called Captain Kangaroo. Brannum joined him as the only other human cast member, Farmer Greenjeans. Created by Keeshan himself, "Captain Kangaroo" became the longest-running children's host in television history. In the course of time he has been awarded six Emmys, three Gabriels, and a Director's Award in 1986 from Ohio State University. Also the recipient of two Peabody Awards for excellence in youth programming, Keeshan says his goal has always remained the same: "To make the child viewer feel good about him- or herself. Children can withstand all kinds of deprivation, all kinds of maltreatment, if they just know they are loved by someone who cares."

In addition to the Captain and Mr. Greenjeans, there was a larger cast, which included at various times: Cosmo Allegretti, as Dancing Bear and later Dennis, a bungling apprentice; puppets Mr. Moose and the Bunny Rabbit; Larry Walls, as Mr. Baxter; Debbie Weems; Carolyn Mignini; and puppeteer Kevin Clash and his friends Artie and Ralph.

The shows previously shown daily on PBS after nearly three decades of morning programs on CBS, were 65 edited versions of those shows previously televised by CBS between 1982 and 1984, and were distributed to public television beginning in 1986 by the Interregional Program Service, a Boston-based syndication company.

Bob Keeshan.

Although some changes had been made since the Captain first opened the doors to the original Treasure House more than 30 years ago (most notably in the colorless setting and in the addition of the Grandfather Clock), the essence of the revived "Captain's Place" basically remained the same. Featuring a number of different segments, programs have included the Captain and his friends in a variety of humorous skits (sometimes as other characters), poetry readings, storybook portrayals, music, animal visits, and two filmed-on-location segments, entitled "Look What's Happening Now" and "Kids Like You." In 1978 comedian and educator Bill Cosby began appearing occasionally on the show as host of a segment called "Picture Pages."

Entertainment was always the main purpose of the show, with educational "life-oriented" lessons woven into each program. Over the years, sketches played an important part in inspiring children to use their abilities while encouraging their natural curiosity. Whether engaging in wry banter, reading a story, or fielding a hail of Mr. Moose's Ping-Pong balls, Captain Kangaroo maintained a relationship with both children and adults which withstood the test of time.

In recent years, Keeshan has reached out to a somewhat older children's audience with "CBS Storybreak" on Saturday mornings, a series designed to present original adaptations of literature to young people. He has also become a leading spokesman for groups advocating children's causes. In the 1980s he testified before a U.S. Senate Judiciary Committee hearing on television violence and campaigned against tobacco industry advertising aimed at encouraging children to start smoking.

As always, Keeshan had the well-being of children in mind when he jumped to public television after decades with CBS, following the network's decision to shift the program from its longtime weekly slot to 6:00 A.M., to make room for an additional hour of morning news. "It's cruel and unusual punishment to ask a child to get up that early," he says. Moreover, Keeshan has always enjoyed the fact that traditionally one-third of his audience has been mothers watching the show with their children—and it is not nice to be cruel to mothers, either.

Curiosity Shop

After years of delighting audiences all over the world with those wonderful Warner Brothers cartoons, animator Chuck Jones created as well as hosted this live 60-minute educational series aimed primarily at pre-teens. The ABC show was broadcast at 11:00 on Saturday mornings from September 11, 1971, through September 3, 1972. It was moved to 11:00 on Sunday mornings on September 11, 1972, where it remained until September 2, 1973. "Curiosity Shop" opened each program with the arrival of several children eager to learn more about such everyday features of life as food, water, and air. The doors to the Curiosity Shop were then opened, and questions were answered with the assistance of music, films, animation, and at times costumed sequences, incorporated by Jones himself. The show's various segments, combined with its well-rounded subject matter, made this a production well worth the time and effort it took in developing.

Members of the juvenile cast included John Levin, Pamelyn Ferdin, Kerry MacLine, Jerrelyn Fields, and Barbara Minkus, as Gittel, the bumbling but fun-loving witch. Animal regulars included Darwin the Chimp and Eunice, the slippery seal. Puppet characters who shared center stage were Flip the Hippo, the Oogle Thing, Monsieur Cou-Cou, Baron Balthazar, and Professor Trivia. Also presented at various times were the animated adventures of some of America's most popular syndicated comic strips, including John Hart's *B.C.*, Hank Ketchum's *Dennis the Menace,* Phillip's *The Strange World of Mr. Mum,* and the late Virgil Patch's homage to married life, *Big George.* Inanimate objects featured regularly included the "Animal Wall" (which housed homeless animals), a computer that paved the way to the future, and an elevator that transported youngsters anywhere they wanted to go.

Similar to other educational shows produced around the same time, "Curiosity Shop" was created with the goal of teaching kids through fun and facts. Although well received by all, the show fell slightly below network expectations, ranking second in the ratings to CBS's "Josie and the Pussycats," which unfortunately attracted a younger but overall larger audience.

"Curiosity Shop," one of the better educational shows linked to a commercial network, lasted for a total of two seasons on ABC, appearing during its final season on Sunday mornings.

Davey and Goliath

Religion was the theme behind this long-running, 15-minute series produced and created by Art and Ruth Clokey and Associates which was syndicated in March 1961. Davey Hansen, a nine-year-old boy, and his talking dog, Goliath, were clay figures vividly presented on the program through a process known as "innovative animation," a stop-motion technique accomplished by having the figures moved manually, one frame at a time, a fraction of an inch. (The system is similar to that of George Pal's award-winning "Puppetoons" of the 1940s.)

As it did with the Clokeys' more popular Gumby character, the clay animation process reappeared frequently over the years in various other forms, such as the classic Speedy Alka-Seltzer and Brylcreem commercials of the 1950s and 1960s.

Throughout its long, enduring run, "Davey and Goliath" consistently provided children with inspirational messages in well-performed stories of faith and courage. Like most shows based on religious concepts, the series was usually limited to early Sunday mornings, with several episodes often running back to back. While many kids found the show boring compared with the more aggressive programs presented on the commercial networks, parents found its messages to be worthwhile and presented in a tasteful manner without appearing preachy.

Although the programs have covered a wide range of concerns, in most episodes, Davey, Goliath, and sometimes Davey's little sister, Sally, are faced with problems in which their strength depends upon their faith in God. Other common themes have included jealousy, sharing with others, respect for authority, and most, of all, prejudice. One episode in which the issue of prejudice was presented indirectly was entitled "Polka

Dot Ties." Here Davey and his friend Jimmy find all kinds of excuses to dislike the new kid on the block because of a difference in his appearance (the difference is the new kid's passion for polka dot neckties). But Davey's compassion shines through when he realizes that God loves everyone just the same, no matter how they are "dressed."

At one time "Davey and Goliath" was seen over more than 120 stations across the United States, as well as in other parts of the world. It aired on National Educational Television (now known as PBS). Reruns of the program remain a favorite today, on both syndicated and cable networks. The show is considered the sole remaining one of its type, designed to prompt the spiritual curiosity of children. The programs were underwritten and produced by Nancy Moore, through the courtesy of the Lutheran Church and the Church of Latter-day Saints, in cooperation with the National Council of Churches of Christ.

Ding Dong School

One of the first educational shows for preschool children, "Ding Dong School" was hosted by Dr. Frances Horwich, head of the Educational Department at Roosevelt College in Chicago. She was better known to millions of youngsters, however, simply as Miss Frances. The show featured a variety of conversation and instruction in such activities as finger painting, drawing, singing, and make-believe. Although similar shows have since come and gone, "Ding Dong School" was the first to blend the elements of instruction into a well-crafted half hour program.

An award-winning series in its own right, the program was watched at the time by 95 percent of the country's preschoolers. Shows were simple and used very few props, as Miss Frances explained the preliminary stages of art, numbers, and letters ("Paper is what we'll be using today, and that starts with the letter P").

"Ding Dong School" was a forerunner to the "Romper Room" series, a close imitator. Miss Frances focused her attentions strictly on the home audience, only occasionally sharing the studio stage with her collection of puppets, dolls, and pet goldfish. At the end of each telecast children were reminded to use their creative skills, while she sang the closing song, ringing the same handbell with which she opened each show.

Presented daily, the show became an undeniable hit for the NBC network and the first of its type to deal solely with the education of children. But to the dismay of parents, critics, and most of all Miss Frances herself, NBC canceled the series after just four short years. Executive representatives forever in search of larger profits realized that the revenues from daytime versions of the prime-time "big money" game shows would give the network the extra boost it needed to compete fully with the other networks. In 1956 "Ding Dong School," still a ratings winner at the time, was replaced, ironically, with "The Price Is Right." NBC placed "Ding Dong School" at 9:00–9:30 in the Monday through Friday morning lineup. The first show aired on November 24, 1952. The final show aired on December 28, 1956. It was syndicated in February 1959.

Having successfully created a unique children's program and owning the production rights to the series with producer Reinald Warrenrath, Dr. Horwich found a new home in the syndication market in the winter of 1959. Unfortunately, this time the show lasted only a single season. Despite the show's previous achievements, sponsors were now hesitant to support the series, favoring instead more weekday morning programs geared to the larger adult audience.

By the beginning of 1960, "Ding Dong School" was permanently dismissed. It remains today an individual standout in the children's genre.

Discovery

Frank Buxton and Virginia Gibson were the cohosts for this long-running children's documentary series that took its viewers on educational journeys all across the world. Each program focused on a different part of the world, discovering, as the title implied, new faces and places, different cultures and life-styles, and how important each one is in its own way.

Developed by then ABC news and children's program director Jules Pewowar, the series was conceived with the idea of arousing children's interest in the world about them. Pewowar had previously been responsible for the production of "Mr. Wizard," one of the most innovative children's series of all time.

In some programs host Frank Buxton or Virginia Gibson could be seen in areas as remote as Alaska or the Arctic, while in others as near as Cape Canaveral's observatory, providing the audience with a close-up view of the solar system. Certain programs focused on biology, demonstrating through diagrams such organs as the heart and the human brain.

Whatever the premise of each episode, "Discovery" left children with a basic foundation upon which to build more knowledge. Subjects of historical significance and cultural importance were also emphasized, providing much of the show's appeal to parents and educators. For a time it appeared that "Discovery" might be the most informative weekday show on the network. It provided factual accuracy, and many presentations helped familiarize children with the lives and accomplishments of many contemporary heroes.

"Discovery" actually began as a 25-minute weekday program for younger children, presented on an irregular basis. It later attracted the attention of older children as well when it shifted during its second year on the air to Sunday mornings. During the show's final season, after a drop in ratings, it survived mainly as a lead-in to the rerun episodes of "Jonny Quest." Here are the various program schedules for which ABC offered "Discovery": Monday–Friday, 4:30–5:00 P.M., October 1, 1962, through September 6, 1963; Sunday, 12:30–1:00 P.M., September 15, 1963, through December 29, 1963; Sunday, 11:30–12:00 noon, January 5, 1964, through September 5, 1971. "Discovery" was an early effort by ABC to present children with a positive alternative in programming.

Draw with Me see *Jon Gnagy: Learn to Draw*

The Electric Company

Like the immensely popular "Sesame Street" series, "The Electric Company" was also a production of the Children's Television Workshop and was shown daily, Monday through Friday over the PBS network from October 3, 1971, through September 3, 1976. "Sesame Street" was aimed primarily at the preschool audience, but "The Electric Company" was presented on more of an intermediate level, for older children. Programs featured a variety of musical skits, animated segments, and various other elements that combined a rapid pace and the underlying theme of education.

In some segments, cast members parodied other forms of the media in satires that often drew the attention of adults. Stan Lee's *Spiderman*, for instance, was featured frequently, leaping from the comic pages to real life as he battled criminals who constantly took advantage of the English language. "Un-Fu" was a take-off on David Carradine's "Kung-Fu," about a Chinese cowboy who roamed the prairie seeking great knowledge about words that begin with the prefix *un*. Also presented were the adventures of "Letterman," a superspeller who righted the wrongs of grammatical errors perpetrated by his greatest enemy, the Spellbinder. While each presentation focused on mathematics and grammar, visual effects and cultural awareness were also very much in evidence, along with a great deal of sophistication and earnestness.

Comedian and educator Bill Cosby was one of the notable cast members. Others included Rita Moreno (who would eventually receive every major acting award in the industry), Morgan Freeman (whose future included an Oscar nomination for best actor in *Driving Miss Daisy*), Judy Graubart (a veteran of the famed Second City Players), and Skipp Hinhart (who had played the original Schroeder in the 1967 stage production of *You're a Good Man, Charlie Brown*). Other cast members included Lee Chamberlin, James Boyd, Luis Avalos, Danny Seagren, and Hattie Winstor.

"The Electric Company" was shown on more than 160 public broadcasting stations nationwide, presented several times each day for the benefit of older children who might miss a telecast during school hours.

In 1976, after five seasons with PBS, "The Electric Company" halted further production, mainly because of the outside interests of several of the most popular cast members. It continued, however, to rerun throughout most of the 1980s.

Fat Albert and the Cosby Kids

In 1971 a survey conducted by the group Black Efforts for Soul in Television (BEST) concluded that children's programs, for the most part were responsible for conveying "racial and bigoted information." With the notable exception of a few, such as "Captain Kangaroo" and "Sesame Street," BEST further argued that several animated programs that featured black characters, such as "Josie and the Pussycats," "The Jackson Five," and "The Harlem Globetrotters," rarely if ever brought up the subject of race relations. Most of the group's arguments applied equally to popular cartoon characters, such as "Tom and Jerry," "Bugs Bunny," and "The Flintstones," whose producers tended either to encourage stereotypes or to avoid blacks altogether.

In the fall of 1972, the CBS network responded to the group's list of concerns with "Fat Albert and the Cosby Kids." The first show aired September 9, 1972. CBS chose 12:30 on Saturday afternoon to schedule the program and the network kept the show at that spot until the final show aired on September 3, 1984. Produced by the Filmation Industries, and featuring comedian Bill Cosby as host and coproducer, the series became a model for others because of the realism it brought to the stories of a group of black youngsters, who expressed the real feelings of children raised in urban environments. Facing the challenges of modern society, the fully animated characters were based loosely on Cosby's childhood playmates in Philadelphia. Fat Albert, the title character and rotund leader of the group, was a likable giant of a boy whose determination and aplomb, despite obstacles, made him a role model not only for his friends—Bill, Old Weird Harold, Rudy, Mush Mouth Leonard, and Dumb Donald, but for millions of home viewers as well.

Besides being enjoyably funny, most of the shows were presented as basic forums for teaching children about such controversial issues as bigotry, cheating, child and sexual abuse, and dealing with the loss of a loved one, each episode ending with a resolution based on tactfulness and common sense. The lessons in life and the values explored have been thoroughly enjoyed, understood, and appreciated over the years by children of all backgrounds and by some as young as five. Although episodes were primarily intended to inform, stories have also managed to include humor while completely avoiding racial stereotypes. Segments concluded with a summation by Bill Cosby of the program's events, and then a musical interlude, with Fat Albert and the gang performing on a variety of homemade instruments.

The series received much acclaim from parents, educators, and action groups such as BEST and A.C.T. (Action for Children's Television). Produced by Norm Prescott and Lou Scheimer, "Fat Albert" made its debut as a prime-time special in November 1969, hosted by none other than Bill Cosby, who also provided most of the character voices. The show's success eventually led to a regular Saturday morning slot, where it remained a favorite for over a decade. Critics have called it "a show before its time."

Much of the program's long-running success was due to Bill Cosby himself, a man whose sincerity and gentle sense of humor have made him an international favorite with children and adults. A graduate of Temple University, Cosby received his doctorate in education in 1976 from the University of Massachusetts. No stranger to children's television, he has long delighted young viewers using a variety of themes directed toward education. In the fall of 1976, while serving as host of his own 60-minute children's variety series ("Cos," 1976), he led the cast of repertory players for the PBS series "The Electric Company." In 1978 he premiered in a segment of his own titled "Picture Pages" on the "Captain Kangaroo" weekday morning series. "Fat Albert and the Cosby Kids" was syndicated in September 1981.

While he shows no signs of slowing down today, Cosby relishes the fact that his commitment to children's education has received a special place in television history. He is over 50 years of age and still "telling it like it is"—somehow we never get tired of him.

The Friendly Giant

"The Friendly Giant" was educational television's earliest popular children's series. Host Bob Homme was known to millions of early television viewers as the Friendly Giant, a towering figure who entertained children by reading stories, singing songs, playing musical instruments, and chatting with puppets. Friendly, as he was called, lived in a huge castle where he lumbered over miniature props and sets. Created by Homme in 1954, the series was designed to provide preschool children with familiar, easy-to-read naptime stories, which always began with "Once upon a time, not long ago. . . ." In the tradition of other such pioneers as Paul Tripp and Bob Keeshan, Homme managed to convey feelings of good cheer and self-expression.

During its first five years, "The Friendly Giant" was broadcast live Monday through Friday from the University of Wisconsin's education station, WHA, and distributed by the network channel in Ann Arbor, Michigan. In 1959 Homme continued the series with the Canadian Broadcasting Corporation in Toronto, where it was presented as before in a series of 15-minute formats. In the fall of 1962, repeats of the programs broadcast in Canada between 1959 and August 1962 were presented on the affiliated NET station through the beginning of the 1969–70 PBS television season. The first show was televised October 10, 1955; the final show appeared September 24, 1970.

The ground-breaking series eventually inspired such high-quality shows as the long-running "Mr. Rogers' Neighborhood" and "Sesame Street" during the changeover period from National Educational Television to the Public Broadcasting System.

The Great Space Coaster see *chapter 8,*
"Puppets, Marionettes, and Dummies"

Hot Dog

Intending to introduce young children to modern technology, this unique series combined everyday wonders with the visual gags of such top-rated comics as Woody Allen, Jonathan Winters, and Joanne Worley. "Hot Dog" was meant to inspire curious children, and the topics of the programs ranged widely. The show was cited by critics, educators, and parents for considering such basic topics as "what drinking water consists of" and "how many trees it takes to make a single baseball bat."

The series was coproduced by Frank Buxton, previously recognized for his narration on the "Discovery" series, and Lee Mendelson, one of the key producers of the CBS Charlie Brown/Peanuts specials.

Although the NBC show, with its fine mixture of comedy and education, won critical acclaim, disappointingly it failed to attract enough of an audience—because of its time slot (Saturday, 12:30–1:30 P.M.), it was often preempted in favor of major sporting events. "Hot Dog" was canceled after just one year (the program was offered September 12, 1970, through September 4, 1971), but not before it received the 1971 Peabody Award for best children's educational show.

Hot Fudge

Produced by Detroit's WXYZ, in cooperation with the Lexington Broadcasting Service, "Hot Fudge" featured a variety of education, comedy, and social themes for children of all ages. Bob Elnicky's racially mixed Mits Puppet, was featured, providing children with 30 minutes of inspirational messages through gentle skits, songs, and stories. Interacting with puppets Mona, Seymour, Stacy, Homer, Jeffrey, Caz, and Mr. Kootch were live actors Ron Coden, Yolanda Williams, and Larry Santos, an excellent cast who provided the show with a unique blend of wit and satire. Ron Coden, for one, played a variety of characters from Mr. Nasty to Detective Tomato. He also appeared in skits with Yolanda Williams and Larry Santos parodying the worlds of entertainment and politics.

Many of the stories also revolved around Seymour, the show's principal puppet, who helped to confront children's greatest fears, apprehensions, and concerns. Seeking solitude in his secret hiding place, an empty treehouse, Seymour faced problems common to children of all ages and backgrounds, such as peer pressure, and how to deal with it properly.

Like "The Great Space Coaster," "Hot Fudge" became one of the better educational shows not affiliated with PBS, a situation that changed after the debut of "Sesame Street" in 1969. Presented weekly in most cities, "Hot Fudge" was syndicated in 1976 and was picked up by over 100 local stations across the United States in just its second year on the air. The show remained on the air until 1980. Shown in an era when television executives and programmers were looking for new ways to educate and inform, "Hot Fudge" remains one of the best.

In the News

This long-running CBS newscast series, developed especially for children, was presented five times for two and half minutes every Saturday morning for over a decade. Excerpts presented news on a children's level, which helped them to understand the world better and the problems faced by adults. The program was produced by CBS's own news team and narrated by Christopher Glenn. It appeared at various times on Saturday from September 11, 1971, through September 3, 1983.

Jon Gnagy: Learn to Draw / Draw with Me / You Are an Artist

This show was hosted by Jon Gnagy, a bearded, self-taught artist who was the first television celebrity to encourage children's creative abilities by demonstrating to them the fundamentals of drawing. Gnagy first began his on-the-air lessons in 1946 in a series of one- to five-minute segments designed to fill air time between programs. In 1950 he was offered a regular contract by CBS to begin a weekly series of instructional programs, 15 to 30 minutes in length. Using his own knowledge of art, Gnagy taught by having children at home draw along with him in a simplistic manner. Step by step, he created on canvas such familiar objects as mountains, animals, and fruit, without the slightest bit of complexity. But his shows eventually attracted as many critics as young viewers. Many complained that Gnagy's approach to children was "domineering" and presented on too high a level. Gnagy responded by stating that his purpose was only to get as many children as possible to begin a sketching pattern all their own. His function was only to encourage, to help beginners turn their drawings into something more inventive by following the few simple steps he offered.

Despite the criticism, Gnagy gained many fans, and he endorsed a series of art supplies that bore his name and likeness. With his trademark theme song, the "Minute Waltz," Gnagy was presented off and on throughout the 1950s on CBS and NBC and in different time slots.

Marlo and the Magic Movie Machine

Laurie Faso served as host for this 60-minute Sunday morning children's series that focused on educational topics. As Marlo, Faso delighted children with a variety of selected movie clips, both old and new, cartoons, guessing games, and historical profiles. A main feature was the Magic Movie Machine, computer designed to provide the answers to fun, trivia, and general knowledge questions. Syndicated nationally from 1977 through 1979 through WFSB, of Hartford, Connecticut, the series became one of the few shows of the 1970s conceived specifically to convey information both significant and trivial.

While most of the show's fun relied on segments featuring highlights from an earlier era, celebrity photos and an animated segment entitled "Adventures of Sweet Pickles" also provided a great deal of appeal. The enthusiastic voice of Marlo's computer was provided off-screen by Mert Koplin. In the premiere episode, the Movie Machine helped children to identify objects whose names begin with the letter *B*. Also included as a first in a series of famous profiles was a story on inventor Thomas Edison.

Parents were often more familiar with the show's subject matter than their children. They found the series delightful, as they responded correctly in Marlo's games involving the identity of celebrities.

During the show's first season, programs were featured in a full hour format. The show was cut to 30 minutes for its second and third years on the air.

Mr. I. Magination

Paul Tripp was Mr. I. Magination, the series host and tour guide on a 30-minute train trip of fun, music, and make-believe. Assisting him on the journey to "imaginationland" were his wife, Ruth Enders, and his friends Ted Tiller, Joe Silver, and Richard Boone. A forerunner of the much more successful "Captain Kangaroo" and "Mr. Rogers'" series, "Mr. I. Magination" became extremely popular with youngsters despite the CBS network's claim that the show was not worth the time it took to produce.

The series was designed to encourage as many youngsters as possible to express themselves more completely by acting upon their own fantasies. As Mr. I. Magination, complete with engineer's overalls and cap and homespun philosophy, Tripp created a comfortable imaginary environment in each program which stimulated participation by the home audience. Sketches, which usually included music, songs, and puppets, were paced to hold the attention of children from preschool to the primary level. While some of television's early children's show hosts found it necessary to perform before a live studio audience, Mr. I. Magination relied only on the indulgence of the home viewer. The show succeeded in creating a colorful world of make-believe that also dealt with the kind of true-to-life experiences that children often encounter.

"Mr. I. Magination" was scheduled for Sunday nights at 7:00 until 7:30 on CBS. The first show aired on May 29, 1949. It remained in this programming slot until it was canceled on June 16, 1951. When the series was first canceled in 1951, critics, who admired the show, along with parents, staged a huge public demand for its immediate return to the air. The series became one of the first to be revived by a loud public outcry. As a result, the show returned to CBS on Sunday nights at 6:00, where it remained from January 13, 1952, through April 13, 1952.

Previously presented on Sunday evenings (at a time when several networks concluded their broadcast day at 8:00 P.M.), "Mr. I. Magination" was switched to Saturdays in 1952. Still at CBS, the program was broadcast from 1:00 to 1:30 P.M. beginning on April 19, 1952, through June 28, 1952. Unfortunately, this time, because of the growing Saturday morning schedule of programs featuring live dramas and cowboy heroes, the series lasted only for two months, this time leaving the air for good.

Tripp, creator, producer, and writer for the series, was only 23 when the show debuted in 1949. When it completed its run in 1952, he hosted two other local children's shows and took various roles on both screen and stage. He was also responsible for a series of children's books, which he co-wrote. His most popular book is the beloved *Tubby the Tuba*.

Mr. Rogers' Neighborhood

Creator Fred Rogers is the host of this long-running 30-minute Monday through Friday series geared primarily toward younger children. From the early years of PBS, Mr. Rogers, with his warm and caring manner, has been an inspiration to educational television, because of his methods of reaching children both as an educator and as a friend. "Mr. Rogers' Neighborhood," using fun, activities, and make-believe, has helped children over the years to understand themselves better. "I want every child to know that he or she has something lovable and worth expressing," Rogers has said many times.

In addition to serving as host of the series, Rogers also produces and provides the manipulation and vocals for most of the puppet characters. Other cast members have included Betty Aberlin, as the charming Lady Aberlin; Joe Negri, as the town handyman; Don Brocket, as Fire Chief Brocket; associate producer David Newell, who played Mr. McFeely of the Speedy Delivery service; François Clemons, as Officer Clemons; and Bob Trow, "Bob Dog," who assisted Rogers with the puppet vocals.

Fred Rogers.

"Mr. Rogers" originally aired for 15 minutes a day in Toronto, Canada, as a local favorite before making its 1967 debut (May 22) in the United States on National Educational Television. Rogers, an ordained minister of the United Presbyterian Church, had previously worked on local television as early as 1955, when he first introduced his easygoing manner to television's first generation of viewers in a 15-minute daily series entitled "The Children's Corner." Throughout his career, Rogers has always focused more on children's uniqueness than on their cognitive skills.

Many of the programs have centered on children's innermost fears and emotions (jealousy, envy, fear of the dark, and so forth). "Our main goal," Rogers has said, "is to confront children with what bothers them the most." A typical episode may show Mr. Rogers as he visits various neighbors, helping them cope with such disappointments as broken toys and alienation from friends or siblings. Since its debut on the air more than 25 years ago, the show has continuously received praise from enthusiastic parents, educators, and critics. During the early years of his career in local television Rogers first introduced his cast of puppet characters, who would eventually become familiar to over two generations of viewers. Among the inhabitants of the "Land of Make-Believe" are the incorrigible King Friday XIII, Lady Elaine Fairchild, the shy Daniel, the Striped Tiger, and Henrietta Pussycat.

Upon completion of "The Children's Corner" in 1962, Rogers joined with the Canadian Broadcasting Corporation in Toronto for a new daily series, entitled "Misterogers." In 1963, he established a full half-hour version of the series, broadcast in Pittsburgh over the Eastern educational network. When funds for the series ran out, audiences made a considerable effort to return it to the air. Thanks to a grant from the Sears Roebuck Company and the Public Broadcasting Service, the program was launched over most of the affiliated national education stations, as a staff of additional writers, producers, and associates was assembled. "Public television has been an instrument for me to be a professional worker for families with your children," Rogers has commented. "It must always be an expression of our highest idealism as well as an instrument for our positive creative powers." Like "Sesame Street," "Mr. Rogers' Neighborhood" has long been a children's institution for expression and learning.

Mr. Wizard / Watch Mr. Wizard

Don Herbert served as host to what has been called the best of the instructional shows for children. As Mr. Wizard, science instructor, Herbert was the first to conduct scientific experiments on the small screen. The show itself was an experiment that would last for over 20 years. As popular on Saturday mornings as "Mighty Mouse" or "Jerry Mahoney," Mr. Wizard was assisted in each presentation by a variety of enthusiastic child actors who shared his 30 minutes of science knowledge with children who watched at home. A landmark series that provided an in-depth look at the basic principles of natural science, "Mr. Wizard" examined such everyday elements as air and water and their interactions with paper, glass, string, and balloons. Although many of Herbert's experiments employed step-by-step directions, a few produced unexpected results during live productions and children at home had to be given an appropriate explanation.

The series, presented during most of its run on Saturday mornings, encouraged thousands of eager youngsters to take an active interest in science; it also became one of the most highly praised shows by critics, educators, and parents. It was one of the most eagerly awaited events of the week, as it proved by the mid–1950s, when teachers began encouraging use of the program as an academic requirement for its safety and preventive measures. Most important, however, "Mr. Wizard" set a high standard for the basics of educational technology which has rarely appeared since.

Produced with a limited budget, "Mr. Wizard" was aired over the NBC network as a nonprofit public affairs program. It was reported that at one time the series drew an estimated 800,000 viewers each week, with the majority between the ages of 9 and 15. After nearly 15 years on the air and over 3,000 experiments, "Mr. Wizard" was canceled in 1964, in favor of programs geared to a much less mature audience.

A science major from the Teacher's College of Wisconsin, Herbert first took an interest in broadcasting while working as a tour guide at the NBC Rockefeller Plaza. After a brief stint in the Air Corps Herbert returned to NBC, this time, however, as a radio artist and writer, and he provided the listening audience with tips on nutrition in a health series that he himself created. With the dawn of the space age, Herbert realized that children's curiosity about the wonders of natural science could provide him an excellent opportunity in the new medium of television. Thus began "Mr. Wizard, Science Instructor," or "Watch Mr. Wizard," as it was most commonly referred to in most television markets.

In 1971 Herbert returned as Mr. Wizard for another season and a younger generation of children, some unfamiliar with his old series. Unlike the earlier shows of the 1950s and 1960s, many of the new programs used fire and inflammable materials, which required a great deal of parental guidance.

After more than 40 years in educational broadcasting and research Herbert is today the author of four books on science, and he continues his work in a new series of syndicated shows produced specifically for cable networks that cater to informative children's programming.

The earlier series was a production of Jules Pewowar. Here is a complete programming history of NBC's "Mr. Wizard": Saturday, 5:00–5:30 P.M., March 3, 1951, through May 5, 1951; Saturday, 6:30–7:00 P.M., May 12, 1951, through February 23, 1952; Saturday, 7:00–7:30 P.M., March 2, 1952, through February 6, 1955; Saturday, 4:30–5:00 P.M., February 13, 1955, through July 2, 1955; Saturday, 11:30–12:00 noon, July 9, 1955, through December 31, 1955; Saturday, 12:30–1:00 P.M., February 4, 1956, through March 4, 1956; Saturday, 5:00–5:30 P.M., March 11, 1956, through April 1, 1956; Saturday, 5:30–6:00 P.M., April 8, 1956, through June 3, 1956; Saturday, 12:30–1:00 P.M., June 24, 1956, through September 9, 1956; Saturday, 5:30–6:00 P.M., September 16, 1956, through October 28, 1956; Saturday, 5:00–5:30 P.M., November 4, 1956, through December 2, 1956; Saturday, 12:30–1:00 P.M., December 9, 1956, through March 3, 1957; Sunday, 2:30–3:00 P.M., March 11, 1957, through June 10, 1957; Sunday, 3:30–4:00 P.M., June 17, 1957, through September 2, 1957; Sunday, 1:00–1:30 P.M., September 9, 1957, through June 8, 1958; Sunday, 4:00–4:30 P.M., June 15, 1958, through August 3, 1958; Sunday, 1:00–1:30 P.M., October 5, 1958, through December 28, 1958; Sunday, 11:30–12:00 noon, April 5, 1959, through May 2, 1960; Saturday, 1:00–1:30 P.M., May 15, 1960, through September 3, 1961; Saturday, 12:30–1:00 P.M., September 10, 1961, through January 28, 1962; Saturday, 12:00–12:30 P.M., February 4, 1962, through September 1, 1962; Saturday, 12:30–1:00 P.M., September 8, 1962, through October 6, 1962; Saturday, 1:30–2:00 P.M., October 13, 1962, through March 2, 1963; Saturday, 12:00–12:30 P.M., March 9, 1963, through September 28, 1963; Saturday, 2:00–2:30 P.M., October 5, 1963, through December 14, 1963; Saturday, 8:00–8:30 A.M., December 21, 1963, through April 5, 1964; Saturday, 12:30–1:00 P.M., April 12, 1964, through September 6, 1964; Sunday, 12:30–1:00 P.M., September 13, 1964, through July 11, 1965; Saturday, 12:00–12:30 P.M., September 11, 1971, through September 2, 1972.

The New Zoo Review see *chapter 8,*
"Puppets, Marionettes, and Dummies"

Nova

The wonders of science are vividly explored in this critically acclaimed series presented over the PBS network. Presented at various times in both a 60- and 90-minute format beginning in 1974, the program has informed children over the years about the mysteries of natural science and the environment through film documentaries centered on such topics as space, geography, and ecology. Other programs have explored such general topics as hobbies, the U.S. Postal Service, and how raw materials are produced and exported. Stories have often helped children to understand the world better through real-life adventures, capitalizing on their natural attraction to the environment.

In one program scientists at major observatories in Hawaii prepared to view the "eclipse of the century," which occurred in July 1991. The experiments conducted by four major teams from NASA attempted to demonstrate for the audience the actions of the sun's magnetic field. Another show was a tour (1989) of "the hidden city," New York City's aqueduct system, considered "invisible" until a breakdown. Even the concept of life has been introduced in several well-taught segments for older children, as well as preschoolers who are just beginning to make sense of the world around them.

As with such documentary series as "Wild Kingdom," parents have praised "Nova" for its consistency in conveying values. Over the years "Nova" has received the funding and support it deserves from the American Association for the Advancement of Science. The series is a production of PBS-affiliate WGBH in Boston, which is responsible for a number of other educational series broadcast over the PBS network.

Pryor's Place see *chapter 7, "Kindly Hosts and Hostesses"*

Reading Rainbow

A Gallup poll conducted several years ago predicted that almost half of all Americans, particularly children, would read more in the future than they do today. The poll further indicated that parents who read to young children will help stimulate them into reading themselves much sooner and to gain advantages throughout their entire lives.

Unfortunately, television-watching has had a negative effect on children's reading habits. Statistics confirm that by the time a child graduates from high school he or she will have spent more than 15,000 hours watching television, in contrast to 11,000 hours of English, spelling, and reading in both the home and the classroom. In short, television is more enjoyable to young people.

In 1983, with this thought in mind, the people at PBS debuted "Reading Rainbow," a half hour show designed specifically to encourage children to read and become better readers. Hosted with enthusiasm by actor LeVar Burton, each program consisted of stories, films, and discussion designed to encourage children to search for the suggested storybooks at stores and libraries. Burton himself entices children with his encouraging introductions as he analyzes their opportunities for critical thinking; he concludes each presentation with a good thought or idea. A welcome but relatively new face to children's television, Burton made his acting debut as the young Kunta Kinte—the African great-great-great-great-great-grandfather of writer Alex Haley in the award-winning 1977 television miniseries "Roots." He has starred since in many dramatic presentations and appears as a regular on the syndicated "Star Trek: The Next Generation."

"Reading Rainbow" themes have helped children learn to overcome their innermost fears and prejudices. Prior to reading the book *All Colors of the Race*, by Arnold Adolf, Burton visits a farmer's carnival where mimes of all sorts freely communicate with one another without words. Marjorite Weinman Sharmat's *Gila Monsters Meet You at the Airport* examined an experience that most children face at one time or another, moving away and the sadness it often entails. And before going into Thatcher Hurd's *Momma Don't Allow*, about a musical alligator, Burton introduces children to the frightening reptiles and the myths surrounding them from the bayous of Louisiana.

Generally concise and entertaining, even to the most unsophisticated viewers, "Reading Rainbow," like the books it presents, offers a level of literary excellence that has been praised by the critics. Presented daily (Monday through Friday) in most cities, "Reading Rainbow" remains one of the most highly acclaimed educational shows of its kind.

Sesame Street

During television's early years, educational shows were often presented in such a straightforward and uninspiring manner that many young viewers felt more forced than inclined to watch. The transition of National Educational Television to the Public Broadcasting System changed that November 10, 1969, with the premiere of just one series: "Sesame Street." Created and developed by Joan Ganz Cooney, executive director of the then newly conceived Children's Television Workshop, the hour long show was originally designed for inner city preschoolers. In due course the series became an institution of educational entertainment with children of all ages and backgrounds.

Through various methods of teaching, with the frequent use of songs, amusing skits, and familiar puppets, "Sesame Street" quickly rose to the top of everyone's list as an international favorite, enjoyed by nearly as many adults as children. Throughout the show's long history the names of its cast of characters, both human and "Muppet," have remained familiar. Generally shown Monday through Friday (but shown in some cities seven days a week), episodes have tried to teach children everything from the basic alphabet to simple math. Lessons have also been offered in foreign languages, based upon a principle of "sight on sound" association. No other children's show to date has taught so vividly while rarely reminding children of its primary objective: "selling" them on learning.

Although the show has managed over the years to gain an enormous amount of support from various adult groups, critics of the early shows were not all kind. Some complained about its "speedy delivery," as well as the large assortments of formats used in a single program. These critics thought children were for the most part "missing the point entirely" and that the show encouraged a new generation of "speed freaks"—this at a time when American children were already caught up in political and cultural turmoil. It was this "fast-paced delivery," however, as well as its biting satire, that made "Sesame Street" not just an outstanding series but the winner of every major award that both television and educational organizations had to offer. It also appeared all over the world, translated into a variety of different languages.

Dramatic creations with human qualities, the late Jim Henson's "Muppet" characters have been popular with millions of youngsters for over two generations. Among the original Muppets were Bert and Ernie, a juvenile version of the Odd Couple; Oscar, the lovable grouch; the dessert-craving Cookie Monster, and his cousins Telly, Grover, and Harry; and perhaps the most beloved muppet of all, Kermit, the Sesame Street News–reporting frog. Others have included game show host Guy Smiley; Polly Darton and Prairie Dawn, country-western singers; the Twiddle-bug family; Elmo Monster; the befuddled Mr. Johnson; the amazing Munford the magician; Bruno the trash man; the bigger than life Mr. Snuffle-upagus; Count von Count; whose hobby is counting everything; and the ever-amusing Forgetful Jones, and his lady friend, Clementine, and horse, Buster.

But of all the Muppets on the show, the biggest and most popular is Big Bird, a ten-foot canary whose inquisitive nature and natural innocence make him resemble a six-year-old child. Originally performed by the series' chief puppeteer, Frank Oz, Big Bird, like Oscar the Grouch, has been played for many years by Carroll Spinney.

"Sesame Street"'s multitalented human actors have included Bob McGrath, as Bob; Will Lee (1969–83), as Mr. Hooper; Loretta Long, as Susan; Matt Robinson (1969–73) and Roscoe Orman (1973–), as Gordon; Sonia Manzano, as Maria; Emilio Delgado, as Luis; Northern J. Calloway (1970–89), as David; Alaina Reed (1976–86), as Olivia; Linda Bove (1984–), as Linda; and Allison Bartlett (1988–), as Gena. The characters on "Sesame Street" might be considered two dimensional, but the nature of the program requires them to be. To serve various educational functions, the principals must perform in both a dramatic and an informative way. For them to do so is both complementary and contradictory.

In its own way, "Sesame Street" exemplified in its early years the cultural awareness movement associated with the late 1960s. Previously, children's educational programs limited participation by minorities, the poor, the disabled, and the hearing impaired. Today, with its inclusion of all different groups, the show continues to be successful. The show has also helped to establish the PBS network as the most successful in fine programming for children.

Today's Special

"Today's Special" was originally designed to encourage children to reflect on their innermost feelings and experiences and on their relationships with adults. Although using the form of a puppet fantasy series, the show in fact focuses on children's feelings, like fear, anxiety, and self-esteem. Episodes centered on an empty department store and its inhabitants: Jody (Nerene Virgin), an attractive female display artist; Sam (Bob Dermer), the night watchman; Muffy (Nina Keogh), a rhyming puppet mouse; and Jeff (Jeff Hystop), a mannequin who comes to life with the magic words *Hocus-pocus-ala-ma-gocus*. Musical skits and stories revolve around the durable relationship among the four friends, each with a different background, and on their dependence and loyalty to one another.

One of the newer PBS daily programs enjoyed by today's children, "Today's Special" was also shown periodically over cable's Nickelodeon, a network devoted primarily to children's programing and to classic television reruns. Produced and directed in Canada by Clive Vanderburgh, "Today's Special" managed to create a unique formula, similar to those of such long-running favorites as "Captain Kangaroo" and "Mr. Rogers."

Since its premier in 1987, the series had been well regarded by adults for outstanding entertainment and for its topics worthy of family discussion which have involved safety, responsibility, and drugs and alcohol. Programs were also included topics of general interest in arts and crafts, where professional guidelines and suggestions were provided to promote children's creativity. Although informative for kids of all ages, the show was of a particular interest to younger children.

"Today's Special" appeared at intervals Monday through Friday on PBS, with long lapses between presentations. Unfortunately, the network has been unable to give the half hour show a regularly scheduled time slot and the show was cancelled in 1992.

Vegetable Soup / Vegetable Soup II

"Vegetable Soup" was the first children's series designed specifically to deal with the subject of race relations. Produced by Charles Thomas and Norma Davidoff, the program consisted at various times of both 15- and 30-minute forums that emphasized, on children's level, issues of prejudice and bigotry, while providing perspective into ethnic conflicts around the world.

Featured on the animated thought-provoking segments was the voice of actor James Earl Jones, as host Long John Spoilsport, for "Adventures in Saniland." Singer-actress Bette Midler supplied the voice of Woody the Spoon, who helped demonstrate the art of preparing such delicacies as sukiyaki and rice, spaghetti and meatballs, corned beef and cabbage, and ham hocks and black-eyed peas. Live segments featured such familiar actors as Ricardo Montalban, Rita Moreno, and Pat Morita, who talked to children, with the assistance of music and puppets, about career opportunities for minorities like themselves.

The show was one of the most innovative new Saturday morning shows for kids to come along for a time, and many criticized program directors for scheduling the program at a very early hour. Most syndicated affiliates aired the program between 6:00 and 7:00 A.M., to avoid interfering with top-rated Saturday morning favorites.

The series was produced in cooperation with the New York State Education Department. Yanna Kroyt Brandt was executive producer. "Vegetable Soup" was made available for viewing by the public broadcasting network while still being featured in various syndication markets. During its second season the series was retitled "Vegetable Soup II." A third season consisted entirely of reruns from the previous two. It was broadcast in syndication from 1975 through 1978.

Wild Kingdom

Zoologist Marlin Perkins was once engulfed in the bone-crushing coils of a huge anaconda while filming a segment of "Wild Kingdom" as thousands of home viewers watched. In another program he was attacked by a charging seal who feared for the safety of her pups. Such was the risk often involved in the filming of each week's show, created by

Perkins, who described the capture of wild animals while telling viewers about their natural environment. Although similar shows appeared over the years, none has been able to depict more vividly than "Wild Kingdom" the unpredictability of animals being captured in their natural habitat.

Shown on both NBC and affiliating syndicated networks for over a quarter of a century, "Wild Kingdom" was one of television's most entertaining and informative documentary series. Sponsored for most of its run by the Mutual of Omaha Insurance Company (a business enterprise that became virtually synonymous with the series), the show was enjoyable, with little or no adult assistance, to most child viewers. Although Perkins was responsible for hosting and narrating most of the programs, other participants have included Jim Fowler, Stan Brock, and Tom Allen. Here is the programming history for "Wild Kingdom": Sunday, 6:30–7:00 P.M., January 6, 1963, through September 7, 1969; Sunday, 7:00–7:30 P.M., September 14, 1969, through April 11, 1971; Saturday, 6:00–6:30 P.M., September 18, 1971, through September 5, 1973. The show was syndicated in October 1973 and remained on the air until 1984.

Marlin Perkins (1900–86) first began his zoological studies as early as 1921. In 1946, while serving as curator for Chicago's Lincoln Park and and the St. Louis Forest Park zoos, he began broadcasting his observations over local Chicago station WBKB. By 1950, his discussions of animal behavior caught the attention of NBC affiliates that were looking for someone to host a series about animals at zoos across the country. Entitled "Zoo Parade," this show featured Perkins, with cohost Jim Hurlbut, for seven years on late Sunday afternoons as a lead-in to the week's prime-time programming schedule. "Wild Kingdom" became the direct descendent of "Zoo Parade," focusing on travels in Africa and India, rather than on animals doing cute tricks for peanuts.

Enlightening and perceptive, "Wild Kingdom" remained the most durable documentary series on television. Reruns can still be seen occasionally on both syndicated and participating PBS networks.

You Are an Artist see *Jon Gnagy: Learn to Draw*

Zoom

Reminiscent of the "revised" "Mickey Mouse Club" of the 1970s, "Zoom" featured a cast of seven talented youngsters, each with different origins, whose goal was to inform through fun and frolic. The programs, sponsored by the WGBH Educational Foundation, featured a potpourri of songs, skits, and games that promoted the joy of being a child. "Zoom" was distinguished by a delightful, fast-paced atmosphere that created a language all its own. Incorporated into each of the programs were such "Zoom"-related topics as "Zoomaroma," "Zoom-games," the "Zoom play" of the week, "Zoom-doodles," and an informative segment on arts and crafts entitled "Zoom-a-do."

The show also became one of the first on PBS produced primarily for entertainment rather than education. Often, "Zoom" even rivaled "Sesame Street" for popularity, reaching more children's homes than any other PBS series at the time. A series that encouraged viewer mail, "Zoom" reportedly received between 15,000 and 20,000 letters a week from children who had their own story ideas for the show.

"Zoom" was produced and distributed by WGBH in Boston. Fun, vibrant, and exhilarating, "Zoom" represented quite a change from the traditional shows PBS had formerly brought to television. Notably, the series did not require the regular guidance of an adult, unlike other shows of this type.

Unfortunately, funding for "Zoom," which often had a larger budget than most PBS presentations, became more and more difficult to obtain. By the end of 1978, one of the network's most distinguished educational/variety shows concluded its run of original productions. Well worth repeated showings, its last two seasons on the air (1979–80) consisted entirely of reruns.

Here is the programming history for "Zoom" which appeared on PBS at various times in various cities: Sunday, January 9, 1972, through September 1, 1979; Monday–Friday, September 9, 1974, through August 18, 1978; Sunday–Friday, August 20, 1978, through October 20, 1978; Monday–Friday, October 23, 1978, through November 17, 1978; Monday, Wednesday, Thursday, Friday, November 20, 1978, through December 22, 1978; Sunday, January 7, 1979, through September 2, 1979; Sunday–Friday, September 9, 1979, through January 4, 1980; Sunday, January 6, 1980, through April 13, 1980; Sunday–Friday, April 20, 1980, through September 21, 1980.

7. *Kindly Hosts and Hostesses*

Many years before Pee Wee Herman, television managed to maintain an equal balance of programs with live and animated characters. Kindly adults once appeared on television in all varieties, from elderly uncles and clowns, to grown-up kids and Mouseketeers. These friendly, funny people with the sunshine smiles became as much a part of early television as black and white and the 15-inch screen. Some became enormously popular with time. Year after year they contributed a talent to meet the demands of a eager young public. Some sang songs, others introduced stories, while a few relied on puppets and off-beat characters. But the concept was essentially always the same: a familiar relationship based on distinctive styles and talents.

Today these shows are only a memory.

The "Bozo" Shows
Bozo the Clown / Bozo's Big Top — The All New Bozo Show / Bozo's Fun House — The Bozo Show

Bozo the Cown was the most familiar, if not the most successful, of the children's television hosts. The long-running syndicated variety show was the invention of producer Larry Harmon, whom, contrary to popular opinion, never actually appeared as Bozo. Instead, he developed the idea of featuring a different (but essentially the same) Bozo the Clown host on local television stations across the country, each serving as master of ceremonies for a 30-minute program of games, prizes, and cartoons.

"Bozo the Clown" was first syndicated in 1956. The show became such a success that by the early 1960s several dozen stations featured former radio announcer Frank Aurunch as the most familiar of Bozo the clown actors, with the Boston station WHDH producing more than 100 shows for national syndication. Besides serving as host, Aurunch made numerous public appearances as the clown, most notably in 1966 at the New York World's Fair, on behalf of both the United Nations and the UNICEF Foundation.

By the mid–1960s through the 1970s, more than 240 stations in more than 40 countries carried the Boston syndicated series, often under titles as "The Bozo Show," "Bozo's Fun House," "Bozo's Big Top," or "The All New Bozo Show." In most of the programs children of different ages competed on stage in the day's big contest for awards and prizes. Also included regularly were comic segments with Bozo interacting with local cast members and supporting actors also dressed as clowns or other funny characters. These skits somewhat resembled the earlier shows of the 1950s and 1960s which featured Bozo in a series of animated adventures also produced by Larry Harmon. In several markets the cartoons were featured independently, often hosted by local celebrities, rather than Bozo himself.

Both Bozo the host and the series have been very popular over the years. The character has maintained his popularity with all kinds of children. The series can still be seen periodically on Chicago station WGN, channel 9.

Dusty's Treehouse

Stu Rosen starred as the title character in "Dusty's Treehouse." Presented on weekdays, the show was set in a clubhouse where Dusty led children through a daily program of songs, stories, and skits that often dealt with realities of life. Dusty was often assisted by the Tony Urband Puppets: Maxine, the boisterous crow; Scooter, the ambitious squirrel; and the inquisitive Stanley, the spider, who somewhat resembled "Sesame Street"'s Big Bird.

Beginning locally on Los Angeles station KNXT and syndicated in October 1975, "Dusty's Treehouse" became a favorite over a few syndicated networks on the West Coast. In the 1980s, though, many children had the opportunity to see the show for the first time on cable's Nickelodeon channel.

"Dusty's Treehouse" earned a number of television's most prestigious awards for excellence in children's programming.

Lunch with Soupy Sales see *The "Soupy Sales" Shows*

The Magic Cottage

This early children's favorite was presented on the old Dumont network, produced live as audiences watched from outside the windows of New York's Wanamaker department store. Pat Meikle starred as the series hostess, a teacher and artist who sketched animated characters and presented them in daily serialized episodes along with a variety of games and contests. The cartoons, still pictures with movable limbs, told stories with nonviolent themes.

The show was produced by Meikle's husband, Hal Cooper, who had previously created a similar children's series entitled "The T.V. Babysitter." This series starred Pat Meikle as a fairy princess hostess who told naptime stories to children with the help of an animated English-speaking pigeon named Wilmer.

"Magic Cottage" was the children's show where "everything and anything can happen and does happen." For two years at a time when television was not yet widespread, "Magic Cottage" offered 30 minutes of daily, good-natured programming, with little competition from other networks. It was broadcast Monday through Friday at 6:30 from July 18, 1949, through February 9, 1951.

Regrettably, it is rarely remembered today.

The Mickey Mouse Club /
The New Mickey Mouse Club

"The Mickey Mouse Club" was at one time the most popular children's daily variety show, and it is still considered a favorite by television's first generation of children.

Walt Disney and his famous animated characters were already known to movie audiences around the world by the time the series arrived on television on October 3, 1955. Premiering at a time when television executives were seeking new gimmicks to attract children. "The Mickey Mouse Club" made its mark in television history for a number of reasons. First of all, the show made its debut on the same day as another noted favorite, "Captain Kangaroo," which appeared hours earlier on CBS. But what really made headlines was that "The Mickey Mouse Club," in just a few short weeks, managed to overwhelm the reigning "Howdy Doody Show" in the daily ratings. This eventually forced the freckle-faced puppet and all his Doodyville pals to move to Saturday mornings for the remainder of the show's run.

The program was hosted by everyone's favorite uncle, former actor

Jimmy Dodd, and the "Mouseketeers," a group of child performers whose trademark was a set of Mickey Mouse ears and T-shirts with their names on them. Another adult, Disney animator Roy Williams, was also featured, as big "mooseketeer" Roy. Dodd served as the show's daily master of ceremonies, leading the group through songs, dancing, newsreels, sketches, mouse cartoons, and a number of thrilling made-for-television serials like "Spin and Marty," "The Hardy Boys," "Clint and Mac," "Corky and White Shadow," and "Annette."

Shows opened regularly with Mickey himself in an animated segment introducing the format of the day's program. Although the premise remained basically the same, the series was constructed to highlight a general theme for each day of the week. Monday was "Fun with Music Day," presenting the Mouseketeers in a variety of favorite song-and-dance routines, including "A Fallen Star" and "The Tramp Ballet," in which the Mouseketeers, in costume, demonstrated "what the well-dressed hobo will wear." Tuesday was "Guest Star Day," and such noted celebrities as cello-playing comedian Morey Amsterdam would appear most frequently. Wednesday was "Anything Can Happen Day," and most anything did occur, from a Mickey Mouse News report on events of interest around the world, to an art session with "mooseketeer" Roy Williams. Another segment often featured on Wednesdays was the live adventures of Sooty, a French hand puppet with a knack for playing the piano. Thursday was "Circus Day," and the Mouseketeers, dressed as circus performers, introduced some of the greatest acts under the Big Top. Friday was "Talent Roundup Day." Here the Mouseketeers ended the week wearing Western gear, as they played host to youngsters performing for a television audience for the very first time.

There were also returning segments, such as the filmed adventures of "Spin and Marty," starring Tim Considine and Dave Stoltery, and "The Hardy Boys," with Considine and Tommy Kirk as the teenage supersleuths Frank and Joe Hardy. Another recurring segment featured the animated Jiminy Cricket in a splendid series of educational discussions of such topics as reading, safety, and responsibility.

Produced for ABC by Bill Walsh, "The Mickey Mouse Club" originally appeared for 60 minutes during its first two years on the air—at 5:00 P.M. until September 1, 1957. On September 4, 1957, it was trimmed to 30 minutes, since Disney's new "Zorro" series was scheduled immediately afterward. Last-minute changes, however, moved the swashbuckler to a weekly slot, at 8:00 P.M. on Thursdays. "The Mickey Mouse Club" remained at the 5:00 P.M. program slot until it was canceled on September 24, 1959.

Among the talented young Mouseketeers were Bobby Burgess,

Cubby O'Brien, Karen Pendleton, Darleen Gillespie, Sharon Baird, Tommy Cole, Lonnie Burr, Doreen Tracey, Johnny Crawford, Don Grady, and, the most popular of all, Annette Funicello. Only a few of them went on to develop their careers beyond the series. Dancer Bobby Burgess appeared later as a regular on Lawrence Welk's television show; little Cubby O'Brien went on to become a first-class drummer, appearing over the years with a number of big-name bands. Johnny Crawford later costarred with Chuck Conners as Mark in the popular Western "The Rifleman" (ABC, 1958–63); Don Grady played Fred MacMurray's son Robbie on the long-running sitcom "My Three Sons" (ABC, CBS, 1959–72). But perhaps the greatest success story was that of Annette Funicello, the bikini-clad heroine of a series of teenage beach movies, in which she played opposite such male leads as Frankie Avalon, Bobby Rydell, and Tommy Kirk. In addition to being a Mouseketeer, Annette was also featured on the program in 1957 as the star of her own dramatic serial, "Annette," in which she costarred with Tim Considine and Roberta Shore. It was a romantic tale, with all the elements associated with "coming of age," such as friendship, rivalry, and jealousy.

By the end of its first season, "The Mickey Mouse Club" had drawn more than 10 million viewers per day, more than any other afternoon show had ever drawn. The series was a great ratings success; it also helped to make the Mattel toy company the country's leading manufacturer of children's toys featuring the likeness of Mickey and several of the Mouseketeers. There were mouseke-ears, mouse-guitars, Mickey jack-in-the-boxes, mouseke-T-shirts (which bore the Mickey Mouse emblem), mouseke-books of all types, plus other items that featured such other Disney characters as Donald Duck, Goofy, Pluto, Jiminy Cricket, the Three Little Pigs, and many lesser-known characters, who, along with Jimmy Dodd and the Mouseketeers, appeared in songs and stories in a series of recordings distributed by Capital records. The Mouseketeers themselves were often seen outside the series, endorsing such kid-related products as Skippy peanut butter, Baker's chocolate drink, and Chocks one-a-day vitamins.

Although much of the show's success belonged to the talented group of youngsters known worldwide as the Mouseketeers, it was their leader, Jimmy Dodd, who won the respect and admiration of children everywhere. His easy-going manner, musical skills, and use of proverbs created an atmosphere comfortably entertaining to children of all ages. It was even rumored that as Dodd lay near death in a semicoma, he continued to provide wise advise to those who cared for him in his final days.

Unfortunately, "The Mickey Mouse Club" was an innocent victim of the times. African Americans and other minorities began to demand equal representation in the media. This error of omission was corrected in 1976 when the series was revived as "The New Mickey Mouse Club," as a new set of Mouseketeers included many African and Asian American faces. Unfortunately, the new series lacked the charm and originality that had made its predecessor such a hit.

When the original "Mickey Mouse Club" finally left the air in 1959, it was rerun in syndication three years later (1962–65) in more than 100 television stations across the United States. It was syndicated once more in 1975 (just one year prior to the new version), where for one year it became hugely successful all over again with a new generation of children who had never seen it before. "The New Mickey Mouse Club" was aired in syndication from 1976 until 1979. "The Mickey Mouse Club" remains vividly remembered today by many grown-up Mouseketeers.

Pee Wee's Playhouse

Pee Wee Herman, the childlike persona of comedian Paul Reubens, was the host of this likably odd children's series, which eventually became one of the biggest Saturday morning hits of the 1980s. Each week Reubens ran wild as the frantic Pee Wee Herman; the show followed a comic format utterly confusing and complicated. One of the calmer segments featured vintage cartoons from the 1930s and 1940s, from several studios as obscure today as the cartoons themselves. Although heavily edited for time reasons, the cartoons were often the the best excuse for watching the program.

Although the show originally seemed to parody the Saturday morning hosts of yesterday, it became evident after a while that Reubens had real rapport with the children's audience. At times he was even said to have compared himself (although not very convincingly) to such figures as Buffalo Bob Smith and Captain Kangaroo — a view disputed by the majority of adults today who grew up with television in the 1950s and 1960s. While Pee Wee's performances often seem contrived from start to finish, his naturalness provided much of the same kind of charm that Buffalo Bob and others had had.

In its own unusual way, the series managed to encourage children to have fun by expanding — as Pee Wee does — their own creative imagination. In a colorful and animated world of make-believe Pee Wee conversed with such inanimate objects as "Flori the Floor" and "Cheery the Chair," as well as such off-beat characters as Reba, the "good news only" mail carrier, and a puppet named Randy, whose face resembled a toilet bowl.

Paul ("Pee Wee" Herman) Reubens and friend.

Although some adults chose to ignore the show's harmless vulgarities, others criticized Pee Wee for his immature nature and his lack of redeeming qualities. Most critics, however, applauded the series for its amusing concept and for being new and different. While the show as a whole might not have been to everyone's liking, Reubens at least revived the concept of a live Saturday morning host.

After making his debut appearance as Pee Wee Herman on such popular talk shows as "David Letterman," Reubens, catching television audiences off-guard, soared to new heights in popularity, starring in such films as *Pee Wee's Big Adventure* and *Big Top Pee Wee*. The huge success of his first film launched him squarely into a Saturday morning slot in 1986, and he became something of a cult favorite with many kids, as well as some adults. Others featured on the series included former Shakespearean actor William Marshall as the "King of Cartoons," Suzanne Kent as "Miss Renee," Larry Fishburns as "Cowboy Curtis," and director John Paragon as the voices for Pee Wee's pet fish "Jambi" and "Petri." From September 13, 1986, through September 4, 1988, "Pee Wee's Playhouse" was broadcast by CBS on Saturday from 10:00 to 10:30 A.M. On September 11, 1988, the show moved to 11:30 A.M. on Saturday. The final show aired on July 20, 1991.

Produced by Paul Reubens and Bob Birnbaum, the series reached a hiatus halfway through the 1990–91 season, and was canceled, mostly because of a sudden drop in the ratings. The final decision to cancel, however, came as a result of Reubens's arrest at a Florida adult movie theater on July 26, 1991, on charges of indecent exposure. Insisting upon his innocence while maintaining a low profile, Reubens, supported by such entertainers as Bill Cosby, Joan Rivers, and Cyndi Lauper, has made only a few public appearances since. Upon learning of the charges, CBS officially dropped the show's remaining episodes (currently in reruns), as did the Disney-MGM Studios in Florida, where a Pee Wee video series had been planned as part of a national theme park tour.

Encouraged by both friends and fans to continue his career, Reubens did appear as a guest presenter at the 1992 MTV Music Video Awards to a thunderous standing ovation. Feeling confident for the first time in a long while, Reubens reverted to his Pee Wee character, teary-eyed but with the spirit of a professional, as he opened his remarks by asking, "Heard any good jokes lately?"

The Pinky Lee Show

Former burlesque comic Pinky Lee (born Pincus Leff) first brought his energetic brand of slapstick humor to television in 1951 in the weekly musical variety series "Those Two" (NBC, 1951–53), in which he co-starred with actress Vivian Blaine. It was three years later, however, that the lisping comedian made his biggest mark in television as the host of his own variety show for children.

Pinky Lee related better to children than had any other performer, for he spoke to them on their level. Having previously been guided by such authoritative adult figures as "big brother" Bob Emery, children regarded Pinky less seriously, perhaps more as a misbehaving older sibling with a flare for the silly and mischievous. Dressed in the checkered hat, coat, and baggy pants that became his trademark, Pinky opened his shows by driving a miniature automobile onto a stage with a live audience of children. After a silly introductory song-and-dance number that began "Yo ho, it's me, my name is Pinky Lee," Pinky spent the next 26 minutes playing games, telling stories, and wreaking havoc that involved everyone in the studio, from the audience of kids to the series regulars, both humans and puppets.

One of the most memorable things about the show was the way Pinky, a master in the art of improvisation, caught his staff members off-guard in a series of brilliantly done candid performances. In one show, for instance, Pinky sneaked silently behind a curtain to reveal an unsuspecting janitor doing his job, maintaining an empty sound stage. Today this trait is often associated with such popular comedians as David Letterman and Garry Shandling.

Apart from all the clowning, Pinky Lee also had a serious side. In a regular segment of the program entitled "Mr. and Mrs. Grumpy," Lee played "Pinky the Clown," an Emmett Kelly/Charlie Chaplin type of character, whose part he performed with much pathos. In one particularly touching episode, the Grumpys moved away and left the lonely Pinky behind; it was rumored that both the studio audience and the television crew were reduced to tears.

Also featured on the show were regulars Roberta Shore, Mel Koontz, Barbara Lake, Jane Howard, and Jimmy Brown.

The success of "The Pinky Lee Show" drove the lovable funny man to become one of the hardest working artists in the business. His show was originally broadcast daily immediately preceding the "Howdy Doody Show." But after taking a huge portion of the daily ratings in just his second season on the air, he included Saturday mornings in his already hectic schedule.

"The Pinky Lee Show" was shown on NBC at the following times: Monday–Friday, 5:00–5:30 P.M., January 4, 1954, through May 11, 1956; Saturday, 10:00–10:30 A.M., March 5, 1955, through June 9, 1956.

In addition to hosting his own show, which was broadcast from Los Angeles, Lee was flown to the East Coast every weekend to serve as cohost of "The Gumby Show," filmed at NBC's New York location. In 1957 Lee took over the job of sole host of the program. On September 20, 1955, while taping a live show, Pinky Lee collapsed before his studio audience; the children laughed, convinced it was all part of the act to which they had become so familiar. News releases stated that the comedian had suffered a heart attack, but in reality it was a combination of exhaustion and a neglected sinus condition. Lee was strongly advised by his doctors to slow down his schedule or accept the consequences, an ultimatum to which he unwillingly acquiesced.

Unfortunately, while he was recuperating, his daily show suffered tremendously in the ratings, partly because of his absence, but also because of the growing popularity of "The Mickey Mouse Club" on a competing network. His daily show was eventually canceled in 1956, replaced by reruns of "I Married Joan," while the "Howdy Doody Show" (also suffering in the daily ratings) occupied the show's vacant time slot on Saturday mornings. With only "The Gumby Show" remaining, Lee began to show signs of real weariness. By the beginning of the 1957–58 season, "The Gumby Show" was replaced by Hanna-Barbera's "Ruff and Reddy." For additional information about "The Gumby Show," see the entry in "Puppets, Marionettes, and Dummies" on p. 186.

Pinky Lee, a grand host and master showman, well remembered today by a generation of baby boomers, continued to make occasional guest appearances on both local and network television throughout the next decade.

Pip the Piper

Developed mainly to attract younger viewers, this 30-minute fantasy series, created and hosted by Jack Spear, became a favorite with older children as well. Jack Spear was the ever smiling Pip, the whimsical minstrel of mirth. He captivated youngsters weekly with his magic flute, whose notes led the way to the land of Pipertown, a place high in the clouds where harmonious instruments grew on trees and music was the universal language.

Pip was accompanied through the wonderland of Pipertown by Miss Merrynote, played by Spear's real-life wife, Phyllis Spear, and by Lucien Kaminsky, as Mr. Leader, the nominal head of the mirthful city, who wore a band leader's uniform. Kaminsky also played a variety of occasional roles, such as Paul the Pirate, Laurel the Lion, and Professor Oompah, the music instructor.

Each week the series was presented to children without the usual formula of incorporated animation, guest stars, or a live studio audience. The show relied instead on the talents of its fine cast of adults, who appeared to take great pleasure in coordinating the entire 30 minutes of fresh story ideas with happily executed performances.

Story segments involving Pip and the others were usually associated with a particular holiday or special occasion. "Story Land Day," for instance, often found Pip and his friends preparing for their roles as popular fairy tale characters. On "Do Something Nice for Someone Day," Pip and Miss Merrynote were featured in one episode burying a treasure chest for a despondent Paul the Pirate, who had never experienced the good fortune of digging one up. Other themes used such holiday traditions as carving a jack-o'-lantern for Halloween and planting a tree on Arbor Day.

"Pip the Piper" was produced in lavish color by Jack Miller on ABC on both Saturday and Sunday mornings at 11:30 from December 5, 1960, through May 28, 1961. The show switched over to NBC during its second season (June 24, 1961, through September 22, 1962), where it remained on Saturdays at 9:30 until its departure in 1962.

One of the few new shows of the era to appear in color, "Pip the Piper" remains a surprisingly timeless program, with episodes that could hold their own against many of today's children's shows that involve actors in live skits and musical backgrounds. Unfortunately though it was thoroughly enjoyed, it is rarely remembered today.

Pryor's Place

Attempting to imitate such fellow comedians as Bill Cosby, Richard Pryor starred in this series as a guide to 30 minutes of fun and knowledge. Like most children's shows that featured celebrities, "Pryor's Place" provided the stage for Richard Pryor to recreate some of his best improvisations from his early years as a stand-up comic. His characterizations of the "Friendly Wino" and the "Reggae Musician" gave children advice and humor. Coproduced by Sid and Marty Krofft, the series was another in a long line of programs that emphasized social norms and moral values, a characteristic used more than any other in educational television today. Costarring with Richard Pryor were Akili Prince, in weekly flashbacks as the comedian as a child growing up in Peoria, Illinois; Marla Gibbs as his elementary school teacher, Miss Jones; the Krofft Puppets; and singer Ray Parker, Jr., who performed the show's opening theme song. "Pryor's Place" aired on Saturday at 10:30 A.M. from September 22, 1984, through June 15, 1985, on CBS.

Pryor, an odd choice for a children's television host, initially became interested in the idea of his own series after several successful guest appearances on such popular favorites as "Sesame Street" and "The Electric Company." Despite the apprehensions of many a concerned adult familiar with Pryor's type of comedy, the show's formula surprisingly became a winning one, receiving not only good ratings but good reviews as well. Nevertheless, the show was destined to last for only a single season, partly because of a disagreement between Pryor and Sid and Marty Krofft over control of production. Pryor had just previously signed a five-year $40 million contract with Columbia Pictures. The money went toward the creation of the Pryor Company, in which Pryor was to be solely responsible for the production of four pictures a year in the range of $5 to $6 million. In addition, Pryor had also agreed to star in at least three of the films during the contract, which would include a series of live concerts. Along with a healthy share of the profits, his annual gross would be somewhere in the neighborhood of $35 million. The Krofft brothers, responsible for a number of successful Saturday morning kids' shows, felt that Pryor's deal with Columbia demonstrated a lack of commitment to a weekly television series.

Often considered a comedian of unlimited versatility, but noted mostly for his "raw" humor, Pryor has proved to be just as successful behind the scenes. In the 1970s he was one of the chief writers for several of the "Lily Tomlin Television Specials" and for the critically acclaimed Mel Brooks film classic, *Blazing Saddles* (1974).

What could have been one of the greatest triumphs of his career, his 1977 NBC prime-time series "The Richard Pryor Show," was canceled after just two short months on the air because of a dispute involving the censorship of material the network considered too offensive. In May 1980, Pryor's life nearly ended in a drug related accident that set him aflame. Often calling himself his "own worst enemy," Richard Pryor remains professionally inactive today, a victim of multiple sclerosis. Considered by many to be one of his best endeavors, the short-lived "Pryor's Place" is a bright spot in Pryor's career.

Shelley Duvall's Faerie Tale Theatre

They say there is something very special about watching big-name celebrities portraying favorite storybook characters, a gimmick that dates back to the 1930s when Judy Garland first thrilled audiences playing Dorothy in the L. Frank Baum masterpiece, *The Wizard of Oz.* This same quality can be seen in the cable production of "Shelley Duvall's Faerie Tale Theatre." A successor to the 1950s "Shirley Temple's Storybook," the show, hosted produced, and occasionally starring Miss Duvall, made its debut on Showtime in 1982 with a beautiful collection of children's popular favorites and with that little something extra to attract members of the entire family. In 1987, while the series was still producing new 60 minute episodes, reruns were telecast over the PBS network. The show still appears on an irregular basis there today.

With storytelling becoming one of the most popular of revived art forms, the series is generally refreshing in its modifications of the original stories. Popular actors, singers, and actresses obviously enjoy themselves in such familiar tales as "Pinocchio," "The Three Little Pigs," "Beauty and the Beast," "The Dancing Princess," "The Snow Queen," and "The Frog Prince," to name a few, and they are fun to watch.

On the down side, Duvall appears to relish the fact that much of her audience is made up of adults who enjoy watching the show with or without their youngsters, and some episodes contain material directed more to them than to children. In "Annie Oakley," for instance, there are enough puns to make the episode resemble "Saturday Night Live." In response to "Little Red Riding Hood," many parents complained to Showtime about Malcolm McDowell's rather frightening portrayal of the wolf (this episode was later reedited to downplay the performance).

Having become known to movie audiences for her roles as the perfect Olive Oyl in Robert Altman's *Popeye* (1980) and as Jack Nicholson's terrified wife in *The Shining* (1980), Shelley Duvall grew popular as a children's hostess as a result of her film work. During the filming of *Popeye*, she and costar Robin Williams (the perfect Popeye) convinced producers at Showtime to support the off-beat idea of presenting a children's series that would feature unlikely guest stars in an array of equally unlikely characterizations. The show began production in 1982 and became a huge success, drawing good reviews and attracting the services of such renowned screenwriters as Jules Feiffer.

Having appeared previously on the Disney Channel, the series continues to be popular today on PBS. Many of Miss Duvall's friends and fellow actors have agreed to appear on the program as a favor to her, asking only rock bottom fees, an odd situation considering that it is their performances that have made the show a success: Paul Simon, in "Simply Simple;" Billy Crystal, as the wisest pig, in "The Three Little Pigs"; James Earl Jones, as the genie, in "Aladdin's Lamp"; Little Richard, in "Old King Cole"; and Cyndi Lauper, as a frustrated Mary, with the overgrown Woody Harrelson as her "little lamb." These are just a few of the stars who have lent their support to Duvall and the program.

Today both CBS and NBC are considering the Duvall productions for a new Saturday morning slot, sometime in the near future. Duvall, ever the children's entrepreneur, remains as busy as ever, recording children's albums and preparing episodes for a new PBS series entitled "Kids in Motion."

Shirley Temple's Storybook / Shirley Temple Theater

Shirley Temple became known to millions all over the world in the 1930s as the cute, dimpled star of more than a dozen successful films for 20th Century–Fox. These films made her just as popular with the next two generations when they were revived for television in the 1950s and 1960s. But Temple has rarely appeared on television as an adult, except for her successful but short-lived children's anthology series "Shirley Temple's Storybook," also known as "Shirley Temple Theater."

A forerunner to Shelley Duvall's popular "Faerie Tale Theatre," the show featured the talented actress as hostess, narrator, singer, and occasional star in a variety of 60-minute live-action films developed by Henry Jaffe as adaptations of children's popular stories, fairy tales, and Mother

Goose rhymes. Featured almost exclusively on the program as favorite storybook characters were celebrity performers, many who had yet to achieve actual stardom. Carol Linley, for instance, a relative unknown at the time, appeared as the title character in "Rapunzel," costarring Agnes Moorehead and John Kerr; Sebastian Cabot was the subject of "The Emperor's New Clothes;" Jonathan Winters introduced his comic wit to the series in "The Land of Oz"; and E.G. Marshall played the lead in "Rip Van Winkle." But it was the series opener (January 12, 1958) that attracted the attention of many, as actor Charlton Heston shed his Moses image (from *The Ten Commandments*) to lend a commanding performance as the Beast in "Beauty and the Beast." Another splendid performance was that of Shirley Temple herself, who was featured as Little Bo-Peep in "The Story of Mother Goose," with Elsa Lancaster in the title role.

Nicely acted and well produced, stories were presented with just enough tongue-in-cheek attitude to attract adult viewers as well as children. Regrettably, the show was often overwhelmed in the weekly ratings since it faced such stiff competition as "Lassie" and the first half hour of the Western "Maverick" (ABC, 1957–62). Produced by William Asher, the show made its debut as "Shirley Temple Theater" in 1960 (Sunday, 7:00–8:00 P.M., September 18, 1960, through September 10, 1961), after previously appearing on NBC beginning in 1958 as "Shirley Temple's Storybook" (Sunday, 7:00–8:00 P.M., January 12, 1958, through December 21, 1958). Programs from the 1958 season were rerun in 1959 on Monday nights on ABC (7:00–8:00 P.M., January 12, 1959, through December 21, 1959). Both versions of the series were eventually rerun in syndication briefly in the 1960s.

Shirley Temple Black, still dimpled and attractive, now spends most of her time as a U.S. ambassador. She managed to avoid being crushed by early fame, unlike so many other Hollywood kids of her day. Although she has not appeared in front of the cameras for years, she seems content in her favorite role today of wife, mother, and grandmother.

The Singing Lady

Ireene Wicker was known to the thousands of early television viewers as "The Singing Lady." The Sunday evening favorite, like the long-running radio show that began in the 1930s, was created, written, hosted, and performed by Miss Wicker herself. During the show's entire 30 minutes, Wicker cheerfully related stories of historical significance as well as fairy tales that combined themes of morality and fair play. She was aided by the Suzari Marionettes, who appeared as the characters in her stories, each nicely presented with a variety of splendid storybook art and songs that Wicker herself performed. Despite the inconveniences of live television, the flow of the material was very smooth. This was an outstanding feat, considering that many of the productions were performed quite spontaneously.

ABC aired "The Singing Lady" at 6:30 P.M. on Sunday from November 7, 1948, through August 6, 1950. On September 27, 1953, the show was returned to ABC on Sunday morning at 10:00. The show held that program slot until March 21, 1954. "The Singing Lady" was enjoyed by audiences of both the young and the young at heart. After her first show was canceled in 1950, Wicker returned to the air three years later in a similar format, presented this time earlier in the day for children, on Sunday mornings.

Ireene Wicker has seldom appeared on television since the 1950s, but she was often heard singing her familiar children's songs, as her long-running radio program continued over the airwaves into the mid–1970s.

Small Fry Club

Hosted by television's first "big brother" for young viewers, Bob Emery, "Small Fry Club" was the first offering in the children's market. Actually called "Big Brother Bob" by his loyal followers, Emery presided over the daily activities of cartoons, contests, and tips involving both nutrition and safety, set in a friendly clubhouse. Although shows basically maintained the same format throughout the week, Tuesdays were devoted mostly to "Movies for the Small Fry," as Emery spent much of the show narrating silent and educational films.

A pioneer in the art of conversing with children, Emery had a straightforward manner, which was different, from that of many of his successors, who relied on children's reactions to funny situations. On a typical show, a bespectacled Emery would enter, often overdressed, in a business suit, reminding kids of the importance of a balanced breakfast and to avoid such bad habits as nail biting, thumb sucking, and not brushing teeth. This was often followed by a Van Beuren Studio cartoon presentation, such as "Brownie Bear" also known as "Cubby Bear," "Dick and Larry" (also known as "Tom and Larry," though with no resemblance to the popular MGM characters), and "The Little King." Each of these was a fine example of early black-and-white animation, characterized by a bouncy musical score, visual gags, and melodramatic plots like those of a silent film comedy.

The program was the first to initiate viewer mail, providing kids an opportunity to compete for various prizes that included membership cards and sweaters with big, bold lettering read across the top, SMALL FRY CLUB, BIG BROTHER BOB EMERY. These contests were devised in fact to estimate the viewership, since there was no other way at the time to tell just who and how many were watching the program. Presented over the old Dumont network, "Small Fry Club" reportedly drew over 75 percent of the viewing audience at a time when there were fewer than 25,000 television sets in households nationwide. Bob Emery helped generate more than 150,000 requests for membership, and by 1950 he helped to sell more than 10,000 television sets, heralded as he was by critics as "a big success in children's video."

Leaving a clear path for others to follow, with various degrees of success, Bob Emery left television in 1951 to revive the format of a radio show over New Bedford's WBSM. Here he was free to broadcast at a much earlier hour, when elementary school teachers and pupils could take time out from lessons to listen to the program. The new radio show lasted for nearly a decade.

The show is still remembered today by dedicated fans from television's first generation of viewers. "Small Fry Club" appeared at the following times, always Monday through Friday: 7:00–8:00 P.M., March 11, 1947, through April 12, 1947; 7:00–7:30 P.M., April 15, 1947, through January 3, 1948; 6:00–6:30 P.M., January 6, 1948, through June 15, 1951.

Smilin' Ed's Gang / Smilin' Andy's Gang

Children's favorite story-telling host, elderly Ed McConnell, brought his popular 30-minute children's series "Smilin' Ed's Gang" to NBC television seven years after it was first introduced to radio audiences. For nearly a decade, children looked forward to Smilin' Ed's weekly clubhouse meetings, far better than most shows of the era mainly because of the memorable cast of puppet and live characters. Included on the program at various times were Midnight the Cat, Squeaky the Mouse, the mischievous Froggy the Gremlin, comedian Billy Gilbert as a frustrated professor, and Shortfellow the Poet, played by Alan Reed (later the voice of Fred Flintstone). Also featured was a filmed adventure segment, "Gunga Ram, the Jungle Boy." Set in East India, serial-type episodes involved Gunga Ram and his friend Rama (Vito Scotti), and their dangerous missions for their leader, "his Highness," the Maharajah (Lou Krugman). Sponsored just as it had been on radio by Buster Brown shoes, the series was produced and directed by Frank Ferrin.

Having become associated over the years with lively children's entertainment, Ed McConnell was easily persuaded to share his talents, moving his programs at various times from network to network. The series began at NBC, airing at 6:30–7:00 on Saturday from August 26, 1950, through May 19, 1951. Then the show was picked up by CBS for the 10:30–11:00 A.M. Saturday slot, running from August 11, 1951, through April 11, 1953. "Smilin' Ed's Gang" then moved to ABC for a 10:30–11:00 A.M. broadcast from August 22, 1953, through April 16, 1955. But following the sudden death of Ed McConnell in 1954, the show was forced to make several drastic changes at the start of the 1955 season. With the second half of the 1954 season, shown mostly in reruns, the show began to falter in the ratings for the first time.

Though a lovable figure like Ed McConnell would be hard to replace, the decision to hire the equally likable Andy Devine proved to be a wise one. Already well known to children from his previous comic role as Wild Bill Hickok's sidekick, Jingles P. Jones, Andy Devine easily adapted to his new role as children's host, although reruns of his old series were still being shown in syndication and his character likeness as Jingles, was still being featured on boxes on Kellogg's Sugar Pops. Although the name of the series was changed to "Andy's Gang," also known as "Smilin' Andy's Gang," the format and its characters basically remained unchanged. New segments included story-teller Uncle Fish Face and the adventures of Puddles the Pup. Devine hosted the show for its remaining five years on the air, where it was again featured over the NBC network. "Smilin' Andy's Gang" ran on Saturday at 9:30–10:00 A.M. from August 20, 1955, through December 31, 1960.

Both McConnell and Devine were highly regarded by children and parents for their story-telling abilities. On several of the programs the host read tales of adventure to children from a giant storybook. While McConnell was especially successful with sounds and facial expressions, Devine had a gravelly voice and interacted humorously with both the studio puppets and the off-camera audience.

Both formats of the long-running series were thoroughly enjoyed and well-remembered by millions of grown-up Smilin' Ed and Andy's Gang members today who helped them both in every program by singing the show's opening commercial jingle for Buster Brown shoes.

The "Soupy Sales" Shows
The Soupy Sales Show /
Lunch with Soupy Sales

Comedian Soupy Sales (born Milton Hines) originally brought his off-beat humor to television as early as 1953 with a local series titled "Soupy's On," which appeared on Detroit station WXYZ. An immediate success, the show caught the attention of Detroit's local ABC affiliates, and Sales then became the host of his own 15-minute network series for children, "The Soupy Sales Show," in 1955. Here the comedian was shown daily for 15 minutes as a summer replacement for the vacationing "Kukla, Fran, and Ollie." ABC aired this show Monday through Friday at 7:00 from July 4, 1955, through August 26, 1955. The spirited Sales was then given the opportunity to host another local show, this time from Los Angeles, before returning to ABC in 1959 with a new Saturday afternoon 30-minute series originally entitled "Lunch with Uncle Soupy," before the network settled on "Lunch with Soupy Sales." This show appeared on Saturday at 12:00 from October 3, 1959, through April 1, 1961.

Sales, a natural-born funnyman with an expressive face and a gift for pantomime, became a slapstick revelation to over two generations of youngsters. Dressed in a crumpled top hat and floppy bow tie, Soupy had a show different from most children's favorites, because of the comedian's ability to follow such trite comic formulas as pie throwing and caricature and use them to good advantage. Among the program's company of stock players were Soupy's two larger-than-life-size dogs, White Fang and Blacktooth, both shown only from the paws down; Herman the Flea; Marilyn MonWolf; and Pookie the Lion, who often assisted in costume while Soupy read fairy tales to the audience. Corny puns and dialogue, songs, silent films, sketches, and nutrition tips for children were all a regular part of the series, presented on a sound stage without a studio audience.

In 1962 the show was moved from Saturday afternoons to prime time on Friday evenings, proving that Sales's appeal with adults was nearly as strong as it had been all along with children. Returning once again to the original title "The Soupy Sales Show," the program remained basically unchanged, except for the addition of weekly big-name stars, who appeared in cameo roles. Featured on the receiving end of Soupy's custard cream pies were such stars as Frank Sinatra, Dean Martin, Sammy Davis, Jr., Steve Lawrence, Perry Como, Jimmy Durante, Tony Curtis, and Bob Hope. Guessing what star would be knocking on the door to Soupy's clubhouse each week became one of the most memorable aspects of the program. Another involved the sound of unpretentious laughter from Soupy's invisible crew of background technicians. "The Soupy Sales Show" in the new format was broadcast from January 26, 1962, through April 13, 1962, on Friday in the 7:30–8:00 P.M. slot. This show was shown in syndication from 1965 through 1967 and from 1979 through 1980.

In 1965, as a joke, Soupy invented a new dance called "the Mouse," which he demonstrated to a national audience on the "Ed Sullivan Show." Amusingly, the song he performed with the dance became a hit record.

After the cancellation of his network series, Sales hosted a daily local show from New York which was sold to syndication less than a year later. In 1979 he served as host to another syndicated 30-minute children's show, with much of the same nonsense as before only this time in color.

In the mid–1980s, Soupy, still clowning, served briefly as host of a widely syndicated weekend radio program called "The Soupy Sales Moldie Oldie Show," and avid fans could detect on it a touch of vintage comedy from his television shows of the 1950s, 1960s, and 1970s.

Always the rubber-faced charmer with the boyish innocence of an overgrown adolescent, Sales once jokingly advised a group of young admirers to mail him "the little green pieces of paper" they found in their parents' pocketbooks. The prank, which he improvised with 30 seconds left on the program and nothing to do, cost him a two-week suspension without pay. Fortunately, he was reimbursed by children who took him seriously. In less than two weeks after the broadcast Sales received over $20,000 (mostly in play money). Somehow the incident only added to the endearing goofiness that Soupy Sales is best remembered for today.

The Uncle Al Show

Appearing locally in Los Angeles for nearly ten years prior to their network debut, Al and Wanda Lewis were the friendly cohosts, creators, and producers of this 60-minute Saturday morning participation series aimed primarily at younger children. Using the familiar "Following the Leader" as its theme song, the show used a carnival-type setting ideal for capturing the imagination of children. Uncle Al played the accordion, guitar, and ukulele at various times, while participating children danced and played so naturally that it seemed as though they never realized they were being filmed.

Uncle Al's real-life wife, Wanda, portrayed the lovely Captain Windy, a flying Wonder Woman type with unique abilities. Thanks to her, many male adults showed a sudden interest in the type of programs usually only children watched on television. Actress Janet Greene also appeared from time to time, playing Cinderella, as did Larry Smith and his funny hand puppets. As "Pip the Piper" would do a few years later, shows often highlighted seasonal occasions. In March 1959, for instance, an Easter show featured such characters as "Eggbert the Easter Egg" and "The Whistling Rabbit."

Uncle Al's blend of music, story-telling and, entertaining instructional segments eventually made the show an even bigger attraction for adolescents. Considering that the show relied little on incorporated segments, guest stars, or various comic elements to maintain a huge following, "The Uncle Al Show" was a rarity even for its day. Unfortunately, ABC did not share viewers' enthusiasm and canceled the program after just one season on the air. The show was broadcast Saturday from 11:00 to 12:00 P.M. beginning on October 18, 1958. The final show aired September 19, 1959.

"The Uncle Al Show" was one of the last Saturday morning children's shows to highlight a studio audience of young children who were being entertained by adults, a sign of the passing of television's first era and a preview of things to come.

The "Uncle Johnny Coons" Shows
Life with Uncle Johnny Coons /
The Uncle Johnny Coons Show

Ventriloquist Johnny Coons served as host and solo performer on this 30-minute Chicago-based live children's variety series. Along with his larger-than-life-size wooden dummy George and invisible dog "Blackie," Coons served as master of ceremonies for various stories, cartoons, and silent films, featuring at various times the comedy shorts of "Our Gang" and comedians Harry Langdon and Bobby Vernon. Playing himself in a variety of comedy routines throughout each program, Uncle Johnny had a subtle but inspired sense of humor that combined with a studio audience of free-spirited children to place the "Uncle Johnny Coons Show" in a class all by itself.

Like others in the genre, Coons had his own distinctive trademarks, which included an oversized derby hat and glasses. Unlike most others, he occasionally appeared in different outfits to fit a variety of different characters, including Cowboy Johnny, Fireman Johnny, and Safari Hunter Johnny. Bruce Roberts was the announcer. Coons provided all the other voices for the show's characters, who were heard off-screen, such as Blackie and Joe, the Friendly Giant. Coons also appeared as Uncle Johnny in various commercials for the shows sponsors, Swift Premium and Lever Brothers.

Critics called Uncle Johnny Coons the "Pied Piper of children's television." The show was produced by Jamel Green and was originally entitled "Life with Uncle Johnny Coons" when it made its CBS Saturday morning debut in 1954. It aired on Saturday at 10:00–10:30 A.M. from September 4, 1954, through December 3, 1955. The title was changed to "Uncle Johnny Coons," or "The Uncle Johnny Coons Show," when the series was presented over the NBC network during its second season. The broadcast schedule was 12:00–12:30 P.M. on Saturday from March 5, 1956, through December 1, 1956.

John David Coons had been a familiar face and voice for children since the early 1950s. He was first seen locally on a 15-minute weekday afternoon program entitled "Noontime Comics." In 1952 he provided the puppet voice for Uncle Mistletoe in a syndicated series televised on Chicago's WGN network. In the early 1960s, he was heard once again as the narrator of a ten-minute educational series entitled "The Funny Company." He also provided the voice for Space Mouse on the "New Woody Woodpecker Show."

As with most live children's shows of the 1950s, ticket demands for "The Uncle Johnny Show" were overwhelming. Coons, along with other children's show hosts worthy of the same respect, was held in high esteem by children, who watched his show faithfully. Sadly, these very hosts, who enjoyed taking their work so seriously, later became the target of mindless parody and ridicule some 20 and 30 years later, by the likes of "Uncle Croc's Block" (ABC, 1975–76) and "The Uncle Floyd Show" (syndicated, 1980). These shows clearly intended to poke fun at the grand old masters whom children once saw as the real heroes of Saturday morning television.

8. *Puppets, Marionettes, and Dummies*

Puppet characters have always made a major contribution to children's television. Even today, part of the industry still depends upon "Muppets," puppets, and costumed adults to improve the quality of children's programming. At one time, however, these types of shows were the center stage of children's programming. Even the commercials were filled with popular wooden characters who easily convinced youngsters that "Nestle's makes the very best" or "The best candy on earth comes from Mars."

Though most of these shows depended on a live host, in many instances the puppets themselves became extremely popular. The producers of these shows were well aware that puppets were indeed the quickest if not the easiest way to get the attention of most children. Perhaps that explains why puppet characters are more prevalent today in educational shows than in any other type.

The Banana Splits Adventure Hour / The Banana Splits and Friends Show

This Saturday morning farce from the Hanna-Barbera Studios featured 60 minutes of live comedy, with a variety of songs, skits, cartoons, and serialized adventure segments. Acting as hosts were four life-size rock musician puppet characters in animal costumes called the Banana Splits. The group consisted of Fleegle the Beagle, Drooper the Lion, Bingo the Gorilla, and Snorky the Baby Elephant. They performed slapstick sketches in addition to rock songs (prerecorded) that created a revolution in both the music industry and in the life-styles of young people of the 1960s.

Also featured at various times were cartoon segments: "The Hillbilly Bears" (formally a segment on "The Atom Ant Show," NBC, 1965–67), "The Three Musketeers," and "The Arabian Knights." The latter was a series of action-adventure cartoons produced for the program by William Hanna and Joe Barbera. Live filmed segments included the serial adventures "Danger Island" and "The Micro Adventure." Produced by Richard Donner, "Danger Island" was the continuing saga of a small group of explorers in search of a lost city. Donner would become more familiar to audiences later as the producer and creator of the new *Superman* movies, featuring Christopher Reeve in the title role. "The Micro Adventure" was an animated version of the movie *Fantastic Voyage* (1966), in which the heroes were reduced to the size of micro-organisms. Another in the line of Hanna-Barbera Productions, the show was presented by one of the team's first sponsors, Kellogg's cereals of Battle Creek. "The Banana Splits Adventure Hour" appeared on NBC's Saturday morning schedule at 10:30–11:30 from September 7, 1968, through September 5, 1970.

Although the Banana Splits were not puppets in the true sense, they led to such similar series as "The Skatebirds" (CBS, 1977–78) and "H.R. Puf-n-Stuf" (NBC, 1969–71). The latter was one of the first Saturday morning productions created by brothers Sid and Marty Krofft. The show's concept even helped set the stage for the immensely popular "Sesame Street" series, which premiered on PBS a year later.

"The Banana Splits," in a way represented the changing times of the late 1960s. No longer would puppets be innocent, diminutive little characters manipulated by adults, but rather expressive and sophisticated figures, as intelligent and wise to the ways of the world as adults. Even today, the escapades of the Banana Splits do not seem especially dated.

Vocals for the series were provided by Paul Winchell (Fleegle), Daws Butler (Bingo), Allan Melvin (Drooper), and Don Messick (Snorky). In 1971, the show was shortened to 30 minutes and repackaged for syndication, along with several other Hanna-Barbera favorites, and retitled "The Banana Splits and Friends Show." The repackaged version of the show was shown in syndication from 1971 through 1975. It is still rerun periodically over Chicago's WGN cable network.

The Bigelow Show see *The Paul Winchell Shows*

Burr Tillstrom's Kukla and Ollie see
The "Kukla, Fran, and Ollie" Shows

Cartoonies see *The Paul Winchell Shows*

Diver Dan

Breaking away from the traditional puppet shows was the soggy ten-minute live serial adventures of Diver Dan. Frank Freda, who always appeared in full diving gear, starred as the title character, whose fondest wish was one day to meet the mermaid Miss Minerva (Suzanne Turner), who reigned over the Sargasso Sea. Although Freda and Turner were the only human regulars, they were never featured together in the same scene.

Although the title of the show referred to a live character, it quickly became clear that the fish marionettes were the real stars. Included among these characters were Finley, the haddock, who served as messenger between Dan and Minerva; Sea Biscuit, the sea horse; Skipper, the kipper; Scout Fish, a migrant from the Indian Ocean; Glowfish, who lived in the bottomless pit; Goldie, the goldfish; and a bongo-playing beatnik fish named Gill Espie. Also present were the villains, the evil Baron Barracuda, and his cigarette-chomping henchman, Trigger-happy Fish. In many of the episodes, Baron commanded Trigger, "Call me Baron, you chowderhead!" To which Trigger replied, "Okay, Baron, you chowderhead." Vocals for the marionettes were all provided by Allan Swift.

Episodes, all set under the sea, involved both Dan's and Minerva's attempts to protect the fish from the Baron's plots to rule the sea. When not focused on Dan, scenes were set outside Minerva's seashell palace, where she contacted both Dan and the other fish by a shell-o-phone kept close to her throne.

"Diver Dan" was syndicated by Young Productions through ITC Entertainment Corporation in 1960. Often shown daily on an independent basis through the 1960s, the shows usually became a regular part of the local "Romper Room" series. In some cities, however, the whole show revolved around Diver Dan's adventures, with several episodes at a time hosted by local celebrities disguised as sea captains, Aquamen, and sailors. In Sacramento, California, the series was presented over station KCRA as "Diver Dan's Treasure Chest."

Although the segments were short on plot and imagination, kids nevertheless found the show entertaining. It remains one of the most memorable of the era.

Fireball XL-5

This British science fiction series was one of the first television shows to use live-action animation in a process known as "super marionation." Developed by Gerry Anderson, the technique used modern plastic puppetry with hidden wires. Reminiscent of children's live-action shows of an earlier era, the series was set in Space City, a solar system patrolled by galaxy policemen who were led by Captain Steve Zodiac, pilot of the jet fighter Fireball XL-5. Other marionette cast members included Lieutenant 90, Steve's friend and fellow pilot; Professor Metric, the team's brilliant head scientist; Commander Zero, the city's controller; and Venus, Captain Zodiac's copilot and love interest. The Space City patrolmen were forever at odds with such foes as the Briggs brothers and Mr. and Mrs. Super Spy. Voices for the characters were provided by David Graham, Sylvia Anderson, and Paul Maxwell.

Each of the 30-minute shows was presented with a special richness unequaled by any other Saturday morning show at that time. It aired 10:30–11:00 on NBC from October 5, 1963, through September 25, 1965. The show provided a pleasant change of pace, and it was able to cash in on the popularity of espionage films. The puppet actors might have appeared crude, but they were effective enough to be complimented by critics, who heralded the marionation process as "a step above virtuoso." Gerry Anderson had previously experimented with the marionation technique in his first series, "Supercar" (syndicated, 1961). However, the process showed little promise because the wires were clearly visible to the viewer. But this problem diminished with each series, from "Fireball XL-5" to "The Thunderbirds" (syndicated, 1967).

The series was produced for Saturday mornings by Gerry and Sylvia Anderson and was distributed by the ITC Television Corporation.

The Great Space Coaster

This 30-minute hit puppet series, with educational elements, became a favorite weekday morning program with children of the 1980s. Shown locally at various times, "The Great Space Coaster" was enjoyed by children of all age groups but was especially popular with older children who had grown weary of "Sesame Street." Similar to that very series, "The Great Space Coaster" featured a pleasant variety of songs, stories, and animation, presented by humans and the Kevin Clash "bigger than life" puppets. The series was one of the few educational and entertaining programs of the era that was not affiliated with PBS. This type of program largely disappeared from the networks after the premiere of "Sesame Street" in 1969.

Featured on the show were human regulars Emily Bindiger as Fran, Chris Gifford as Danny, and Ray Stevens as Roy. The trio served as hosts and performers in a fantasyland of such unsubtle puppet friends as Baxter, a magical dog constantly hounded by a villainous carnival barker named M.T. Promises; Gary Gnu, a no "g-news" newscasting gnu; Goriddle Gorilla, an uneven-tempered purple-faced ape who bore a remarkable resemblance to "Sesame Street's" Oscar the Grouch; Knock-Knock the Bird, whose favorite hobby was telling knock-knock jokes; and Edison the Elephant, who spoke through his long, echoing trunk.

The show, with its light and lively atmosphere, introduced youngsters to both educational and cultural themes through its variety of filmed segments and gentle skits. One episode in particular that caught the interest of many viewers featured Fran, Roy, and Danny journeying in the Space Coaster to places of fun and interests and their adventures were filmed live as they sang and danced with children of different backgrounds and life-styles. Another popular feature of the program involved the casting of such celebrities as Valerie Harper, Cleavon Little, Mark Hamill, Sally Struthers, Kathleen Turner, and "Mean" Joe Green in cameo roles.

The series was sponsored by Kellogg's cereals during its first season and was produced in affiliation with Sunbow Productions. "The Great Space Coaster" was syndicated in 1981.

The Gumby Show / Gumby

Long before comedian Eddie Murphy appeared in costume on "Saturday Night Live" to parody a once-familiar little clay figure, "Gumby" was introduced to children on "The Howdy Doody Show" before becoming a series of its own in 1957. Not really a puppet, Gumby was actually a combination of live animation and stop-motion photography, a technique that showed him moving slightly from one frame of film to the next. A novelty on television, like George Pal's Puppet-toons of the 1940s, "The Gumby Show" was produced by Art Clokey, who was also executive producer for the "Davey and Goliath" series a few years later.

Episodes of "Gumby" usually involved the character and his claymates in clever misadventures that ranged from the unusual to the predictable. In one, for instance, "The Witty Witch," Gumby and his horse, Pokey, set out on a trip to a mysterious forest where they became involved with the doings of a witch they mistook for a kindly old woman.

Then there was one entitled "The Puppy Dog School," where Gumby's dog was sent to school to learn to speak words other than the one he already knows, *nope*. In a particularly clever ending, the dog somewhat attains the goal by learning to say *nope* in more than five different languages.

Bobby Nicholson, who at one time played Clarabell the Clown on "The Howdy Doody Show," appeared as original live host of "Gumby," Scotty McKee, when the show made its Saturday morning debut on March 23, 1957. NBC offered this show at 10:30–11:00 on Saturday until November 16, 1957. Programs began with Scotty welcoming children and viewers to his Funshop where he presented the adventures of his most popular character, Gumby. When Nicholson left the program midway through the season, he was replaced by comedian Pinky Lee for the remainder of the series. For additional information about Pinky Lee as the host of "Gumby," see "The Pinky Lee Show" on page 168.

By an odd twist of fate, the short-lived "Gumby" series was one of the unpopular shows of the 1950s to be revived some 30 years later for new audiences. The show was syndicated in 1985. Gumby had also become something of a cult figure with many adults who enjoyed him as children. Although unparalleled in quality, the new series was characterized much too often by contrived plots that lacked the energy of modern competitors. In turn, much of the enthusiasm viewers felt for the original show was absent with regard to the new "Gumby" show of the 1980s. The revival of the character, however, did provide a new opportunity for several other children's favorites of the same era to become familiar to today's new audiences. Among these old favorites were the tremendously talented Shari Lewis and her puppets and the remarkable Don Herbert as Mr. Wizard, both of whom are still featured periodically today.

H.R. Puf-n-Stuf

"H.R. Puf-n-Stuf" was the first in a long line of Saturday morning programs produced by the brothers Sid and Marty Krofft. As "Banana Splits" had done a year earlier, this series starred adult-size puppets as the featured characters. Thirty minutes long, the show centered on the adventures of a little boy named Jimmy and his magic flute, Freddie, who become stranded on an enchanted island. Mayor H.R. Puf-n-Stuf, a lovable dragon, presided over the colony, which was made up of equally strange looking but likable characters (all in complete puppet oufits).

A contrast to the friendly characters was an evil witch named

Witchiepoo who became obsessed with adding Jimmy's flute to her collection of magical possessions. Episodes involved Jimmy's attempts to escape the island with the help of Puf-n-Stuf and his friends. Jack Wild, who had previously starred as the Artful Dodger in the Broadway musical *Oliver Twist,* played young Jimmy, while actress Billie Hayes, memorable for her role as Mammy Yokum in both the film and the stage productions of *Li'l Abner,* was Witchiepoo. They were the only human characters in the cast.

Although the show was mildly successful, enjoying a three-seasons run, it generated many imitators, which began to fill the Saturday morning schedule. Most of them were also produced by the Kroffts, such as "Lidsville" (ABC, 1971–73), "The Bugaloos" (NBC, 1970–72), and "Sigmund and the Sea Monsters" (NBC, 1973–75), which offered variations on the old fairy tale in which the hero encounters incredible odds as he fights a diabolical force. While many younger children continued to watch the Krofft productions with glee and enthusiasm, older children tended to find the pace a bit slow and the stories too repetitive to sustain their interest.

"H.R. Puf-n-Stuf" appeared on NBC for two consecutive seasons (September 6, 1969, through September 4, 1971) on Saturday morning from 10:00 to 10:30. After a year's absence it returned to the air for a single season on ABC, appearing at 11:30–12:00 noon on Saturday from September 9, 1972, through September 1, 1973.

The "Howdy Doody" Shows
Puppet Playhouse Theater / The Howdy Doody Show / The New Howdy Doody Show

Considered by many the most popular children's show in the history of broadcasting, "Howdy Doody" made its debut on December 27, 1947, as "Puppet Playhouse Theater." Featured by NBC only once a week for 60 minutes on Friday at 5:30, the show provided lively entertainment that centered around a little freckle-faced marionette named Howdy Doody and his wooden friends and neighbors. Howdy Doody appeared on television under the program title "Puppet Playhouse Theater" from December 27, 1947, through August 12, 1948. Created and hosted by Howdy's mentor, former radio broadcaster Bob Smith, the show, originally with a circus-like atmosphere, was one of television's first big hits and became a virtually unparalleled national phenomenon.

Smith had formerly served as host to a local Saturday morning radio program for kids entitled "Triple B Ranch." Set in a Western atmosphere

"It's Howdy Doody time!"

(a change "The Howdy Doody Show" would later undergo), "Triple B Ranch" included a Mortimer Snerd–type character named Elmer who, when greeted by Smith, would reply, "Well, Howdy Doody!" When approached by NBC producer Martin Stone to gather material for a new children's puppet series for the fall of 1947, Smith decided the name of the lead character would be "Howdy Doody," the phrase to which kids had become most accustomed. The character, originally an awkward-looking country bumpkin type, came to life after the first few weeks of the program. Smith, also a ventriloquist, had initially conversed with the unseen puppet with the voice of Elmer by means of a telephone or a walkie-talkie, or by conversations through a hidden closet.

Although Howdy's face would eventually appear on everything from lunchboxes to Welch's jelly jars, it bore little resemblance to that of the original wooden marionette created by Frank Paris which audiences finally saw after the first few weeks of the series. Because of a contract dispute with the network, Paris soon walked away from NBC, taking the Howdy Doody puppet with him. The new one, designed by Thelma Thomas and Scott Brinker, had a pixie, freckled face (one freckle for each state of the union), a red bandana, a checked shirt, and a pair of cowboy boots; this puppet became an American fixture, closely associated with television's first generation of viewers. Howdy's new face was explained to kids as being the result of plastic surgery, to make him better looking.

Buffalo Bob Smith and Howdy Doody.

Kids accepted the explanation without question, and the show quickly became a national hit. The show was also a factor in the early sale of television sets nationwide.

Beginning August 15, 1948, the show was featured Monday through Friday for 30 minutes as "The Howdy Doody Show," airing on NBC at 5:30. Howdy, having originally called his mentor "Mr. Smith," now addressed him as "Buffalo Bob," a title Smith created for the show's new version in reference to his alleged pioneer heritage. From the show's early days, Bob was assisted in every program by a horn-honking, seltzer-squirting, lovable, speechless clown named Clarabell Hornblow. Sporting a zebra-striped outfit and a carrot-top hairdo, Clarabell was played by a succession of actors, beginning with Bob Keeshan in 1947. When Keeshan abandoned the role in 1951 to pursue a show of his own (*see* "Captain Kangaroo," chapter 6, "Informative Shows"), he was replaced by actor Bobby Nicholson. In 1954 Nicholson appeared as another character on the program, Cornelius J. Cobb, the Howdy Doodyville town storekeeper. This left the part open for Lew Anderson, who next played the role, until it left the air in 1960. Of all the many characters, both human and puppet, who appeared regularly throughout the program, Clarabell achieved a level popularity of that never slipped below that of the show's stars, Howdy Doody and Buffalo Bob.

Howdy's other friends and neighbors included marionettes Phineas T. Bluster, Doodyville's cantankerous mayor, responsible for many a sinister scheme; Dilly Dally, Howdy's less intelligent counterpart and friend who often fell prey to the schemes of Mr. Bluster; the Flub-a-Dub, a strange little animal who wore a flower pot hat and claimed to be a combination of seven animals all rolled into one; Captain Windy Scuttlebutt, a salty sea captain; brothers Hide and Zeke Bear; Lizzie the Dinosaur;

Buzz Beaver, a character who appeared in several of the earliest shows as a participant in the evil plans of Mr. Bluster; Sandra Witch, a licensed broom pilot; and John J. Fadodoozle, America's number one—boing, boing, boing—private eye.

Bob Smith supplied the voice of Howdy himself by prerecording conversations and songs he had with the puppet. Other voices provided for the characters over the years included those of Allan Swift, Herb Vibrin, Bill LeCornec, Dayton Allen, and Paul Frees. Bill LeCornec was featured in a variety of roles, including Dr. Sing Song and Oil Well Willy. His most familiar, however, was the gullible Indian "Chief Thunderthud," whose favorite expression, when exasperated, was "Cowabunga." Actress Judy Tyler starred as the chief's beautiful princess, SummerFall-WinterSpring. Unfortunately, during the show's tenth season, Miss Tyler was the victim of a fatal auto accident. Interestingly, her character had originally appeared as a puppet during the show's very first years on the air.

Others in recurring roles included Dayton Allen as Ugly Sam the Wrestler and Alene Dalton as the beautiful Story Princess. During the show's sixth season (1954) Western character actor Gabby Hayes and radio celebrity Cowboy Bison Bill briefly took turns as hosts when Bob Smith suffered a mild heart attack, the result of overexertion. On a few occasions Howdy's look-alike brother and sister, Double Doody and Heidi Doody, were featured on the program.

Each of the Howdy Doody shows included a live studio audience of children, who sat in a section of the stage known as the Peanut Gallery. Programs began as they shouted the answer to the question Bob asked at the start of every telecast:"Hey, kids, what time is it?" "HOWDY DOODY TIME!" The show relied heavily on the appeal of Buffalo Bob Smith, who had a tantalizing, articulate personality. He often included songs, consisting of words to the wise, which played an integral part in the storyline of each episode. Smith was also an accomplished musician, who played well a variety of instruments, from the piano to the accordion.

Creating television's first popular kids' show was not without its share of responsibilities. Witnessing the growth of television, as the network gradually expanded to more than 150 markets, Smith explained that each new station was welcomed to the show with an on-the-air salute. Other on-air promotions included a Howdy Doody smile contest, a look-alike contest, and a 1948 "Howdy for President" contest, which featured Howdy's new face on campaign buttons distributed by request to kids all across the country.

Although the show also became very popular with adults, some felt it lacked a genuine redeeming quality. But these critics overlooked the fact that many of the stories contained indirect messages of vital significance, such as sharing or telling the truth. In addition, Smith also publicized national safety awareness themes, such as the American Auto Association's national campaign song, "Don't cross the street with your feet but with your eyes." "We strove for parental approval and were very selective in our choice of commercial sponsors," Smith later stated in a press release for the Fries Entertainment Corporation. "Backed by clients like Colgate and Kellogg's, we taught children the importance of such personal habits as brushing their teeth and eating a good breakfast, but we would not sponsor any colas because dentists and doctors were against them."

"The Howdy Doody Show" continued to run five days a week until June 1, 1956 when it fell prey to the competition of "The Mickey Mouse Club" on ABC. The show then became a fixture on Saturday mornings for the remainder of its run. NBC aired the show from 10:00 to 10:30, beginning on June 16, 1956. Like all successful live children's shows of the day, "Howdy Doody" was in great demand for tickets. According to one popular story, pregnant women stood in line to register their unborn children for a seat in the Peanut Gallery. The show was produced by Robert Muir and written by Edward Kean.

Howdy and his friends made their final farewell in an hour-long broadcast on September 30, 1960, after 13 years and 2,434 television performances, more than any other television program in the history of NBC. At the very end of the telecast, a for once serious Clarabell the Clown at last broke his long silence, saying tearfully, "Goodbye kids."

Howdy Doody has never been forgotten over the years. His place in television history is assured, and the show continues to resurface periodically, everywhere from college campuses to nostalgia conventions, where Buffalo Bob is often asked by enthusiastic admirers to speak. Even today, kids who were not around when the series aired have become familiar with the puppet and all his friends through the memories shared by their parents and grandparents who once enjoyed the show.

In 1976 Bob Smith made an attempt to revive the series with a new cast in a syndicated updated version called "The New Howdy Doody Show." Regrettably, it failed to recreate the success it had achieved some 30 years earlier. In 1987 the show celebrated its fortieth anniversary with a two-hour reunion special featuring Howdy and most of the original gang in a fond look back into the past. When asked recently how he would describe his pioneer days on the frontiers of television, Smith chuckled heartily, grinned his Buffalo Bob grin, and summed it all up by saying, "Exciting, very, very exciting."

In the Park

Paul Ritts and his wife, Mary Holliday Ritts, were the puppeteers and the creative force behind this 30-minute Sunday afternoon series hosted by Bill Sears. In the tradition of such favorites as "Kukla, Fran, and Ollie," Sears conversed in every program with the various Ritts hand puppets, from a serene area on a park bench. From that location the premise of each show would be established, along with the distinct personality of each puppet character, who inspired tales of humor and morality.

Some of the puppets were the wide-eyed Sir Geoffrey the Giraffe, who was somewhat reminiscent of the Flub-a-dub from "The Howdy Doody Show"; Albert the Chipmunk, who chatted frequently with Sears from a hollow window of his treehouse; Calvin the Crow, a likable little character whose bad habits were presented in order to steer children away from smoking, boasting, and lying; and Magnolia the Ostrich, a gentle soul who spoke with a Southern accent and whose common sense provided a sharp contrast to Calvin.

Much of the show's charm stemmed from the way the stories allowed viewers to relate their own experiences to those of the puppet actors. Themes involving such topics as jealousy, friendship, and rivalry were tactfully woven into each program without sacrificing storylines and plots to preachy dialogue.

"In the Park" originally began as a local 15-minute series telecast live over Philadelphia's CBS affiliate station WCAU. The network series was later produced by Charles Vanda, responsible for the children's circus favorite, "The Big Top," which ran on CBS for seven seasons. Although "In the Park" was the only series in which the Ritts Puppets appeared as the starring characters, several of the puppets did reappear later in support of such other programs as "Exploring" and "The Pink Panther Show." Magnolia also appeared briefly in several scenes talking to Jerry Lewis in the 1961 comedy *The Errand Boy*. Bill Sears, the show's elderly and distinguished live resident, had previously been featured in the short-lived series "Kid Gloves" (CBS, 1951), where he served as both host and referee for abbreviated boxing contests featuring youngsters from the age of three and up.

Scheduled for 12:00–12:30 P.M. on Sunday, the show ran from December 9, 1951, through May 31, 1953. The series, one of the best puppet shows ever produced for television, was featured on CBS for a total of one and a half seasons before it faded away into obscurity.

Johnny Jupiter

This imaginative series, which featured a space-age puppet as its star, was presented in two versions, beginning with the first for three months over the old Dumont network. (The show aired on Saturday at 7:30–8:00 P.M. from March 21, 1953, through June 13, 1953.) Episodes focused on the interplanetary conversations via television screen between Johnny, a visitor from the planet Jupiter, and earthling Ernest P. Duckweather (Vaughn Taylor), a janitor in an isolated television station who first made contact with the alien by accidentally switching on a hidden telescreen. Johnny was accompanied on his journeys by his traveling companions and fellow hand puppets B-12 and Major Domo, a robot.

Initially presented for only a brief period, the show was then picked up by ABC, with Will Wright in the role of Duckworth and an additional live cast that included Pat Peardon as Duckworth's girlfriend and Cliff Hall as his frenzied boss, Mr. Frisbee. ABC offered this show on Saturday at 5:30–6:00 P.M. from September 5, 1953, through May 29, 1954. In this version of the series, Duckworth was featured as a clerk in a general store with a passion for electronic equipment. Whenever he found the time (which was often), he would sneak away to the back room to contact the Jupiterians over an electric television device he invented for this purpose.

Produced by Martin Stone, both versions provided a refreshingly different kind of program in which the puppets parodied everything from the Eisenhower administration to the new American space program. Carl Harms gave the puppets their mobility while Gilbert Mack supplied the voices. Although both versions were presented on Saturdays the second was shown in several markets on Sunday afternoons.

Like many other early live television shows, the production quality of "Johnny Jupiter" suffered by comparison with today's shows, with muffled dialogue and scratchy sound. If these programs were to be presented to audiences today, in their purest original form, it would probably be difficult to sustain the audience's interest. But the show was not without its share of charming effects. The program never failed to give both children and adults a pleasant dose of fantasy, along with feelings of good cheer and tranquility. Scenes of the tiny puppets dancing to life on a gigantic television screen were a delight, despite any technical shortcomings.

Although seldom remembered today, "Johnny Jupiter" is considered a children's television classic.

Judy Splinters

Twenty-one-year-old ventriloquist Shirley Dinsdale first introduced her wooden friend Judy Splinters to local Los Angeles television audiences in 1948. The program then was shown nationally from June 13, 1949, through October 14, 1949, on NBC at 7:00–7:15 P.M., Monday through Friday, as a summer replacement for the "Kukla, Fran, and Ollie" series. In her teen years Dinsdale had performed on such popular radio programs as "The Eddie Cantor Show" and "Nelson Eddy's Music Hall" (where she and the puppet harmonized simultaneously). "Judy Splinters" consisted of 15 minutes of whimsical stories and songs with an undeniable appeal to small children.

When "Kukla, Fran, and Ollie" returned to NBC for the 1949 fall season, "Judy Splinters" continued to air in the evenings, Monday through Friday, for a full 30 minutes (6:00–6:30), and included an added variety of games, prizes, and conversation between Shirley and her pigtailed prodigy. "Howdy Doody" producer Robert Muir served as executive producer for the series, which was written by Miss Dinsdale herself. NBC offered "Judy Splinters" at the 6:00 P.M. time slot from October 24, 1949, through June 30, 1950.

In an industry that depended heavily upon first impressions, Shirley and Judy had a unique presence. Dressed most of the time in similar outfits, they caught the attention of audiences of all ages. As the first television actress ever to receive an Emmy Award (for Best Children's Show), Miss Dinsdale, it appeared, was fast becoming one of the medium's most important female figures. Unfortunately, her career was overshadowed by a string of successors whose shows offered children a much wider range of entertainment. Even though she had received television's most prestigious award, very few offers came her way after the cancellation of her show in June 1950.

Although "Judy Splinters" was well within the usual standards of shows produced during this period, early videotapes of the program have disappeared, and are regarded as lost, destroyed, or buried so deeply in the NBC vaults that they have become quite obscure. Today, with nostalgia a popular pastime, it would be interesting to see Shirley and Judy as guests on a network talk show with such other female groundbreakers as Fran Allison, Shari Lewis, and Joan Ganz Cooney. As pioneers in children's television, they could have valuable thoughts and comments to offer on children's television of the 1990s.

The "Kukla, Fran, and Ollie" Shows
Kukla, Fran, and Ollie /
Burr Tillstrom's Kukla and Ollie

Many adults and children enjoyed Burr Tillstrom's hand puppets Kukla, the bulb-nosed clown, and Ollie, the lovable long-toothed dragon. The series was hosted by the delightful and charming Fran Allison and was seen in various lengths and formats. Nearly everyone who watched was convinced that Tillstrom's puppets had suspended reality.

Originally creating the puppets solely for display purposes during the 1930s World's Fair, Tillstrom, a puppeteer since childhood, first brought Kukla and Ollie to local television in 1947 on a program entitled "Junior Jamboree," where he provided the voices for both puppets. Chicago NBC affiliates were so impressed by his ability to manipulate the puppets singlehandedly that they gave him a network series of his own the following year.

As the show increased in popularity so did its cast of puppet characters, who often had names that matched their personalities as well as their odd looks. Some of these characters were Fletcher Rabbit, Beulah Witch, Madame Ooglepuss, Colonel Winbag Crackie, Ollie's little niece, Delores Dragon, and the dim-witted Cecil Bill. Segments of the show focused on the escapades of the "Kuklapolitans," who performed on lavishly set stages or platforms productions ranging from plays and stories to operettas, each usually providing a worthy message to kids. Kukla, whose name is derived from a Russian word meaning *doll,* served as the group's founder and lead thespian.

Although most of the puppet productions looked like an updated Punch and Judy show, they offered sheer delight to audiences of all ages. The first of several puppet troupes that led the way toward such puppet-related programs as "Sesame Street," the Kuklapolitans acted on their own, with little or no interference from humans. Fran Allison simply served as moderator.

Burr Tillstrom was a lead role model for such successors as the great Jim Henson, who carried on in even grander style; for this reason alone Burr Tillstrom's work outshines that of most other puppet shows of the era. While such timeworn antics might not interest today's sophisticated young audiences, Kukla, Fran, and Ollie's charm and charisma once helped to establish a creative, harmonious pattern in an era filled with such worries as the Korean War, the McCarthy "red" scare, and social and political oppression.

At the same time, the show's great appeal still derived mainly from the gentle but erratic conversations among its stars, Kukla, Fran, and Ollie. The charming Miss Allison, who maintained a constant smile throughout the series, joined the program just as it made its move to the NBC network. She had also been appearing at the time as a regular on the then popular "Don McNeill Breakfast Club" radio show. In at least one segment in each of the programs, the talented Miss Allison provided audiences with a song, either alone or with the aid of her puppet comrades.

"Kukla, Fran, and Ollie" was dropped by NBC in 1954 shortly after a move from weekdays to Sunday afternoons. But public demand for the show's return was so strong that it was revived in a somewhat limited version by ABC for another three seasons. Beulah Zachary, after whom Beulah Witch was named served as the show's executive producer for both network presentations. Here is the programming history for "Kukla, Fran, and Ollie": Monday–Friday, 7:00–7:30 P.M., NBC, November 29, 1948, through August 23, 1952; Sunday, 4:00–4:30 P.M., NBC, August 25, 1952, through June 13, 1954; Monday–Friday, 4:00–4:15 P.M., ABC, September 6, 1954, through August 30, 1957.

In 1961 the show returned to NBC in a daily 15-minute format retitled "Burr Tillstrom's Kukla and Ollie." This show aired Monday through Friday at 4:45–5:00 P.M. from September 25, 1961, through June 22, 1962. Although they followed the original formula, the puppets carried on this time without Fran Allison. Miss Allison did rejoin the puppets, however, in the late 1960s for two seasons over the public television network, and once again in the 1970s when the trio served as hosts for nearly a decade on "The CBS Children's Film Festival." (See entry for "The CBS Children's Film Festival" on page 12.)

Tillstrom and his puppets continued to show up in later years in guest spots, specials, commercials, and public service announcements. Their unique version of good clean family entertainment has remained popular with at least three generations of viewers. Burr Tillstrom passed away in 1985, but he has won a permanent place in the hearts of millions. The various shows starring Kukla, Fran, and Ollie remain as great classics from television's golden age.

Lamb Chop's Play-Along see *The Shari Lewis Shows*

Lucky Pup

When most people think of puppet characters from the 1940s and 1950s, the names Howdy Doody, Kukla and Ollie, and Jerry Mahoney are usually the first that come to mind. But some also found the antics of Lucky Pup amusing. With an ear for dialogue like no other puppet series, past or present, "Lucky Pup" is little more than a memory today.

The series was presented daily for 15 minutes at 6:30 P.M. in serial-style episodes, with a continuing story that usually began on Monday and concluded on Friday. In many instances several of the daily programs were reedited for the 30-minute Saturday program which aired at 6:00 P.M. Hosted by Doris Brown and recorded in early kinescope, the show was produced by Hope and Morey Buin, a husband-and-wife team, who also served as the show's chief puppeteers. Miss Brown was the only human foil for a group of puppets whose stories took place in a circus setting—which perhaps is why the show's sponsor, the Good and Plenty Candy Company, also associated itself with a circus atmosphere.

One of the show's puppets was Lucky, a handsome little dog with an equally handsome $5 million inheritance. Lucky was the star performer of the Buin Circus. Jolo the Clown was Lucky's friend and ever present protector, Foodini the Great was the villainous magician who constantly schemed to try to claim the pup's fortune; he was aided in his vile attempts by his faithful but inept accomplice Pinhead. Although Lucky Pup was clearly the show's star, children preferred the mischievous clowning of his nemesis, Foodini, which prompted television's first spin-off series in 1951, "Foodini the Great," on ABC. Both shows and their characters enjoyed moderate success with viewers of television's first era. CBS offered "Lucky Pup" to viewers from January 1949 through June 24, 1951.

The Muppet Show

Jim Henson's Muppet characters have been amusing both children and adults ever since the mid–1950s. Learning his craft from such influential figures as Edgar Bergen, Burr Tillstrom, and Bil Baird, the young Jim Henson first introduced his group of socklike puppets on a local Washington syndicated program entitled "Sam and Friends," presented on station WRC from 1955 to 1963. In 1969, after appearing regularly in children's commercials and on such popular adult shows as "Ed Sullivan," "Jimmy Dean," and "The Tonight Show," the expressive puppets became an important part of the newly developed "Sesame Street" series for the public broadcasting network. It was through "Sesame Street" that the characters, now known the world over as the Muppets, would become as familiar to viewers as members of their own families.

In 1976, the Muppets consisted mainly of leader Kermit the Frog,

Fozzie Bear, the Cookie Monster, Miss Piggy, Crazy Harry, and Slater and Waldorf, a pair of old coots who expressed their opinions of the show from the balcony. At this time, they appeared in their own weekly variety show of comedy and songs, with big-name guest stars taking turns as host. Produced by ITC Entertainment, "The Muppet Show" allowed Henson and company to demonstrate their accomplishments in integrating live actors with puppets, both small ones and others the size of full-grown adults. In their construction and personality, the Muppets were in a class by themselves.

The most popular of Muppets was Kermit the Frog. An inspiring figure since the premiere of "Sesame Street," Kermit served as the show's master of ceremonies and host to such continuing segments as "The Great Gonzo," "The Muppet Newsflash," "The Muppet Laboratory," where a wacky new invention was presented every week, and "Pigs in Space," where Miss Piggy headed the crew of the starship *Swine Trek.* Created by Frank Oz specially for "The Muppet Show," Piggy gained a degree of popularity that soon rivaled Kermit's. Together these two provided the basis for many of the show's running gags and regular segments. One involved their "on again, off again" relationship. Obsessed with Kermit, Miss Piggy often sang love duets with the guest stars in an effort to capture his affections.

With Henson and Oz providing most of the character voices, the Muppets succeeded in providing the show with an unusually high level of sophistication and humor that proved a pure delight to audiences young and old.

The syndicated series (September 1976–1981) was shown on different networks in different time slots over more than 100 local stations across the United States. The show nearly made its debut on ABC, but the network hesitated, assuming the show would not go the distance with adult viewers. Unfortunately, their decision cost them a smash hit series, for within just a few short months, "The Muppet Show" became the most popular first-run syndicated series in the history of television, eventually spinning off several equally successful motion picture sequels: *The Muppet Movie* (1979), *The Muppets Take Manhattan* (1984, directed by Frank Oz), and *The Great Muppet Caper* (1988).

The show was syndicated for rebroadcast in February 1982 and reruns of "The Muppet Show" are still shown on over 50 stations across the United States today. The show achieved a level that made Jim Henson, who passed away unexpectedly in 1990, a national treasure.

The New Howdy Doody Show
see *The "Howdy Doody" Shows*

The New Zoo Review

Despite its tantalizing title, "The New Zoo Review" was another in a long line of programs meant primarily to provide preschoolers with entertainment and some education using live-action puppets and humans. Featured were the show's producer and host, Douglas Momary, as "Doug," and Emily Peden, as "Emily Jo." Other cast members, who appeared in life-size puppet outfits, included Yanco Inone as "Freddie the Frog," Larri Thomas as "Henrietta the Hippo," and former Mouseketeer Sharon Baird as "Charlie the Owl." Created by Barbara Atlas, the show introduced youngsters to cultural and educational themes through songs and gentle skits.

Because of a limited production budget, the show was technically inferior to many of those previously mentioned. Even though the actors themselves appeared to be having a grand time, the series failed to attract sufficient numbers of viewers. Perhaps if the show had been produced many years earlier viewers would have been willing to overlook its deficiencies. But this was the 1970s, an age of advancement and social protest when television opened its doors to a much broader vision that appealed particularly to young people.

Still in all, "The New Zoo Review" dealt effectively with children's emotions, like fear, greed, and trust, and in many instances acted them out in a manner that young children could easily comprehend. Many parents especially admired the program for its relevance, often finding the antics of its adult-size puppet stars amusingly naive.

Coproduced by Stephen Jahn, the series was one of the few newly syndicated shows of the 1970s produced with young children in mind. Presented on a first-run basis for three years (1972–1975), the show is still available in reruns to both cable and syndicated networks that provide children's entertainment. The program was endorsed by the National Education Association.

The Paul Winchell Shows
The Bigelow Show / The Speidel Show / The Paul Winchell Show / Winchell and Mahoney / Cartoonies / Winchell and Mahoney Time

Ventriloquist acts have been a children's favorite since the very beginning of television's so-called golden age. Señor Wences and his funny hand puppets entertained millions of children during his performances on "The Ed Sullivan Show," while Jimmy Nelson and his dummies Danny O'Day and Farfel the Dog also delighted audiences with their regular appearances on "The Texaco Star Theater," as well as their numerous Saturday morning commercials for Nestle's Quik. But none to date has ever provided more continuous enjoyment than Paul Winchell and his dummies Jerry Mahoney and Kuncklehead Smiff, a team that became one of the most popular acts in the history of television.

As early as 1943, a young Paul Winchell became familiar to radio audiences as a regular on the "Major Bowes Amateur Hour," after initially appearing on the program as a contestant, winning a prize of $100.00. In 1947, after a series of irregular guest appearances on the old Dumont network, he costarred with a master mind reader named Dunniger on NBC's "The Bigelow Show." It was not until 1950, however, that Winchell gained international success as the host of his own prime-time variety series called "The Speidel Show" (the title referred to the show's sponsor). With its variety of comedy and songs, the show had a regular cast, whose members included Dorothy Claire, Jimmie Blaine, Sid ("A-l-l Righty") Raymond, and a very young up-and-coming comedienne by the name of Carol Burnett. This show aired at 8:00–8:30 P.M. on Monday on NBC from September 18, 1950, through August 31, 1953. By the fourth year of the series, Winchell had gained such a following that the name was changed to "The Paul Winchell Show," and Fab detergent products replaced Speidel watches as the sponsor. This NBC vehicle for Winchell's talents appeared on Sunday at 7:00–7:30 P.M. from September 13, 1953, through May 23, 1954.

Although the show gained international fame for its mild comedy and its fine cast of regulars, its chief appeal came mainly from the dialogues between Winchell and his wisecracking dummy, Jerry Mahoney.

Winchell had taught himself the art of ventriloquism at a very early age and his original hand-carved version of Jerry won him the admiration of audiences both locally and abroad. The first television version of Jerry was made by a professional puppet carver named Frank Marshall. To contrast with the impudent puppet, Winchell later created his dim-witted nemesis, the equally lovable Knucklehead Smiff.

In 1954, Winchell gathered up both dummies and moved to the Saturday morning slot in a new series that featured a live children's audience. The NBC series was called "Winchell and Mahoney" and appeared Saturday mornings at 10:30–11:00 from November 20, 1954, through February 25, 1956. The show was much as it had been before, focusing its attention this time directly on the children, with a flair for films, games, and contests in which winners would receive products from the show's sponsors, Schwinn bikes and Tootsie Roll candies.

In the fall television season of 1956, Winchell and Mahoney did a brief stint as hosts of ABC's "Circus Time" (see the entry for "Circus Time" on page 95) before moving to the network with their own new series, "The Paul Winchell Show" the following year. This version featured newcomer Frank Fontaine, several years before he would become better known to audiences as a "Jackie Gleason Show" regular, Crazy Guggenham. Presented on Sunday afternoons at 5:00–5:30, the program had every kid in the country familiar with the team's opening theme song, "Scottie-wattie-doo-doo," as well as with their closing, "Friends We'll Always Be." ABC offered this show from September 29, 1957, through April 3, 1960.

Not surprisingly, this was yet another case in which the dummy outshone his mentor. Reportedly, Jerry Mahoney received tons of fan mail each week from adoring young children who found his appealing qualities to be amazingly lifelike.

Generously undaunted, but attempting to emphasize the range of his other talents, Winchell appeared just as often on television in the early 1960s but now he appeared alone. He was frequently seen as a guest contestant on such game shows as "What's My Line?" and "I've Got a Secret" and on popular sitcoms like "The Beverly Hillbillies" and "The Dick Van Dyke Show," where viewers had the opportunity to witness his extraordinary talents as a comedian.

Still, Winchell managed to stand by for the networks as a possible Saturday morning replacement, and such an instance occurred when ABC canceled the reruns of "Top Cat" in April 1963. For the first time in almost three years, Winchell was once again featured with his popular dummies, Jerry and Knucklehead, as they served as hosts to the midseason replacement series, "Cartoonies" (Saturday, 12:00–12:30 P.M., ABC, April 13, 1963, through September 28, 1963). In 1965 the trio appeared in a new hour-long syndicated weekday morning series entitled "Winchell and Mahoney Time."

Toward the end of the 1960s, Winchell lent his talents to the world of animation, providing the voices for various Hanna-Barbera characters, as well as to many commercials featuring cartoon creations, from hungry Tootsie Pop–chomping owls to scrubbing bubbles. Perhaps his most famous voice, aside from those of Jerry and Knucklehead, was that of the evil Gargamel, on the Saturday morning cartoon series "Smurfs." In 1972 Winchell appeared once again as he and Jerry served as hosts on one season of the NBC children's game show "Runaround." (See the entry for "Runaround" on page 130.)

A kind man, and known as a great humanitarian, Winchell always found the time to visit children's hospitals and to appear at associated benefits whenever possible. Until his recent death, he was very interested in later years in medical technology; he is credited with the development of an artificial heart.

In 1982 television's first Jerry Mahoney and Knucklehead Smiff dummies were presented to the Smithsonian Institution by Paul Winchell himself, leaving behind many fond memories and making a final closing on one of the most enduring acts in children's television.

Puppet Playhouse Theater see *The "Howdy Doody" Shows*

Rootie Kazootie

Rootie Kazootie was the star hand puppet in this series, which entertained kids for four years at various times over both NBC and ABC. Following a format similar to that of "The Howdy Doody Show," Rootie, the Little Leaguer with the tilted baseball cap, was joined by human regulars Tod Russell and John Vee as the show's hosts. Other puppets included Polka Dottie, Rootie's little girlfriend; El Squeako Mouse, a Mexican rodent; Poison Zoomack, Rootie's archenemy; and Gala Poochie, Rootie's faithful little dog.

Originally presented daily for 15 minutes, the show was centered on the Rootie Kazootie Club, which was made up of fun and music and continuing story episodes that usually began on Monday and concluded on Friday. The show aired at 6:00 P.M. on NBC from December 9, 1950, through November 1, 1952. Episodes involved Rootie and his friends in all sorts of humorous escapades, which they eventually worked through by the week's end. The pace and variety of the continuing segments were meant to get children to return to the program daily. In keeping up with the times, the series also emphasized such important, thought-provoking themes as sharing, honesty, and friendship.

When NBC canceled "Rootie Kazootie" in the fall of 1952, the show was picked up almost immediately by ABC and presented on Saturday mornings at 11:00 for another two seasons (December 22, 1952, through May 7, 1954). Extended to a full 30 minutes, this version of the program included youngsters from the studio audience, who answered questions asked by Tod, Rootie, and the other puppets on such topics as popular science and American history. Another popular feature of the Saturday show was vintage shorts from the silent era starring such favorites as the Keystone Cops, Charlie Chase, and Edgar Kennedy.

Rootie, so named because of his constant rooting and tooting on his kazoo, and all his puppet friends were operated by Paul Ashley and Frank Milano. Ashley, a puppeteer by trade, appeared later on many local shows featuring his other puppets. He is also credited for creating the new Howdy Doody puppet, making public appearances with Bob Smith today. "Rootie Kazootie" at one time was so popular that ten-cent membership requests to the "Rootie Kazootie Fan Club" once brought a response of more than 19,000 letters in just one week.

The Shari Lewis Shows
Shariland / The Shari Lewis Show / The Shari Show / Lamb Chop's Play-Along

When "The Howdy Doody Show" left the air in 1960, perky ventriloquist Shari Lewis was given the difficult task of following one of the greatest children's acts so far in the history of television. She began working in television in 1953, when, at the age of 18, she hosted a local network series entitled "Fun 'n' Facts." This show was followed the next year by "Shari and Friends," in which she first demonstrated her amazing vocal skills by introducing her sock puppet friends Lamb Chop, Charlie Horse, and Hush Puppy. In 1957, after several well-received guest appearances on the popular "Captain Kangaroo" weekday series, Lewis was cast in a short-lived network summer replacement series, which she created, called "Shariland." But it was not until three years later when she was chosen to fill the void left by "The Howdy Doody Show," that she was truly able to demonstrate talents, in her new series, "The Shari Lewis Show." "The Shari Lewis Show" was broadcast on NBC at 10:00–10:30 A.M. from October 1, 1960, through September 28, 1963.

On this program, produced by Robert Scherer, Lewis delighted youngsters every Saturday morning with her refreshingly different style of stories, songs, and of course conversations with her spirited trio of puppet friends, each distinguished by a completely different personality. Lamb Chop was the epitome of childhood innocence, Charlie Horse was the know-it-all wiseguy, and Hush Puppy had the charm and grace of a Southern gentleman. In many of the shows, Shari was often featured singing with the puppets, miraculously moving her voice among them from lyric to lyric. Also featured on the program were Ronald Radd as Mr. Goodfellow, Shari's neighbor, and Jump Pup, a life-size puppet figure in a dog suit, played by Jackie Warner.

Each episode blended informative tidbits with the usual fun and mirth found in such shows. The difference was that the characters presented topics like jealousy and overcoming fear and adversity without the usual contrivance. For example, in one episode, Jump Pup brings out the cowardliness of the town bully, Billy Bully, who is then held accountable for terrorizing Lamb Chop and her small friends.

While "The Shari Lewis Show" provided pleasurable entertainment for young viewers, it also exposed the talents of guest actors who were just starting out in television. Both Dom DeLuise and Barbara Feldon made their debuts on the show, while actor Fred Gwynne appeared in character as Officer Francis Muldoon one day before the premiere of his first television series, "Car 54, Where Are You?" (NBC, 1961–63).

Lewis also appeared often with her puppets in children's commercials, where she pitched such products as Cracker Jack and Bubble Bath. She also continued to make guest appearances after her Saturday morning show left the air in 1963, often performing alone on prime-time drama and comedy programs. In 1975 Shari Lewis returned to television with a new syndicated 30-minute series entitled "The Shari Show."

Today, Miss Lewis, still busy and attractive, continues to showcase her many talents. She has become a best-selling author of a series of children's storybooks designed to encourage children's imaginations and to provide basic elements of cultural literacy. In addition, she has performed in and conducted more than 100 symphony orchestra concerts across the United States, many of which have been presented to children over the cable networks. In 1991 she once again returned to television on a regular basis in a new PBS series entitled "Lamp Chop's Play-Along." Throughout her long and distinguished career, Shari Lewis has devoted herself to the happiness and welfare of millions of children everywhere, including her own.

The Speidel Show see The Paul Winchell Shows

Time for Beany see Beany and Cecil, chapter 2, "Cartoons"

The Whistling Wizard

Marionettists Bil and Cora Baird became very popular in the 1950s and 1960s for several shows that featured their likable marionette characters. One of their most popular shows, "The Whistling Wizard," involved the adventures of a boy named J.P. and his horse, Heathcliff, who are transported to an enchanted island in search of the legendary Whistling

Wizard. Supporting characters among the Bairds' familiar cast of marionettes were Flannel the Mouse, Charlemane the Lion, the vile and wicked Spider Lady, and of course the Wizard himself, who, like the Wizard of Oz was not actually a wizard at all but a leprechaun named Dooley.

Imagination in its purest form, the show was a wonderful fantasy, from the acting of the puppets to the moves of the camera, to create a magical, timeless little tale that greatly appealed to children of all ages. The show received high marks from critics, as well as parents who enjoyed watching the show with their children. It was to become one of the first children's shows designed exclusively for the early Saturday morning time period. CBS offered this half hour show at 11:00 from November 3, 1951, through September 20, 1952.

The show's starring puppets were only a few of the many stringed characters the Bairds worked with in their numerous appearances on early television. Besides becoming regulars on such influential adult programs as the "CBS Morning Show," with Walter Cronkite, the Baird marionettes also appeared in many series and specials, which varied from 15- to 60-minute formats. Some of the most familiar were "The Bil Baird Show" (CBS, 1953), "Peter and the Wolf, with Art Carney" (ABC, 1958), and "Life with Snarky Parker" (CBS, 1950). The latter, which also featured J.P. and Heathcliff, was directed by a bright, aspiring young actor and director named Yul Brynner.

Willy Wonderful

This puppet series, produced by Bracken Productions, was originally released in 15- and 30-minute episodes. It featured the adventures of a youngster named Willy Wonderful (whom everyone called "little Willy") and his dog, Ellwood. Together they shared a tent with Willy's godfather, Phineas Q. Throckmorton, manager and partner in Major Catastrophy's Traveling Circus Menagerie. Other hand puppets included Major Catastrophy himself, Elinor the Elephant, Girade the Giraffe, and Willy's man-hungry aunt, Wanda Winkie. Initially shown in 1952 as a program on its own, "Willy Wonderful" soon became an incorporated segment in the local franchise productions of "Romper Room." "Willy Wonderful" continued to be available for syndication through 1960.

As with the Bil Baird marionettes, episodes presented a continuing saga, with storylines designed to capture both fantasy and the human experience without the usual assistance of live performers. Unlike the Baird presentations, and others that focused on humor, "Willy Wonderful" was one of the few puppet shows of its day to become popular without the usual abundance of parody or satire. This absence often left older viewers unable to sustain interest, except for the interplay between Willy's world and reality. Scenes such as Willy's godfather parading about with a huge set of fluttering wings sprouting from his back contrasted greatly with realistic scenes involving Willy's heart-to-heart talks with the Major, as well as other heart-tugging moments that gave the show some of the trappings of a soap opera.

In this early television era, puppets like Willy Wonderful were conceived mainly to designate a certain, mystical type. Children, especially the younger ones, loved them not because of how they looked but because their personalities left basic impressions, apart from anything else that they might have said or done. It really mattered little to Willy's fans what the show's intentions truly were, as long as characters were wholesome and upright.

A relic today compared with "Sesame Street," "Willy Wonderful" was presented with an innocent flair that reflected a more tranquil time. There are few adults today, age 40 and older, who do not remember the series and its pipe organ theme song.

Winchell and Mahoney see *The Paul Winchell Shows*

Winchell and Mahoney Time see *The Paul Winchell Shows*

9. Westerns

During television's infancy, the Western series became the most popular of children's shows. Both children and adults thoroughly enjoyed the seemingly endless hours of nonstop action provided by their favorite sagebrush heroes. Although these horse operas offered different levels of action, each usually featured a cowboy with no problems too big that they could not be handled by a six-shooter of a good old dust-kicking fistfight. In their own way, shows such as "Hopalong Cassidy," "Roy Rogers," "The Lone Ranger," and "Sky King" left their mark on television's first generation of youngsters, with themes far more significant than those of today's animated super heroes.

Although the kiddy Westerns (as they were called) of television's golden age have long since ridden off into the sunset, they shall always be remembered as the first dramatic form of television entertainment for children.

The Adventures of Champion see
Champion, the Wonder Horse

The Adventures of Jim Bowie see *Jim Bowie*

The Adventures of Kit Carson see *Kit Carson*

The Adventures of Rin Tin Tin see *Rin Tin Tin*

The Adventures of Wild Bill Hickok see *Wild Bill Hickok*

Annie Oakley

The "prettiest gun in the West," as she was sometimes called, appeared in the form of actress Gail Davis as the legendary Annie Oakley, a heroine who matched wits with grubby outlaws, wild Indians, and any other villainous adversaries who stood in her path. Annie resided with her kid brother, Tagg (Jimmy Hawkins), in the sleepy town of Diablo, and was assisted in keeping the town free of desperadoes by her friend and comrade, Sheriff Lofty Craig, played by Brad Johnson. Miss Davis had previously appeared in several "B" Westerns and had had character parts on such popular shows in the genre as "The Lone Ranger" and "The Gene Autry Show." It was Gene Autry who decided to give her a chance at stardom with her own series, "Annie Oakley" produced by his Flying A Production Company.

Long before "Sheena," "Isis," or "Wonder Woman," "Annie Oakley" first suggested a new type of sexuality never before seen on television. Pigtailed and standing no more than five foot one, Annie could look attractive while at the same time shooting the wings off a fly blind-folded at six paces. Consequently, in episodes such as the premiere, "Bullseye," and others like "Justice Guns," she often appeared as deadly as she was attractive, convincingly performing feats impossible for other actresses. She was the perfect heroine for the age, holding her own against any leading male figure of the day who flew, fired a gun, or wore a badge.

Already a skilled horseback rider and sharpshooter, Davis performed many of her own stunts, such as the one at the very beginning of the show's opening sequence where she is featured standing on her horse's back at full gallop while firing a Winchester at a target and hitting the bullseye. Like Clark Kent and several other influential figures in children's dramas, Annie at times concluded stories with a friendly wink and smile into the camera as a way of letting viewers know that the last 30 minutes had been strictly for fun.

Second only to "The Adventures of Kit Carson," "Annie Oakley" was rated the most popular new children's Western of 1954, the year of its premiere. However, it was the adults, both admiring men and women, who helped make the series an overall favorite. When production for the series ended in 1956, reruns were syndicated through 1963, while Davis continued to appear as Annie Oakley in traveling circuses, Western shows, and rodeos across the United States and Canada.

Brave Eagle

One of television's most unusual children's Westerns was "Brave Eagle." Set in the Old West, "Brave Eagle" was the first program of its type to feature American Indians in a positive light, showing how the West was "won" from their point of view. The 30 minutes of live-action drama featured Keith Larson in the title role as Cheyenne chief Brave Eagle, whose modern efforts at peace between the races were different from the old.

Although the show tried hard to erase the negative stereotypes often associated the Indians in motion pictures, ultimately it failed. In one episode, for instance, entitled "Valley of Decision," a stubborn settler refuses to let Brave Eagle and his tribe pass through his property in order to harvest their corn. Though the story could have offered a realistic portrayal of the struggle between the cultures, by the end, Brave Eagle, in the spirit of nonviolence, backs away from the conflict, as if to symbolize his acceptance of the place of Native Americans as second-class citizens. Moreover, the show as a whole did little to discourage the negative attitudes of white Americans toward Indians as they appeared in Hollywood films. Although the title character was played by a white actor, the supporting cast, those of true Indian heritage, gave the show a genuine touch of authenticity. Featured were Keena Nomkeena as Keena, Brave Eagle's adopted son, and Kim Winoma as the beautiful Morning Star. Bert Wheeler starred as Smokey Joe, the comical sidekick.

Produced by the Roy Rogers Production Company, "Brave Eagle" initially appeared in prime time for one season on CBS (Wednesday, 7:30–8:00 P.M., September 28, 1955, through June 6, 1956) before going into syndication a year later. Even though it developed something of a cult following, mostly among minorities and liberal-minded critics, most parents encouraged their children to watch Walt Disney's "Disneyland" on an alternate network. Ironically, this show often featured Fess Parker's character Davy Crockett fighting "savage bloodthirsty Indians" for his life. Though conceived with the intention of shedding a bit of light on the Native American experience, the series, in some ways a very fine one, unfortunately contributed to 1950s minority stereotyping.

Buffalo Bill, Jr.

Former child actor Dick Jones starred in this 30-minute Western series produced by Gene Autry's Flying A Productions which was syndicated in October 1955. In this show, set in the lawful town of Wileyville, Texas, around the turn of the century, Bill and his younger sister, Calamity (Nancy Gilbert), had become wards of the town's founder, Judge Ben Wiley (Harry Cheshire), after an Indian ambush resulted in the deaths of their parents. Although the series' theme song referred to Bill as the "son of a son of a gun," in reality he was not related to the original Buffalo Bill Cody.

Having previously costarred as Jock Mahoney's partner Dickie West on "The Range Rider" series, Jones was coaxed into his new role as a 25-year-old prodigy in the Old West by his boss, Gene Autry. Originally thinking that the role would pale by comparison to his old one, Jones rose to new fame beyond his own expectations. Having been billed as "the world's youngest trick rider and roper" since the age of six, the young star was already considered one of Hollywood's finest horsemen. He insisted on doing his own stunts for the series and was featured jumping off of cliffs, diving through shattering glass, and racing through countless breath-taking chase scenes in such episodes as "Trail of the Killer," "Spitfire," and "Kansas City Lady."

In the show's second set of episodes, young Bill became the town marshal, and he spent most of his time bringing lawbreakers to justice and trying futilely to rescue his kid sister from all sorts of "calamities." The series had drawn such a following among young cowpokes at home that with its second season in syndication, it somehow managed to squeeze into the Saturday morning hour that was already filled with cowboy heroes who had previously staked their claims across the networks.

As a child actor, Dickie Jones, as he was called, had provided the voice for Pinocchio in the 1940 Walt Disney classic film of the same name. In later years he showed up in such forgettable Western films as *The Wild Dakotas* and *Requiem for a Gunfighter*. He is still remembered best today by fans of his early television work.

Champion, the Wonder Horse / The Adventures of Champion

The star of this Western series was Gene Autry's "wonder horse," Champion, the first steed to enter the juvenile television horse races, followed closely by Fury and Flicka. In Texas in the late nineteenth century, Champion, once the king of the wild horses, was befriended in the first episodes by 12-year-old Ricky North (Barry Curtis), who lived with his uncle, Sandy, played by Jim Bannon. Like many people in an animal-related series, Ricky was often involved in all sorts of rescue situations that required the heroics of his four-legged friend. Whenever Champion was not busy keeping Ricky out of trouble, he often worked of his own accord with the town marshal by rounding up the likes of cattle thieves and horse rustlers. Champion often accomplished these tasks with the aid of Ricky's faithful German shepherd, Rebel. Champion was actually played by Fella, a look-alike to the equine star, trained by Glenn Randall. He had also appeared with Autry in his own series, "The Gene Autry Show." The original horse from the popular Gene Autry films died in 1944.

The weekly adventures of Champion were created by Gene Autry's own Flying A Productions, which had also created the radio version of the series, from 1949 to 1950.

"Champion, the Wonder Horse" lasted only 26 episodes, ending midway through the show's first season, for it proved no match in the ratings race for "The Adventures of Rin Tin Tin" on ABC. Also known as "The Adventures of Champion," the show aired on Friday at 7:30–8:00 P.M. on CBS from September 30, 1955, through February 3, 1956. Many CBS affiliates preempted the show by as much as two hours, often running it as late as nine or ten o'clock, where it developed a regular adult following. In 1964 the series was rerun with other children's Westerns in syndication.

Circus Boy

With its unlikely title for a Western, "Circus Boy" was another in the long line of popular action stories for children which followed an entirely different drummer. It starred 12-year-old Mickey Braddock as an orphan who traveled across the western United States with a turn-of-the-century circus troupe. Corky earned his keep with the circus as a water boy for Bimbo the baby elephant, which he claimed as his personal pet.

Stories usually centered on Corky and his involvement in the problems of his adult friends and guardians, Big Tim Champion (Robert Lowery), the circus owner, and Joey the Clown (Noah Beery, Jr.), who was the legal guardian of Corky after his parents, the "Flying Falcons," were killed in a high wire act accident. Guinn Williams was also featured as Big Pete, the roustabout. Other well-known character actors who guest-starred on the show included Andy Clyde as the Cimarron Kid, Sterling Holloway as the Great Elmer, Otto Waldis as Old Fritz, Hal Peary as a lighthearted con artist, and Edgar Buchanan in a variety of different roles.

Typical episodes featured threatening encounters with hostile land barons, evil crooks, and trouble-shooting nonconformists as the circus troupe tried to bring a little joy and excitement into the lives of the early settlers. Although lacking the usual amount of gunplay in television Westerns, "Circus Boy" nonetheless managed to maintain its share of brawling, which was so much a part of the genre.

"Circus Boy" made its debut over the NBC network on Sunday nights under the sponsorship of Mars candy bars. Here is the programming history for "Circus Boy": Sunday, 7:30–8:00 P.M., NBC, September 23, 1956, through September 8, 1957; Thursday, 7:30–8:00 P.M., ABC, September 19, 1957, through September 11, 1958; Saturday, 11:30–12:00 noon, NBC, October 11, 1958, through September 5, 1959. The series, distributed through Screen Gem Productions, was featured in syndication throughout the mid–1960s after release in October 1962.

Both Robert Lowery and Noah Beery, Jr., had previously established their careers in films in a variety of credited performances. While Lowery is perhaps best remembered as Batman from the Columbia movie serial, Beery's brush with screen immortality came many years later when he played the father of James Garner in NBC's "The Rockford Files." Mickey Braddock, one of the more gifted television child actors, was probably best remembered later for his adult role as singer Mickey Dolenz on the rock favorite, "The Monkees" (NBC, 1966–68).

The Cisco Kid

"The Robin Hood of the early West" was the title most often given to the Cisco Kid. The character, whose real name was Juan Francisco Delarus, was first presented on the screen in a series of "B" movies produced by Monogram Studios and was played at various times by actors Cesar Romero and Gilbert Roland. But it was not until a young and suave Duncan Renaldo stepped into the role in 1945 that movie audiences began to sit up and take notice.

After five years as the Spanish horseman on the silver screen, Renaldo repeated his role for television, becoming one of the medium's earliest Western favorites. The video version paired Renaldo with veteran character actor Leo Carillo as his comical sidekick, Pancho. Both actors fit perfectly into their roles because like the characters they portrayed they were also of Hispanic descent.

Set in early New Mexico, episodes often involved the duo's well-meaning attempts to assist the poor and downtrodden victims of crooked politicians, scheming con artists, and corrupt officials. Cisco, who always dressed in black, was frequently at odds with the law himself. Inept lawmen, for instance, often looked upon the sombrero wearing stranger as a meddlesome troublemaker until he and Pancho proved otherwise by succeeding within the law where others had failed.

In typical episodes, Cisco and Pancho are framed for the crimes of the real evil-doers. After proving their innocence, the two win the town's respect as heroes. Cisco also became a favorite with many female viewers, and he was featured in many episodes flirting with beautiful señoritas.

"The Cisco Kid" was a creation of romance author O. Henry, who wrote a series of Western novels in the early 1900s. Syndicated on October 3, 1950, and produced in color, the series was a creation of Frederic Ziv's ZIV-TV Productions. Still enjoyed today when rerun on local stations, "The Cisco Kid" is one of the most popular syndicated Westerns of all time.

Cowboy G-Men

Lesley Selander directed this low-budget 30-minute Western series that starred Russell Hayden as no-nonsense government agent Pat Gallagher and Jackie Coogan as his less than serious partner, Stoney Crockett. The two of them in several ways differed from the stereotypical cowboy. Gallagher and Crockett were nineteenth-century undercover agents whose job it was to discover the criminals who posed a threat to the U.S. government. The show was an inspiration for later adult Westerns such as "Stories of the Century" and "The Wild, Wild West." Episodes always involved a plot line in which the agents uncovered espionage activities, as revolutionaries planned to take control of the country.

Sponsored by the Taystee Bread Company and produced in color, "Cowboy G-Men" was syndicated in 1952 and usually featured locally on Saturday afternoons.

Prior to the series, Russell Hayden had become familiar to movie audiences as Lucky Jenkins, one of the many partners of matinee idol Hopalong Cassidy. He later gave up acting for directing, becoming responsible for such adult Western series as "Judge Roy Bean" and "26 Men."

Former child star Jackie Coogan, who had received critical acclaim for his juvenile performances in *The Kid* (1921) and *Tom Sawyer* (1930), went on to appear in another television role for which he unfortunately became better remembered—that of Uncle Fester on "The Addams Family."

"Cowboy G-Men" is another fine old Western that because of its infrequent appearance in reruns is rarely remembered today.

Fury see *chapter 1, "Action-Adventure Shows"*

The Gene Autry Show

Like William Boyd with his Hopalong Cassidy character, singing cowboy star Gene Autry was another former movie celebrity to discover gold "deep in the heart" of television. Although edited versions of his feature films had been around since 1947, his own 30-minute weekly series made its debut in July 1950. Here is the programming history of this half hour CBS show: Sunday, 7:00 P.M., July 23, 1950, through September 27, 1953; Tuesday, 8:00–8:30 P.M., October 6, 1953, through September 30, 1954; Wednesday, 7:00–7:30 P.M., October 6, 1954, through August 7, 1956.

Autry's Melody Ranch, horse Champion, and comical sidekick Pat Buttram became just as popular on television as they had been previously in both motion pictures and on the radio. Notably missing, however, was Smiley Burnette, the actor who usually played Autry's sidekick in the dozens of movies he made for Republic pictures.

In nearly every episode on the series, Gene roamed from his ranch into town, where he often became involved in the lives of people, who needed his help. Ranchers and tired lawmen, for instance, welcomed his assistance in bringing desperate outlaws to justice.

As in many Westerns of the era set at the turn of the century, Autry had his share of gunfights and rough-and-tumble struggles, but unlike most others (with the exception of Roy Rogers), he somehow always managed to look as though his clothes had just returned from the laundry. Gene always got the best of the bad guy, but this was especially satisfying when his enemy was a corrupt, dishonest law official.

One of the earliest television Westerns produced specifically for a children's audience, "Gene Autry" was presented throughout its entirety during the evening hours of prime time. It eventually moved to Saturday mornings in reruns when 54 of Autry's films from Republic were bought and syndicated to various television stations across the country by MCA-TV Film Corporation.

An inspiration to such later television cowboys as Jock Mahoney and Dick Jones, Autry chose to perform most of his own stunts, coming close a number of times to being seriously injured. Autry himself was shown a number of times leaping from the saddle of his horse, Champion, to get a jump on the bad guy.

A gentleman both on and off the screen, Autry set a good example for kids with his cheery attitude and moral code of the Old West, which stated that good cowboys never smoked, took a drink, or told a lie and always helped people (particularly old ones) in distress. Gene Autry became a huge favorite not only with kids, but also with many adult organizations, such as church and teachers' groups.

Singing cowboy Gene Autry from "The Gene Autry Show."

In addition to becoming one of early television's most celebrated personalities, Autry was one of the industry's most consistent businessmen. After the 1950 premiere of his series for CBS, Autry formed the Flying A Production Company, which became responsible for a variety of other popular children's Westerns, such as "Annie Oakley," "The Range Rider," and "Buffalo Bill, Jr.," as well as the first season of the popular adult Western anthology series, "Death Valley Days." He also became stockholder in a chain of early television and radio stations, which helped pave the way for his million-dollar recording of the Johnny Marks Christmas favorite, "Rudolph the Red-Nosed Reindeer," along with "Santa Claus Is Coming to Town." His first gold record, made back in 1935, "That Silver-Haired Daddy of Mine," was followed closely on the charts by his theme song of many years, "Back in the Saddle Again."

Gene Autry has remained constantly busy over the years as a manager, a director, and owner of several flying schools, oil fields, and recording studios. He is still the inspiring force behind his California Angels baseball team. All this represents a significant accomplishment for a starving young fellow who began his career as a singing telegraph operator.

Hopalong Cassidy

Former silent screen actor William Boyd joined early television's roster of stars when his celebrated Hopalong Cassidy movie character first hit the airwaves on NBC, Saturday at 6:00 P.M. on August 8, 1948. (The show remained at this programming slot until December 23, 1951.) After acquiring the television rights to his feature films, Boyd formed the William Boyd Production Company and filmed new 30-minute episodes featuring the popular Western hero. The television series became an overnight sensation, especially among youngsters who had never previously seen a Hopalong Cassidy film.

The idea of recreating the character from the movies on television was indeed a smart move. Not only did it help to further Boyd's career, but it brought the Western drama to a medium where it would be successful for over two decades.

Hopalong Cassidy (called "Hoppy" by his close friends) was the epitome of the traditional Hollywood cowboy hero. Although he dressed in black, his clean-cut image was upheld by his nonviolent approach and his serious effort to set a good example for children's audiences by avoiding such vices as alcohol, tobacco, and the lack of common courtesy. In this way the character set standards that others of the genre closely followed. Interestingly, however, the original character as portrayed in Clarence E. Mulford's novels was a far coarser individual.

Boyd first acquired the name "Hopalong Cassidy" after the character (Bill Cassidy) was hit in the leg by a bullet in the very first Hopalong Cassidy film for Paramount, *Hopalong Cassidy Enters* (1935). He was originally supposed to have appeared as a character from the Zane Grey novels named Buck Peters after just a few films as Cassidy. Kids, however, who made up the large majority of his fans, instantly became hooked on the character with the funny name, thus making Hopalong Cassidy the most consistent role ever to be played by the same actor.

Episodes often found Hoppy traveling around, aiding the local sheriff in foiling the plans of law-breakers. Hoppy was accompanied by his horse, Topper, and actor Edgar Buchanan as his sometimes comical sidekick, Red Conners. Shows ended with Cassidy delivering a personal message to young viewers about safety awareness and individual responsibility. It was rumored that, when the series was presented from 6:00 to 6:30 on Saturday evenings, more than 75 percent of American households were watching, thus making the show the second most popular program on the air, following only Milton Berle's "Texaco Star Theatre."

By the early 1950s, though, with the emergence of such novelty Westerns as "The Lone Ranger" and "Lash LaRue," "Hopalong Cassidy,"

William ("Hopalong Cassidy") Boyd (left), Gabby Hayes (center) and guest star George ("Superman") Reeves making a rare appearance without his cape.

with its thin line of repetitious plots, began to show signs of deterioration. After a while, it became all too evident that the show had run its course. The show was available in syndication from 1952 through 1954. It was syndicated for rebroadcast in 1955.

When William Boyd finally retired from acting in 1952 (he was well into his fifties when the television show first began), he reportedly received over 80 percent in profits from his rights to the shows, as well as an additional amount from the edited versions of his feature films. He also took charge of Hopalong Cassidy Enterprises, which initiated one of the first and biggest commercial tie-ins to feature a television character's likeness. At this project's peak, over 100 licensed manufacturers were bringing Boyd as much as $70 million a year, by featuring Hoppy on such items as imitation gun belts, bicycles with steer-horn shaped handles, flashlights, pajamas, records, coloring books, and even peanut butter.

Reruns of both the Hopalong Cassidy movies and the television series are rarely, if ever, seen today, even on cable networks. Those who do remember the program saw Western melodrama at its best.

Jim Bowie / The Adventures of Jim Bowie

Louis Eldelman and Lewis Foster produced this series about the famous, knife-wielding adventurer of the late nineteenth century, James Bowie. Scott Forbes starred as the only series regular in the title role as the wandering crusader, owner of the historic knife that carried his name and trademark.

Unlike most Westerns, which were set in Texas or Arizona, this one was located in New Orleans in the days when settlers and homesteaders fanned across the American Midwest in search of a better life.

Born in Georgia, Bowie had previously fought in the Spanish-American War in order to liberate the southwestern states. (In one of the show's many contradictions, the real Jim Bowie was killed soon after, along with Davy Crockett, during the battle of the Alamo.) Like Crockett, Bowie was one of America's greatest folk heroes, and his exploits became legendary. Stories often revolved around his encounters with Indians and casual acquaintances, and his confrontations with various enemies, who challenged his skills as a knifeman. The weapon itself was a single-edged curved blade, 10 to 15 inches in length, bearing Jim's name, though in several episodes his brother Rezin was credited as the actual inventor.

Unlike most children's Western-style heroes, Bowie appeared more dapper than daring, and in many instances he kept a sharp eye out for the fairer sex. In an episode titled "The Swordsman," for instance, Jim goes back to New Orleans to settle down and buy an estate, but he soon loses sight of his objective after meeting the estate's pretty owner (Lilyan Chauvin).

Actually the series, presented on Friday evenings, appealed to as many adults as children. It came under repeated attacks, however, from critics and pressure groups who charged that the show encouraged violent acts associated with Bowie's knife. Mostly remembered for its tongue-in-cheek performances, "The Adventures of Jim Bowie" was something of a Friday evening cult favorite for two seasons (Friday, 8:00–8:30 P.M., September 7, 1956, through August 29, 1958) over the ABC network before going into syndication in 1959.

Kit Carson / The Adventures of Kit Carson

Bill Williams starred as the legendary Christopher ("Kit") Carson in this 30-minute syndicated Saturday morning series produced in 1952. Unlike most other Westerns of the era, "Kit Carson" was a television original, never having appeared previously as a regular in movies or on radio. The series, which also featured Don Diamond as Kit's Mexican sidekick, El Toro, was a Revue Production, shot at the old Republic Studios, home of many of the great movie serials and "B" Westerns of the 1930s and 1940s.

Born in Kentucky in 1809, the real Christopher ("Kit") Carson grew up near a stockade fort in Mississippi, where Indian raids were a regular part of his life. When he was 20, he joined an expedition through uncharted territory, through the Mojave Desert to California. While on the trip, the young frontiersman learned his skills as a scout and guide to the Old West which later made him a favorite with early homesteaders. During the great Mexican War, Kit served as a cavalry scout and he was noted for defending Fort Adobe Walls against an Indian attacking force of 4,000.

Elaborating on his reputation, the television episodes continued the Carson saga, with the character acquiring additional skills in trick riding and shooting. Nearly every episode included a scene in which Kit was featured, Indiana Jones style, hanging either from the back of or underneath a stagecoach moving at full speed in pursuit of desperadoes.

A former championship swimmer, Williams had previously appeared in such films as *30 Seconds Over Tokyo* (1944) and *West of the Pecos* (1945). He was later featured as Betty White's husband in the comedy series, "A Date with the Angels" (ABC, 1957–58). His son William Katt has become one of the film industry's most promising young actors, appearing in such films as *Carrie* (1976), *Butch and Sundance: The Early Days* (1979), and *House* (1986), as well as the short-lived but memorable television series, "The Greatest American Hero" (ABC, 1981–83).

During its second season, "The Adventures of Kit Carson" became the most watched children's Western in the country. Consisting of three seasons (syndicated 1953–56) and a total of 106 episodes, the series was a production of directors Richard Irving and Norman Lloyd.

Lash of the West

"Lash of the West" was in actuality a compilation of 15- to 30-minute Western films hosted by and starring former "B" Western star Al ("Lash") LaRue. As with "Death Valley Days," programs ended with LaRue's personal wrap-up segment telling kids about the Old West and the way life used to be.

Lash had little in common with most of his Western counterparts, as far as chivalry, marksmanship, and the usual "squeaky clean" image went. Dressed in black from head to foot, Lash was not all that handsome and was a bit on the short side, standing no more than five foot six, in two-inch lifts. In many of his films, LaRue often appeared more villainous than most of the criminals he ended up bringing to justice.

Despite his shortcomings (including his lack of skill as a horseman), Lash had a gimmick that separated him from all the others and attracted children to the screen. Instead of the trusty shooting iron, Lash had instead a 15-foot bullwhip, which he used with the skill of an expert.

Starting out in films as an outlaw called the Cheyenne Kid, LaRue developed the bullwhip gimmick in an effort to improve his otherwise unappealing image. The idea met with huge success, and LaRue suddenly began receiving dozens of fan letters from approving children.

Although his career in films was brief, and for the most part unmemorable, his television series, first syndicated (1952–53), then shown briefly on ABC (Sunday, 5:00–5:15 P.M., January 4, 1953, through May 9, 1953), then resyndicated (1953–55), later inspired such other novelty-related Western heroes as Whip Wilson, Chuck Connors's Rifleman, and even the similar dressed Richard Boone, with his business cards that read "Have Gun Will Travel."

Al LaRue's real life was often as complicated as his life on screen. After his acting career came to an abrupt halt in the 1950s, he had several encounters with the law, with charges ranging from being drunk and disorderly to the unlawful possession of illegal drugs. He later toured the country with traveling carnivals and sideshows in the guise of a born-again evangelist. Reportedly he is living today in a monastery in Florida. Fortunately, mostly because of his skill with the whip, his character is one of the best remembered of yesterday's cowboy heroes.

The Lone Ranger

The most popular television Western ever produced, "The Lone Ranger" began in the 1930s when a variation of the character first appeared upon movie screens in *The Lone Rider*. A few years later the character was revived for radio by George W. Trendle, owner of Detroit station WXYZ. Although it gained a huge following, "The Lone Ranger" only reached its height in popularity in 1949 when the character and his faithful Indian companion, Tonto, were presented in a new series of half-hour films made for television by Jack Chertok Productions.

Although few actors have managed to capture the public's imagination so vividly with a character, today, when the Lone Ranger is mentioned, only one name comes to mind—Clayton Moore. John Hart played the role during the show's second season, but it was Moore who was destined to become the best of the Lone Rangers.

Following in the bootprints of such inspirations as "Hopalong Cassidy," the Ranger stood for everything wholesome and just, while remaining as quick with his wit as he was on the draw. No matter how rough the action might have appeared, Moore always managed to underplay the violence that later dominated the "adult" Western series.

Off-screen, however, Moore was a bit of a rebel. Because of a contract dispute during the show's second and third seasons, Moore refused to play the part any longer. But he was eventually persuaded to return, on his own terms, when it became evident after just 26 episodes that viewers had not really accepted John Hart in the role. Moore had previously been known for his work in such low-budget movie serials as "Dick Tracy Returns" (in which he played a villainous role), "Jessie James Rides Again," and "The Ghost of Zorro."

Jay Silverheels, a real Mohawk Indian, costarred as Tonto, whose stone-faced presence was very different from that of the traditional comic sidekick. Although the word *Tonto* means "incompetent" in Spanish, the character was in no way a bungler. In fact Tonto was often shown as being nearly as skilled as the Lone Ranger, and just as interested in the rights of Indians as the Ranger was in truth and justice.

Enjoyed by all age groups, "The Lone Ranger" appeared for many years (often simultaneously over various networks) on Saturday mornings and in the early hours of adult prime-time. The show was produced by Jack Chertok until 1954, when it was sold to the Wrather Production Company, which became the copyright owner of the characters for many years.

Throughout the series' run, and for the benefit of new audiences, viewers were occasionally reminded of the show's origin, first presented in the opening three episodes, "Enter the Lone Ranger." It was here that the story of the Lone Ranger first begins as John Reid, sole survivor of a murderous ambush of the Texas Rangers by the Butch Cavendish Hole in the Wall Gang, continued to bring law and order to an unruly West

Clayton Moore as the Lone Ranger and Jay Silverheels as Tonto from the series "The Lone Ranger."

during the mid–1800s. He remains anonymous, allowing the ambushers to believe him dead and wearing a cloth mask made from the vest of his slain brother, Tom, sheriff of the Texas Rangers. Glenn Strange, an actor born to play sadistic villains and bad guys, appeared in several episodes, reviving his role as the Ranger's most contemptible nemesis, Butch Cavendish.

The Ranger is nursed back to heath by Tonto, whom he befriended as a youth. Vowing unlimited devotion to his "kemosabe" (trusted friend) in the pursuit of law and order and justice, he joins the Lone Ranger, and the two became the most memorable team in the history of television Westerns.

Out in the plains, the Ranger, Tonto, and Tonto's paint horse, Scout, find a beautiful but injured white stallion which Tonto declares "white as silver." Eventually recuperating, Silver becomes the Lone Ranger's trusted steed. Several follow-up episodes pointed out that the Ranger and his late brother had been joint owners of a silver mine, which explained the Lone Ranger's means of support (especially since he was always turning down rewards for his good deeds), as well as his endless supply of trademark silver bullets. Because of the Ranger's avoidance of unnecessary violence (he never shot to kill) and his correct use of the English language, parents overwhelmingly preferred the program to others of the genre.

Many of the show's stories were developed and written by Trendle's chief writer, Frank Striker, whose idea it was to introduce young Dan Reid (Chuck Courtney) into the series as the Lone Ranger's nephew, the son of his dead brother, Tom. In several episodes Dan was featured working right along with the Ranger and Tonto, while in others he filled in for Tonto, who sometimes took a leave of absence to attend to Indian affairs. Dan would also appear in another Trendle creation as the grown-up father of another popular crimefighter, the Green Hornet.

A master of both disguise and dialect, the Lone Ranger was able to fool many an adversary with an assortment of disguises that ranged from a grizzled old coot, to a drunken Mexican, to an aristocratic gentleman.

"The Lone Ranger" became not only an overnight success, but also one of the longest running shows in the history of television, producing new episodes while old ones were still being rerun on various networks. In 1956 and 1957 it even spun off two successful Technicolor motion pictures for Warner Brothers, entitled *The Lone Ranger* and *The Lone Ranger and the City of Gold*.

Clayton Moore, like George Reeves of "Superman," became very closely identified with his television role. But much unlike Reeves, who was not really Superman, Moore was very much the Lone Ranger. Years after the show's production ended, Moore continued to make public appearances as the familiar figure. The celebrated actor wears the mask again today after a lengthy court battle with the Jack Wrather Corporation, which obtained a court order in 1979 prohibiting Moore from wearing the mask in public. The company, in association with the series' long-time sponsor, General Mills, was promoting a younger actor for the role in a new movie, *The Legion of the Lone Ranger*.

Jay Silverheels remained somewhat active in the business after the series ended production in 1957. He spent his later years breeding horses and becoming involved with the Bureau of Indian Affairs. He died in 1980, shortly after being acknowledged for a lifetime of achievement with a star that bore his name on the Hollywood Walk of Fame.

Today "The Lone Ranger" continues to be shown in syndication to new generations of children who are otherwise unfamiliar with the television Western. And although there is much that might be considered humorous by today's standards—the hokey dialogue, the repeated plots, the tired musical score—the material still works if for no other reason than the unflinching integrity of the lead characters. An animated version of the series aired on CBS in 1966, running for three consecutive seasons on Saturday mornings. Here is the programming history for "The Lone Ranger": Thursday, 7:30–8:00 P.M., ABC, September 15, 1949, through September 12, 1957; Saturday, 1:00–1:30 P.M., CBS, June 13, 1953, through September 24, 1960; Wednesday, 5:30–6:00 P.M., ABC, September 28, 1960, through September 27, 1961; Saturday, 10:00–10:30 A.M., NBC, September 30, 1961, through September 29, 1962; Saturday, 10:30–11:00 A.M., ABC, March 13, 1965, through September 11, 1965; syndicated, for rebroadcast, 1965.

Clayton Moore, older and much the wiser, can still be seen from time to time as the Lone Ranger. He proudly continues to wear the uniform that made him famous and can be seen everywhere from television commercials, to shopping mall openings, to nostalgia conventions, where little ones innocently ask their parents the famous question, "Who is that masked man?"

The Range Rider

Another television original, "The Range Rider," starred former movie stunt man Jock Mahoney (Jacques O'Mahoney) as the wandering, hard-hitting stranger from the Pecos who rode from town to lawless town, taking the law into his own hands when necessary. He was aided in his efforts at making the West a better place by his teenage partner, Dickie West, played by Dick Jones. The series, another in the line of Gene Autry's Flying A Productions, combined comedy, drama, and action while managing to remain within the boundaries of a children's program. Similar to "The Lone Ranger," "The Range Rider" was a familiar variation on the "lone rider" story in which the hero constantly roams the prairie seeking those who need his assistance.

Appearing in syndication from 1951 to 1954, the series, unlike most other children's Westerns, rarely (if ever) appeared on Saturday mornings. Instead, it was often featured in the early evening prime-time hours before moving to a weekday afternoon slot. During this period the show became something of a hit with mothers as well as preschoolers, who encouraged their mothers to stock up on the products of the show's sponsor, Table Top Frozen Pies.

The six foot four Mahoney was the perfect traditional Hollywood cowboy. He had a stern, dimpled chin and was agile and skillful enough to do his own stunts. A natural athlete, Mahoney began his career in films as a stuntman, often standing in for cowboy heroes like his boss Gene Autry, and others such as Johnny Mack Brown and Randolph Scott. In 1946 he received screen billing for his first role, in *The Fighting Frontiers-*

man, where he appeared as a bad guy. He later appeared in several of the "Three Stooges" shorts in spoofs on legends of the Old West. "The Range Rider" was his biggest claim to fame until 1958 when he starred in the adult Western series "Yancy Derringer" (CBS, 1958–59). In 1962 he appeared as the screen's thirteenth Tarzan in the film *Tarzan Goes to India.*

Although usually remembered today as the late stepfather of Academy Award–winning actress Sally Field, the actor was one of the most enduring stuntmen ever to rise out of Hollywood.

Rin Tin Tin / The Adventures of Rin Tin Tin

Set at Fort Apache in the 1880s, this live-action Western featured the great-grandson of the original canine star of silent films of the 1920s. Costarring was youngster Lee Aaker as an honorary corporal, Rusty, an orphan adopted by the soldiers of Company B, the "Fighting Blue Devils," after being rescued from an abandoned covered wagon with his German shepherd puppy Rinty (short for "Rin Tin Tin").

Rusty followed in the footsteps of a generation of television children who were featured in action series as orphaned and were adopted by various types of adults. This plot element was used so often, to emphasize the plight of orphans, that children appearing with traditional families almost seemed out of place. Aakers was discovered for his role in the show after he appeared in the "Ford Theater" presentation "And Suddenly You Knew," with Ronald Reagan.

Owned and trained by Lee Duncan, Rinty was born into a family of acting canines who provided early screen audiences with heroics never before performed by an animal of any kind. Often receiving star billing, above his human costars, Rinty, in the films produced by Warner Brothers, kept audiences thrilled throughout the 1940s.

Produced by Herbert Leonard for Screen Gem Productions, the series also starred James Brown as Lieutenant Rip Masters, Joe Sawyer as Sergeant Biff O'Hara, and Rand Brooks as Corporal Boone. Leonard had previously served as executive producer for many of the Columbia movie serials, which explained the show's resemblance to the adventure melodramas of the 1940s. Like many children's Westerns of the era, episodes were usually light on plot, emphasizing more heavily the action, which was all that really mattered to children.

In most of the episodes, plots focused on Rusty and Rinty's efforts to assist the soldiers in their continuing battle with enemy forces threatening the lives of those whom the soldiers have sworn to protect.

In one of the show's most popular episodes, "The Legend of the White Buffalo," Jim Brown, an accomplished vocalist, recreates the tale in song that he made popular in the 1940s. The story involved Rusty and Rinty's attempts to track a wanted fugitive in the desert when they come face to face with the legendary giant bison.

Rin Tin Tin was the most popular canine star since Lassie, with qualities well above those of the average animal. Producers and directors of the series made a special attempt to present stories that stressed redeeming qualities, and most of all, bravery. There were scenes in which Rinty fought with animals that were obviously much stronger, and though blood was spilled, Rinty was always undefeated.

"The Adventures of Rin Tin Tin" ran for five consecutive seasons over the ABC network on Friday evenings (7:30–8:00, October 15, 1954, through August 28, 1959), before being rerun on CBS on Saturday mornings (10:00–10:30, October 6, 1962, through September 3, 1966). In 1976 the series was syndicated once again, with Jim Brown appearing in a new color opening segment, with Rinty VII, and telling the original stories of Rin Tin Tin to a group of youngsters visiting the fort.

The Roy Rogers Show

Billed as he was in films as the "King of the Cowboys," Leonard Slye, better known as Roy Rogers, came to television in his own 30-minute series shortly after a lengthy contract dispute with the producers of his old Republic Studio. The handsome singing cowboy star was still the studio's leading box office draw when he decided lock, stock, and guitar to jump into television with his own production company, just as Gene Autry and William Boyd had done a few years previously.

Rogers was accompanied by his wife, Dale Evans ("Queen of the West"); Trigger, his golden palomino; Bullet, the German shepherd wonder dog; and Pat Brady, his comical sidekick, who rode about in a broken-down jeep he called Nelliebelle. At various times the show also featured the Sons of the Pioneers, the singing group with whom Rogers first broke into show business.

Episodes, which were set in present times, provided a unique blend of songs, adventure, and of course plenty of hard-hitting action. Much of the show's action took place between Roy's ranch, the Double R, and the outskirts of the town of Mineral City, where he assisted the local sheriff in capturing and restraining contemporary outlaws. In several cases, Roy also became involved in the affairs of local citizens unjustly accused of breaking the law. In an episode entitled "Peril from the Past," for instance, he comes to the aid of a bank cashier with a secret past who is blackmailed by bandits into helping rob the Mineral City bank. Imbued as the show was with appreciation for morality and reverence, many parents, especially mothers, favored "The Roy Rogers Show" over most others.

Oddly, although Roy and Dale played themselves on the program, there were few hints of their actual marital status, although viewers knew it to be a fact. In most of the show's 104 episodes, they seemed to have a

Roy Rogers.

relationship far more spiritual than sensual. Evidently this was considered more appropriate for a traditional cowboy hero, and it was an excuse to allow for more action and less affection. However, in the show's closing credits, the couple's subtlety becomes less apparent with their rendition of "Happy Trails to You."

If singer Gene Autry was considered the cleanest, best-dressed of television cowboys, Roy Rogers was considered to be in the same league. It was reported that imitations of Roy's $200 sequin-covered buckskin shirts and $1,200 rawhide boots were among the items on the market most requested by children. Other merchandise and toys bearing the likenesses of Rogers and his television family were rumored to have earned well over $30 million. (This does not include profits from such sponsor- related items as Jello gelatin, Nestle's Quik, and Post Sugar Crisp.)

"The Roy Rogers Show" proved to be very popular with children, as well as older family members, enjoying a long Sunday afternoon run on NBC (5:00–5:30, December 30, 1951, through June 23, 1957). Reruns of the program were telecast over CBS on Saturday mornings (11:30–12:00, January 7, 1961, through September 19, 1964). In the fall of 1962

Roy and Dale, along with their old friend Pat Brady, served as cohosts of a 60-minute musical variety hour of country-western favorites.

Roy Rogers, like several of his contemporaries, remained active in the business after his show ceased production in 1957. In addition to setting up his own production company, Roy Rogers' Frontier Productions, he became involved in the distribution of an assortment of Western products, as well as the management and ownership of a chain of family restaurants, real estate, rodeos, and the Roy Rogers Museum, in which the original Trigger and Bullet, stuffed, are on display.

In 1975 Rogers made a brief, ill-fated attempt to return to the screen in the poorly received "Mackintosh and T.J." He was put to much better use when he was allowed to appear as himself once again in a 1982 guest-star role on ABC's "The Fall Guy."

Today Roy Rogers and Dale Evans (who recently recovered from a lengthy illness) like to spend most of their time working as evangelistic leaders of the New Christian Experience.

Sky King

Television's one and only airborne cowboy, Sky King first flew his plane, the *Songbird*, out of the blue Western skys into America's living rooms in 1951. "Sky King" had been a radio program in the 1940s. Actor and real-life aviator Kirby Grant starred as Skylar King, pilot and owner of the Flying Crown Ranch, where he spent much of his time combating evildoers in a small town near the Arizona desert. Sky often worked closely with local law enforcers who needed assistance in apprehending escaped fugitives or hijackers, or rescuing people who got lost in the desert.

Set in the present, the series often seemed more interested in technology than in run-of-the-mill action. Many of the programs highlighted electronic devices, radios, and high-frequency antennas as Sky's most commonly used possessions. Although he rarely fired a six-shooter and resorted to physical violence only as a last resort, kids enjoyed the series, and parents praised its lack of violence.

While managing to satisfy both age groups, the show also presented topics expressing the concerns of an era in which the nation felt profoundly threatened. In the episode "Formula for Fear," for instance, Sky is recruited to track down a gang of foreign agents who have stolen a top-secret formula for poison gas. In another, "Operation Urgent," secret agents devise a clever scheme to penetrate U.S. security; it is up to Sky to prevent them from succeeding. The show was produced by Jack Chertok Productions. Others featured on the program included Gloria

Winters as Sky's niece, Penny; Norman Ollstead as Bob Carey, Sky's friend; Ron Hagerthy as Clipper, his nephew; Gary Hunley as Mickey the ranch hand; and Ewing Mitchell as the town sheriff.

An accomplished musician and vocalist, Kirby Grant first became popular in the 1930s as the conductor of a radio dance band. He later appeared, usually as second lead, in a number of low-budget films for a variety of studios, including Columbia and Universal. While still appearing at nostalgia conventions, he was killed in 1988 in an automobile accident.

"Sky King" was initially presented on NBC for one season before moving the following year to ABC. In 1955 new episodes of the show begin filming in syndication when the Nabisco Cookie and Cereal Company took a renewed interest in sponsoring the series. It became a Saturday morning favorite for many years as shows were rerun on CBS. A total of 130 episodes were made. Here is a programming history of "Sky King": Sunday, 5:30–6:00 P.M., NBC, September 6, 1951, through October 12, 1952; Saturday, 11:30–12:00 noon, ABC, November 8, 1952, through September 12, 1953; Saturday, 12:00–12:30 P.M., CBS, October 3, 1959, through September 3, 1966.

Tales of the Texas Rangers

This refreshingly different 30-minute Western series from Screen Gems featured Willard Parker as Jace Pearson, sheriff of the Texas Rangers, and Harry Lauter as his friend and deputy, Clay Morgan. Enjoyed by children and adults alike, the show featured one of the most interesting concepts ever used in a children's series: it was supposedly based on the 100-year-old files of the Texas lawmen. Pearson narrated as well as starred in each program in which, in one episode, he and Morgan are pursuing cattle rustlers on horseback in the 1860s, and in another episode, they are driving their 1950s Chevrolet to track down oil hoarders or poachers. The chronological variations were unusual but caught the attention of viewers. Episodes similarly ended with an epilogue personally delivered by Pearson.

Some of the modern episodes featured the Rangers as undercover men, cleverly disguised to foil the efforts of enemy agents. In one of their best stories, Pearson and Morgan are recruited to infiltrate a crime syndicate by disguising themselves as gang members: Pearson as a notorious gambler, and Morgan as a slaphappy pugilist. Interestingly, Lauter was recreating the role for which he had previously become well known. Entering television as early as 1949, he was featured quite often in supporting roles, most frequently as the bad guy. After winning fame with television Western fans, he later limited his film work to walk-ons and cameo appearances in such films as *It's a Mad, Mad, Mad, Mad World* (1963) and *The Phynx* (1970). Parker, a former tennis pro and leading man in a number of low-budget films in the 1940s, continued his acting career into the 1960s, appearing in a number of respectable films, including the Westerns *The Lone Texan* (1959) and *Young Jessie James* (1960).

"Tales of the Texas Rangers" was another in the long line of children's action tales from Columbia Pictures' Screen Gems Presentations. It was originally shown on CBS on Saturday mornings from 1956 to 1958. Becoming a favorite with adults the show appeared the following season in reruns on ABC in a variety of evening slots. "Tales of the Texas Rangers" was offered at the following programming slots: Saturday, 11:30–12:00 noon, CBS, September 3, 1955, through May 25, 1958; Thursday, 5:00–5:30 P.M., ABC, October 25, 1958, through December 25, 1958; Monday, 7:30–8:00 P.M., ABC, January 5, 1959, through May 25, 1959.

Wild Bill Hickock /
The Adventures of Wild Bill Hickok

Actor Guy Madison played the title role as the soft-spoken but hard-fisted U.S. marshal of Tombstone, Wild Bill Hickok. The 30-minute series, which made its debut in color in 1951 as the first children's Western made specially for television, also starred gravel-voiced Andy Devine as Wild Bill's jovial sidekick and loyal deputy, Jingles P. Jones ("Hey, Wild Bill, wait for me!").

As with many traditional children's Westerns based on historical figures, Madison's Hickok fell short in comparison to the original appearance of James Butler Hickok, who sported a large handlebar mustache, a shaggy pageboy haircut, and a long overcoat as his trademarks. Further, the real Marshal Hickok also lived to some extent the life of a scoundrel, which accounted for his nickname "Wild Bill." He was said to have died from a gunshot wound to the back while holding a dead man's poker hand of aces and eights.

Guy Madison (born Robert Moseley) spent much of his early career in a string of low-budget films that usually emphasized his rugged good looks rather than hard-hitting action. His revised, clean-cut, clean-shaven presentation of Wild Bill Hickok gave the character an undeniable appeal that set him apart from most other Western characters.

Perhaps the most noticeable difference was the reverse style in which he wore his pearl-handled guns for the effective cross-draw.

Equally fascinating to watch was Andy Devine as his comical partner. He brought to the series a unique kind of humor that lacked the forced quality found in most other children's Westerns. With his name included in the titles of some of the show's funniest episodes ("Jailbird Jingles," "Jingles's Disguise," "Jingles the School Marm," and so on), Devine was able to create many of the show's liveliest moments through a variety of disguises used to thwart various outlaws. Formerly one of film and television's top-rated second bananas, Devine had become very familiar to children, as his Jingles role often coincided with his other role as host of the series "Andy's Gang." In later years he served as honorary mayor of Van Nuys, California, for several terms. Devine passed away in 1977.

Despite the awkwardness posed by their physical differences (Bill was tall and lean, Jingles grossly overweight), and even though they never took themselves too seriously, the duo became the second most popular team in children's Westerns, falling only a few steps behind the Lone Ranger and Tonto. Although many of the show's stories were quite implausible, they delighted children and many adults. Kids especially enjoyed seeing their heroes perform in commercials for the show's sponsor, Kellogg's Cereals. As pitchmen for Sugar Corn Pops, Wild Bill and Jingles became just as famous for their 40-second promotions for the cereal that featured their pictures on the boxes.

In just its second season on the air, "Wild Bill Hickok" became a syndicated favorite nationwide. It grew so popular, in fact, that by the start of its third season, a second episode was featured regularly during the week without costing Kellogg's an extra cent.

CBS had perhaps the biggest reason to brood about the success of the series, for the network had once been given the opportunity to air it on a first-run basis. It was rumored, however, that affiliates doubted that children would accept the concept of a "fat and skinny" cowboy team. Although distributed independently by William F. Broidy Productions, most of the shows were presented on Saturdays and Sundays over many ABC-affiliated outlets across the country.

The rise in popularity of the adult evening Western, however, made it clear by the end of the 1950s that kiddy Westerns were facing the last roundup. Production for many had ceased entirely, and those that were still being shown were reruns of the originals. "Wild Bill Hickok" ended its long syndicated run in 1958, with a total of 120 episodes produced in association with the Screen Gems Corporation. This series and "The Cisco Kid" were the first television Westerns to be produced in color. The show was syndicated for rebroadcast on October 1, 1958.

Guy Madison remained somewhat active in the business over the years primarily by performing and touring occasionally with the European Company of Artists. His show is best remembered today by fans more for its tremendous character appeal than as a tool for merchandise. Unfortunately, "Wild Bill Hickok," although one of yesterday's best loved television Westerns, has rarely become available today for rebroadcasting.

Zorro

For two seasons toward the end of the Eisenhower administration, Guy Williams starred in the title role as the dashing masked swordsman of early California in this swashbuckling Western from the Walt Disney Studios. Set in the mid-nineteenth century, "Zorro" was the story of a crusading defender of Spanish California's poor and downtrodden, the victims of a military dictatorship. In an effort to protect the people from such tyranny, the Spanish nobleman Don Diego donned the disguise of the mysterious caped rider who takes action whenever necessary to fight injustice. Unlike the Lone Ranger, who always wore the mask, Don Diego's secret identity as Zorro was known to his deaf manservant, Bernardo (Gene Sheldon), and to his father, Don Alejandro de la Vega (George J. Lewis). Henry Calvin also costarred as Sergeant Garcia, Zorro's hapless pursuer.

Walt Disney himself served as executive producer for the 30-minute weekly series, which was sponsored, during the family hour, by the Seven-Up Company. ABC offered "Zorro" on Thursday at 8:00–8:30 P.M. from October 10, 1957, through September 24, 1959.

Zorro (who enjoyed marking Z's) might have seemed at first to be just another children's television hero, but it was not long before he won the admiration of the adult crowd as well. The show's high level of swordplay, acrobatics, and breathtaking chase sequences attracted audiences of all age groups, reportedly reaching an estimated 35 million homes each week. The show was even rumored to have been a favorite of Senator John F. Kennedy, the country's next president.

Produced with a children's audience in mind, the Disney version downplayed many of the romantic elements that dominated the popular Tyrone Power film version of the 1940s. Adding to the show's comic formula were the often humorous performances of Gene Sheldon and the burly Oliver Hardy look-alike, Henry Calvin, who later teamed up again to provide fun and merriment in the Disney film classics *Toby Tyler* (1960) and *Babes in Toyland* (1961).

With the popularity of children's Westerns waning by the end of the 1950s, "Zorro" was still one of ABC's top-rated series when it was canceled after just two seasons in favor of the more adult Westerns that emphasized family-oriented stories. But the show quickly reappeared in syndication (October 1959), and as an occasional 60-minute special presentation on the Walt Disney program. Guy Williams went on to become even more familiar to audiences as Dr. John Robinson in the television cult favorite, "Lost in Space" (CBS, 1965–68).

Like rock and roll and the hula hoop, "Zorro" and all of its tie-in paraphernalia will remain as among the most familiar icons of the 1950s. A new version of the series appears today on cable television.

10. Special Presentations

Children's specials are those programs that appear irregularly or in the place of others regularly scheduled. The best ones are eagerly awaited, each providing a thrilling or joyous moment that seems to make the wait worthwhile. While several specials appear annually at a particular time of the year, others are repeated frequently, though still on a limited basis. Many have become the source of some of television's most unforgettable moments. At the very least, these presentations have broken the monotony of television's regularly scheduled programming.

This chapter is as special as the presentations themselves. The five selections here were chosen for their durable entertainment value, because of their characters who have never lost their appeal to viewers.

The Charles Schulz / Charlie Brown Specials

The Charles Schulz "Peanuts" characters have been appearing in our homes since their debut on December 9, 1965, at 7:30 to 8:00 P.M. on CBS. From "A Charlie Brown Christmas" (1965) to "Happy New Year, Charlie Brown" (1985), veteran animators Bill Melendez and Lee Mendelson have produced, in cooperation with creator Charles Schulz, more than 30 "Peanuts" specials, featuring Charlie Brown and all his friends from the popular syndicated comic strip. Several of the shows, particularly such traditional ones as "A Charlie Brown Christmas" and "It's the Great Pumpkin, Charlie Brown," are presented annually, making the programs among the most enduring children's specials in the history of television.

Over the years, children and adults have grown familiar with the cartoons and all the memorable characters: Charlie Brown, the lovable, round-headed loser, the leading figure in each story; the conceited Lucy Van Pelt and her security blanket–carrying little brother, Linus; the tomboyish Peppermint Patty; piano enthusiast Schroeder; the incorrigible Pigpen; Frida, the little girl with the naturally curly hair; Marcy, the bespectacled innocent; Franklin, the hip black kid; and Charlie Brown's amazing dog, Snoopy, and his feathered friend, Woodstock.

Appearing in the comic pages in the 1940s as "Li'l Folks," the strip was renamed "Peanuts" after being sold to King Features in December 1950. Second only to Chick Young's "Blondie," the strip is among the most successful of all time and is published in more than 1,500 newspapers and in foreign countries. Much of the strip's popularity over the years comes from its ability to remind adults of their own childhoods while remaining true to the views of the world as seen through the eyes of little children. Like other cartoonists, Schulz wanted to create a popular strip. But his characters have always been children, with only references to any adult presence.

Each of the television presentations has been produced using an expensive and time-consuming process that is rarely used with shows that appear on a continuing weekly basis. The visual style of the animation is also very close to that of the actual comic strip, and as a result, the programs are far superior to the average cartoon series.

Although the shows are popular today, the idea for them originally met with rejection. Initially failing to realize the impact of the strip on adults, program executives considered the first Charlie Brown pilot to be much too juvenile to be enjoyed by adult audiences. For nearly a year and a half the project sat on the shelf until an advertiser from the Coca-Cola Corporation suggested the "Peanuts" characters for an upcoming yuletide project that the company was planning to sponsor. The original pilot was quickly revamped to suit the needs of the advertisers, but a reluctant CBS still feared the worst. The 30-minute special titled "A Charlie Brown Christmas" aired December 9, 1965, and it became the highest rated prime-time show of its time. Winning good reviews and critical favor, the little story, which focused on the theme of commercialism versus the true meaning of Christmas, captured over three-quarters of the television audience. The single presentation not only won an Emmy for Best Children's Program for 1965, but it also initiated a successful three-way partnership among CBS, Charles Schulz Productions, and the bottlers of Coca-Cola.

Throughout the years other "Peanuts" productions have included the following: "Charlie Brown's All Stars" (June 1, 1966); "It's the Great Pumpkin, Charlie Brown" (October 27, 1966); "You're in Love, Charlie Brown" (June 12, 1967); "He's Your Dog, Charlie Brown" (March 3, 1968); "It Was a Short Summer, Charlie Brown" (September 27, 1969); "Play It Again, Charlie Brown" (March 28, 1971); "A Charlie Brown Thanksgiving" (November 20, 1973); "It's the Easter Beagle, Charlie Brown" (April 9, 1974); "You're a Good Sport, Charlie Brown" (October 28, 1975); "It's Arbor Day, Charlie Brown" (March 16, 1976); "It's Your First Kiss, Charlie Brown" (October 24, 1977); "You're the Greatest, Charlie Brown" (March 19, 1979); "Life's a Circus, Charlie Brown" (October 24, 1980); "It's Magic, Charlie Brown" (April 28, 1981), and "Happy New Year, Charlie Brown" (December 31, 1985).

In addition to the television specials there have been several feature-length films (some of which were later televised by CBS), including *A Boy Named Charlie Brown* (1969) and *Snoopy Come Home* (1972). In February 1973, NBC presented the live Off Broadway theatrical production, *You're a Good Man, Charlie Brown*, starring Wendell Burton in the title role.

In the fall 1983, CBS decided to feature the characters on a weekly basis on Saturday mornings. Surprisingly, the series, "The Charlie Brown and Snoopy Show" lasted only a few seasons. Evidently, children prefer to have their "Peanuts" one at a time.

Cinderella

Actress Julie Andrews made her television acting debut (March 31, 1957, 9:00–10:30 P.M., CBS) in this 1957 musical adaptation of the popular fairy tale created for the screen by Oscar Hammerstein and Richard Rodgers. A highly acclaimed television event, "Cinderella" was one of the most lavishly staged television productions of its time. Directed by Ralph Nelson, the program featured more than 20 dancers, including choreographer Joe Layton, who later staged some of television's most critically acclaimed productions, such as the 1965 Barbra Streisand special, "My Name Is Barbra."

Presented live from New York, the program featured the lovely Miss Andrews, magnificent even in drab clothes. The story opens with "Cindy" feverishly matching wits with her ugly stepsisters. Following the original story as closely as possible, the familiar rags-to-riches tale was particularly enhanced by the casting of Jon Cyper as the Prince, stepsisters Ilka Chase and Alice Ghostley, Edith Adams as the beautiful Fairy Godmother, and Howard Lindsay and Kaye Ballard as the King and Queen. Succeeding with just enough comic touches not to spoil the timeless charm and appeal, the program became an overnight ratings success and a much-awaited rerun event for several years.

In 1965 a restaged version of "Cinderella" was telecast, with Leslie Ann Warren in the title role and Stuart Damon as the Prince. With an expanded budget to allow for even more elaborate sets than the original, production standards reached the highest levels of quality. The costuming, choreography, script, and supporting cast were equally brilliant. From Miss Warren's first appearance as the tattered, mistreated scullery maid, to Pat Carroll's airy portrayal of her stepsister, to Celeste Holm's worldly Godmother, to Walter Pigeon's and Ginger Rogers's King and Queen, the production was a masterpiece from start to finish. This version of the story was also somewhat more sophisticated than the original television version, but it contained the same kind of sentiments, especially when the Prince finally finds the girl of his dreams with the dainty foot.

In 1966 "Cinderella" was rerun once again over the CBS network. It was rerun again in later years, each time with the same effect on audiences as the first time.

Unfortunately, neither version of "Cinderella" quite reached the heights of such presentations as "Peter Pan." Appearing, however, at a time when live television specials of all types were presented frequently, "Cinderella" was one of the true viewing highlights of the 1950s and 1960s.

The Dr. Seuss Specials

Long before the television debut of "How the Grinch Stole Christmas" on December 18, 1966, at 6:30–7:00 P.M. on CBS, kids had been reading Dr. Seuss's books. One of the strangest tales ever conceived by Dr. Seuss was his first, *And to Think I Saw It on Mulberry Street.* In it a bored little boy envisions a series of unlikely events that take place on his desolate little street.

In the mid–1940s, avid readers were first given the chance to see a full treatment of Dr. Seuss on the silver screen, with the Warner Brothers cartoon production, *Horton Hatches the Egg,* immediately followed the next year by *Horton Hears a Who.* It was not until nearly 20 years later, however, that Dr. Seuss came to television with "How the Grinch Stole Christmas," the first in a series of 30- and 60-minute specials. The yuletide tale with a flavor like that of Charles Dickens's *A Christmas Carol,* was animated by Chuck Jones, who had previously been responsible for bringing Seuss's Horton the Elephant stories to the movie screens. The cartoon also featured the distinctive voice of actor Boris Karloff as both the Grinch and the story's narrator. The program has been rerun annually ever since, often following "A Charlie Brown Christmas" on CBS.

Theodor Seuss Geisel, born in 1904, had wanted to become a children's author, but was met with discouraging words from both artists and publishers. Later inspired by the chuckling at his discarded drawing of a flying cow, he spent the next 12 years drawing funny cartoons for an advertising agency. In 1936 he wrote a book of rhymes to match a cast of characters he had created for his first children's tale, *And to Think I Saw It on Mulberry Street.* After many rejections, the book was finally accepted, and Theodor Geisel became Dr. Seuss, a best-selling children's author.

His next tale (although placed on hold until many years later) met with even greater success. The *Cat in the Hat* books had their basis in Seuss's assumption that children were not being encouraged enough to read. An attractive story, remarkably silly but simple enough to appeal to all ages, *The Cat in the Hat* sold over 500,000 copies in just its first year. In 1970 the animated version was presented live over the NBC network, with comedian Allan Sherman providing the voice of the mischievous cat with the striped stovepipe hat and the umbrella. The program also included a variety of other short tales, brought together in a 60-minute program entitled "Dr. Seuss on the Loose."

Again with the assistance of Chuck Jones, several of Seuss's other books were translated to the screen, bringing with them some of the most humorous, unforgettable characters ever presented to a television audience. This unusual array included "star-bellied Sneetches," "north and south going Zaxs," "Grumps," "Humps," and "Whos," with names like "Pontoffel Pock," "Mary-Lou Who," and "Sam-I-Am," who lived in such odd places as "Hungus," "Who-ville," and "Hoober-Bloop," while indulging in such delicacies as Roast Beast, Who Hash, and Green Eggs and Ham. The Peabody Award–winning presentation also recruited such talented voice actors as Hans Conried, Paul Winchell, Bob Holt, Hal Smith, Henry Gibson, June Forey, and Paul Frees.

Dr. Seuss's Pulitzer Prize–winning witticisms have been translated over the years into more than 16 languages, while television reruns of his presentations continue to delight children as well. Although the author is no longer living, his characters remain immortal.

The Nutcracker

Of the several adaptations of E.T.A. Hoffmann's classic tale, the 1958 Tchaikovsky-Balanchine ballet was the first televised version. Endowed with great richness of sight and sound "The Nutcracker" provided audiences with the fantasy of the familiar tale and with the traditional spirit of the Christmas holiday. Edward Villella starred as both the Prince and as the Nutcracker, who first comes to life on Christmas Eve when given as a gift to a lonely little girl. Also featured were other members of the famed New York Ballet who gave an inspired performance to the music of Tchaikovsky.

Focusing far more on music and dance than on the story, the production was enlivened by some striking images with lasting impact. The familiar melodies accompanying the dance of the Sugar Plum Fairies have delighted audiences around the world, allowing listeners to associate the story in their own minds with images from the music alone.

Over the years other interpretations of the ballet have been presented with varying results, but Tchaikovsky's beautiful score remains intact. The 1958 televised version appeared at a time when spectacular live productions were presented on television with greater frequency. The program was a 90-minute live presentation of the CBS network's critically acclaimed "Playhouse 90," which had a reputation for costly productions and unforgettable moments of drama. "The Nutcracker" was first televised on December 25, 1958, at 9:30–11:00 P.M. on CBS.

Written and composed in 1814, "The Nutcracker" represented the height of Hoffmann's musical and literary achievement. A devotee of Mozart, Hoffmann (born Ernst Theodor Wilhelm Hoffmann) originally studied law, but he spent most of his time in Germany supporting himself by writing, composing, and managing provincial theaters. In 1816 he became the chancellor of the court of appeal in Berlin and legally adopted his middle name of *Amadeus*. His compositions continue to occupy a prominent place in both American and German literature.

Although Tchaikovsky's music is often overshadowed today in various updated video versions and in adaptations performed by ballet troupes, the 1958 television presentation of "The Nutcracker" is generally considered the medium's finest production of the children's fantasy.

Peter Pan

Just as the 1950s will always be known as the golden age of television, "Peter Pan" will always be remembered as the special of children's specials. Premiering over the NBC network a few hours before the seventh annual Emmy Awards program, the 1955 two-hour spectacular starred the late Mary Martin in the role that made her a household name. It aired on March 7, 1955, from 7:00–9:00 P.M. Although others have played the part, it is hard to imagine anyone else besides Martin as the little boy who never grew up. Her 120 minutes of songs, charm, and grace represented a turning point in the history of television. Hardly a stranger to live television, the singer-actress had starred in a number of early productions where her strong presence often made her the center of attention. In 1953 she nearly stole the show along with singer Ethel Merman as the two of them performed, on a bare stage, a musical medley for the "Ford 50th Anniversary Show." And in 1957 her splendid portrayal of Annie Oakley in Irving Berlin's *Annie Get Your Gun* made her nearly as famous as her distinguished role as Peter Pan.

Equally delightful was Cyril Ritchard's amusing portrayal of Peter Pan's archnemesis, Captain Hook. It was mostly the combined performances of Martin and Ritchard, along with good production numbers, that made the show the classic that it is today. Actress Kathy Nolan was also featured in the role of Wendy.

NBC's Producer's Showcase and producer Jerome Robbins were responsible for bringing Sir J.M. Barrie's children's classic from the Broadway stage to live television. Based on Barrie's original tale *The Little White Bird*, the play, retold as *Peter and Wendy* in 1911, deals with the adventures of fairies, pirates, Indians, and a group of young boys who follow Peter, the boy who never grew up.

The curious fact that the role has long been performed by women remains inconsequential for most. Maude Evans enjoyed her greatest stage success in the role, followed by Eva le Gallienne in 1929. Le Gallienne perhaps became the most memorable until Martin flew across the stage on invisible wires in 1954. In 1976 a vague attempt to recapture the magic was made on the ABC network, with Mia Farrow and Danny Kaye in the roles of Peter and Captain Hook. Although Kaye fell marvelously into place as the foppish sea captain, Farrow's performance as Peter Pan was somewhat below par, a pale reflection of the glow that Martin brought to the part. In the 1980s, the play was once again revived for the stage, with the role of Peter played by such notable female figures as actress Sandy Duncan and gymnast Cathy Rigby.

For several years the Jerome Robbins television production was eagerly awaited for rebroadcast by children who still believed in fairies as well as by adults who welcomed fine entertainment. In 1960 both Mary Martin and Cyril Ritchard recreated their roles with a new cast in a lavish new color production, with the script, songs, and choreography remaining basically intact. In 1989 the NBC network's rebroadcast of the 1960 version drew an overwhelming response from a new generation of children who had never seen the tale performed on a live television stage.

"Peter Pan" remains today a credit to modern literature and a fine example of classic television at its very best.

Appendix A:
Awards and Citations

Action-Adventure Shows

"The Afterschool/Afternoon Specials" (ABC): Emmy Awards (1972, 1973, 1975, 1976, 1980, 1981); Peabody Awards (1972, 1979, 1983). Producers: David H. DePatie, Fritz Freleng, Martin Taske, William Hanna, and Joseph Barbera.

"Children's Film Festival (CBS): Peabody Award (1967). Albert Lamorisse, producer and director. ACT commendations (1971, 1972).

"Disneyland" (ABC): Emmy Awards (1954, 1955); Peabody Award (1962). "Walt Disney's Wonderful World of Color" (NBC) created and produced by Walt Disney.

"Lassie" (CBS): Emmy Awards (1954, 1955); Peabody Award (1955). Jack Wrather Productions.

Cartoon Shows

"The Charles Schulz/Charlie Brown Specials" (CBS): Emmy Awards: "A Charlie Brown Christmas" (1965), "A Charlie Brown Thanksgiving" (1973), "Happy Anniversary, Charlie Brown" (1975), "You're a Good Sport, Charlie Brown" (1976), and "Life Is a Circus, Charlie Brown" (1980). Charles Schulz, executive producer and creator; Bill Melendez and Lee Mendelson producers.

"Dr. Seuss on the Loose" (NBC): Peabody Award (1970). "Halloween Is Grinch Night" (ABC): Emmy Award (1977). David H. DePatie and Fritz Freleng, executive producers, Ted (Dr. Seuss) Geisel, creator; Chuck Jones animator.

"The Flintstones" (ABC): Golden Dozen Award (1961); Golden Globe Award (1966), for Outstanding Achievement in International Television cartoons. William Hanna and Joseph Barbera, executive producers and creators.

"The Huckleberry Hound Show" (Syndicated): Emmy Award (1959). William Hanna and Joseph Barbera, executive producers and creators.

"The New Fat Albert Show" (CBS): Emmy Award (1980). Bill Cosby, executive producer; Norm Prescott and Lou Scheimer, producers.

"Smurfs" (NBC): Emmy Award (1982). William Hanna and Joseph Barbera, executive producers; Peyo Culliford, creator.

"Star Trek" (NBC): Emmy Award (1974). Norm Prescott and Lou Scheimer, executive producers (animated version).

"Tom and Jerry" (CBS/ABC): Academy Awards (1943–48, 1952). William Hanna and Joseph Barbera, executive producers; Fred Quimby, producer.

"Ziggy's Gift" (ABC): Emmy Award (1982). Lena Tabori, executive producer; Tom Wilson, creator.

Circus and Magic Shows

"The Big Top" (CBS): TV Guide Award (1950), Best New Children's Show.

"Super Circus" (ABC): cited by the National Association for Better Radio and Television (1954), Television's Most Enjoyable Family Program.

Comedy Shows

"Laurel and Hardy" (Syndicated): 1932 Academy Award, for the Hal Roach short, "The Music Box." Leo McCarey, director.

"The Little Rascals" (Syndicated): 1936 Academy Award, for the Hal Roach short, "Boarded of Education." Gordon Douglas, director.

Sherwood Schwartz, creator and producer of such child-oriented series as "Gilligan's Island" and "The Brady Bunch": Emmy Award recipient (1960) for outstanding writing achievement in the field of comedy.

"The Three Stooges" (Syndicated): 1934 Academy Award nomination, for the Columbia short, "Men in Black." Jules While, director.

Informative Shows

"Big Blue Marble" (Syndicated): Emmy Awards (1975, 1978); Peabody Award (1975). Created and produced by Harry Fownes.

"Captain Kangaroo" (CBS): Emmy Awards (1977, 1978, 1981, 1982, 1983, 1984); Peabody Awards (1957, 1972, 1978); Gabriel Awards (1974, 1978, 1982). Bob Keeshan and Jim Hirschfeld, executive producers; Ruth Manecke, producer.

"Ding Dong School" (NBC): Peabody Award (1952). Reinald Werrenrath, executive producer.

"Discovery" (ABC): Emmy Awards (1963, 1964). Frank Buxton, executive producer.

"The Electric Company" (PBS): Emmy Awards (1972, 1976). Samuel Y. Gibbons, Jr., executive producer.

"Exploring" (NBC): Peabody Award (1962). Hosted and created by Dr. Albert R. Hibbs.

"The Great Space Coaster" (Syndicated): Peabody Award (1983). Sunbow Productions.

"Hot Dog" (NBC): Peabody Awards (1970, 1971). Created by Frank Buxton; Lee Mendelson, executive producer.

"Hot Hero Sandwich" (NBC): Emmy Award (1979). Created and produced by Bruce Hart and Carol Hart.

"In the News" (CBS): Emmy Award (1979); Peabody Award (1976). Created and produced by the CBS news team.

"Make a Wish" (ABC): Emmy Award (1973); Peabody Award (1971). Lester Cooper, executive producer.

"Mr. Rogers' Neighborhood" (PBS): Emmy Award (1979); Peabody Award (1968). Fred Rogers, executive producer.

"Mr. Wizard" ("Watch Mr. Wizard") (NBC): Peabody Award (1953). Jules Pewowar, producer.

"The New Fat Albert Show" (CBS): Emmy Award (1980). Produced by Norm Prescott and Lou Scheimer; Bill Cosby, executive director.

"Razzmatazz" (CBS): Emmy Award (1978). Joel Heller, executive producer; Vern Diamond, producer.

"School House Rock" (ABC): Emmy Awards (1977, 1979). Thomas Yoke, executive producer; George Newall, producer.

"Sesame Street" (PBS): Emmy Awards (1969, 1971, 1972, 1973, 1975, 1978, 1979, 1982); Peabody Award (1969). Jon Stone, executive producer; Joan Ganz Cooney, creator, executive director; Dulcy Singer, Al Hyslop, and Dave Freyss, producers.

"Zoo Parade" (NBC): Peabody Award (1950). Marlin Perkins, producer.

"Zoom" (PBS): Emmy Awards (1972, 1973, 1976). Produced at WGBH-TV, Boston.

Kindly Hosts and Hostesses

"Dusty's Treehouse" (Syndicated): Peabody Award (1973). Stu Rosen, host and creator.

"The Uncle Al Show" (ABC): cited by *Saturday Review* magazine as Best New Saturday Morning Children's Show (1959). Al Lewis, creator and executive producer.

Puppets, Marionettes, and Dummies

"The Great Space Coaster" (Syndicated): Peabody Award (1983). Sunbow Productions.

"The Howdy Doody Show" (NBC): Peabody Award (1948). Created by Bob Smith; produced by Robert Muir.

"Judy Splinters" (NBC): Emmy Award (1948). Robert Muir, executive producer.

"Kukla, Fran, and Ollie" (NBC): Emmy Award (1953; 1970 [CBS] for single performance on the "CBS Children's Film Festival"); Peabody Awards (for NBC and irregular PBS series, 1949 and 1964). Burr Tillstrom, creator and producer.

"The Muppet Show" (Syndicated): Emmy Award (1977); Peabody Award (1978). Created and produced by Jim Henson.

"The Shari Lewis Show" (NBC): Peabody Award (1960). Produced by Robert Scherer.

"Time for Beany" (Syndicated): Emmy Awards (1950, 1952). Bob Clampett, creator and producer.

Westerns

"The Adventures of Kit Carson" (Syndicated): cited in 1954 by *Variety* magazine as Television's Highest-Rated Children's Western. Directed by Richard Irving and Norman Lloyd.

"The Lone Ranger" (ABC/CBS): nominated for an Emmy Award in 1954 as Best Western-Adventure Series. Created by George W. Trendle; Jack Wrather Producers.

"Stories of the Century" (Syndicated): Emmy Award (1954). Directed by Lesley Selander.

"The Tim McCoy Show" (Syndicated locally, KNXT–Los Angeles): Emmy Award (1952), Best Children's Show.

Special Presentations

"The Charles Schulz/Charlie Brown Specials" (CBS): Emmy Awards "A Charlie Brown Christmas" (1965); "A Charlie Brown Thanksgiving" (1973); "Happy Anniversary, Charlie Brown" (1975); "You're a Good Sport, Charlie Brown" (1976), and "Life Is a Circus, Charlie Brown" (1980). Charles Schulz, executive producer and creator; Bill Melendez and Lee Mendelson, producers.

"Danny Kaye's Look-in at the Metropolitan Opera," "The CBS Festival of Lively Arts for Young People" (CBS): Emmy Award (1975). Sylvia Fine, executive producer; Bernard Rothman, Herbert Bones, and Jack Wohl, producers.

"Dr. Seuss on the Loose" (NBC): Peabody Awad (1970). "Halloween Is Grinch Night" (ABC): Emmy Award (1977). David H. DePatie and Fritz Freleng, executive producers; Ted ("Dr. Seuss") Geisel, creator; Chuck Jones, animator.

"Jack and the Beanstalk" (NBC): Emmy Award (1966). Gene Kelly, executive producer; William Hanna and Joseph Barbera, producers.

"Peter Pan" (NBC): Emmy Award (1955), Mary Martin, for Best Actress in a Single Performance. Jerome Robbins, producer.

The Red Balloon: Academy Award (1955), for Best Original Screenplay in a Short Subject; Peabody Award (1967), for single presentation on "The CBS Children's Film Festival." Produced and directed by Albert Lamorisse.

"The Runaways" (ABC): Emmy Award (1975). William Hanna and Joseph Barbera, executive producers; Bill Schwartz, producer.

"The Snowman" (PBS): nominated for Emmy Award (1982), for Best Animated Short. Lain Harvey, executive producer; Raymond Briggs, creator.

The Wizard of Oz: Academy Awards (1939) for Best Original Score, and Best Song "Over the Rainbow"; Special Award, to actress Judy Garland for her role as Dorothy. A Victor Fleming Production; Mervin Leroy, producer.

"Yes, Virginia, There Is a Santa Claus" (ABC): Emmy Award (1974). Burt Rosen, executive producer; Bill Melendez and Mort Green, producers.

"Ziggy's Gift" (ABC): Emmy Award (1982). Lena Tabori, executive producer; Tom Wilson, creator.

Appendix B: Landmarks in Children's Television

1947:

March 11 — "Movies for the Small Fry" debuts on the Dumont network. Component series, "Small Fry Club," starring Bob Emery, premieres a month later. The program was the first network show made for children.

April 3 — "Juvenile Jury" premieres on NBC, hosted and produced by Jack Barry.

September 1 — "Judy Splinters" first premieres over local network, starring female ventriloquist Shirley Dinsdale.

December 27 — "Puppet Playhouse" debuts on NBC. The show's stars, Bob Smith and his freckle-faced marionette, Howdy Doody, help it to become television's first popular kids' show.

1948:

August 7 — 30 of the 54 "Hopalong Cassidy" films are edited and sold to television stations across the country. William Boyd, as the title character, begins production of new half-hour films of the Western specifically for television.

August 12 — Ireene Wickers's "The Singing Lady" radio program makes its television debut on the ABC network.

August 23 — "Lucky Pup" debuts on CBS.

November 29 — "Kukla, Fran, and Ollie" debuts on NBC.

1949:

January 16 — "Super Circus" premieres over the ABC network live from Chicago.

January 25 — Shirley Dinsdale voice and mentor of puppet Judy Splinters, becomes the first recipient of television's premiere Emmy Awards presentation for Outstanding Television Personality.

February 1 — Bob Clampett's characters Beany and Cecil come to local syndicated television for the first time in puppet form in "Time for Beany."

249

May 29 – "Mr. I Magination" begins its CBS network run.

June 29 – "Captain Video and His Video Rangers" debuts on Dumont.

September – "Crusader Rabbit," created by Jay Ward, debuts in syndication as the first made-for-television cartoon series.

September 15 – "The Lone Ranger" begins its long run over the ABC network as the first made-for-television children's Western.

1950:

May 28 – The Marlin Perkins series "Zoo Parade" begins its seven-year run over the NBC network.

July 1 – "The Big Top" makes its CBS weekly morning debut. It establishes the traditional pattern for Saturday morning programming for children.

July 23 – "The Gene Autry Show" premieres on CBS as television's second Western series to feature a major film star.

August 26 – Smilin' Ed McConnell and His Gang debut over the NBC network while still being presented on radio. The show will eventually be broadcast as well over both the CBS and ABC networks.

September 11 – "Space Patrol" premieres on ABC, joining a string of action-adventure dramas involving journeys into space.

October 1 – The remaining 24 Hopalong Cassidy feature films from Paramount Studios are edited for the television series.

October 3 – "The Cisco Kid" is syndicated nationally from Frederick Ziv Productions. It is the first television series ever to be filmed in color, with experimental color sets numbering fewer than 100 in the entire United States.

1951:

March 3 – Don Herbert as Mr. Wizard begins his 14-year run on the NBC network. He becomes the most influential educational figure on the air.

April 15 – Film actor Guy Madison makes his television debut as Wild Bill Hickok. Sponsored by Kellogg's Cereals, the show was the first nationally syndicated juvenile Western conceived for television ("The Cisco Kid," which had premiered a year earlier, had previously run as a movie series).

September 16 – "Sky King" first debuts over the NBC network.

October 15 – The Bil and Cora Baird Puppets are featured in their own series, "The Whistling Wizard," on CBS. It was the network's first color series.

December 30 – Singing cowboy actor Roy Rogers becomes the third major Western star to appear on television in his own series.

1952:

October 7 — "Ramar of the Jungle" makes its syndicated debut. It is the first of the action-adventure genre to feature a jungle setting.

October 25 — William ("Hopalong Cassidy") Boyd retires from acting to run Hopalong Cassidy Enterprises, controlling the commercial tie-ins rights to the character.

November 24 — "Ding Dong School" premieres on NBC as the first morning show for preschoolers.

November 25 — "Terry and the Pirates," a popular syndicated comic strip, debuts in television syndication.

1953:

February 9 — "The Adventures of Superman" debuts in syndication through the courtesy of National comics and the Kellogg's Cereal Company. It will become the most continuously rerun children's series ever.

February 10 — "Romper Room" debuts as the first national syndicated franchise series shown individually on local networks.

April 18 — "Rod Brown and the Rocket Rangers," another children's series involving space travel, debuts over CBS.

1954:

January 4 — Comedian Pinky Lee stars as host of television's first comedy-variety series for children. It is presented over the NBC network.

January 5 — Gail Davis stars in the debut of "Annie Oakley," the first juvenile series to feature a female in a starring role.

September 4 — Screen Gems, the television subsidiary of Columbia Pictures, begins its string of 30-minute action films for children with the series "Captain Midnight" over CBS.

September 6 — "Kukla, Fran, and Ollie" moves to the ABC network.

September 12 — The legend of "Lassie" begins its long tenure on Sunday nights on CBS.

October 15 — Screen Gems' second series for a children's audience debuts with "The Adventures of Rin Tin Tin," broadcast on Friday evenings over the ABC network.

October 27 — Walt Disney's first series, "Disneyland," premieres over the ABC network. It will go through various title changes and be featured throughout the next three decades on every network.

November 20 — Ventriloquist Paul Winchell and his dummy Jerry Mahoney begin their first program for children over the NBC network.

December 15 — "Davy Crocket" premieres as a segment of the Walt Disney show called "Frontierland."

1955:

January 17 — Producer Hal Roach's "Our Gang" shorts from the 1930s are syndicated nationally as "The Little Rascals" through Interstate Television Corporation and Allied Artists, syndicators of the Hal Roach Studios.

— "Captain Gallant of the Foreign Legion" debuts over NBC.

— "Uncle Johnny Coons" makes its CBS debut from Chicago affiliate WBBM.

March 7 — Mary Martin stars in the two-hour NBC stage presentation of "Peter Pan."

July 4 — Comedian Soupy Sales stars in the first of a long string of shows that will carry his name. The ABC series served as a summer replacement for "Kukla, Fran, and Ollie."

August 13 — Actor Andy Devine replaces the late Ed McConnell as host of "Andy's Gang."

September 3 — "Tales of the Texas Rangers," from the Screen Gems Corporation, debuts on Saturday mornings on CBS.

September 10 — "The Friendly Giant" debuts and later becomes educational television's first hit series.

September 22 — "The Adventures of Long John Silver" debuts in syndication. It is the third children's action series to gain national sponsorship through the Kellogg's Cereal Company.

September 26 — "The Adventures of Robin Hood," a British export, is presented weekly over the CBS network through the sponsorship of Wild Root Hair Oil.

September 28 — "Brave Eagle" debuts over CBS from the Roy Rogers Frontier Production Company. It is the first series to feature Indians in a favorable light.

September 29 — "Sergeant Preston of the Yukon" is moved from CBS radio to television.

September 30 — Gene Autry's wonder horse Champion gets a shot at his own Western series over the CBS network.

October 3 — Bob Keeshan premieres as the "grandfatherly influential" "Captain Kangaroo" on CBS on weekday mornings, to remain throughout the next three decades.

— Walt Disney's "The Mickey Mouse Club" makes its daily midafternoon debut on ABC.

October 6 — "Sheena, Queen of the Jungle," another popular comic strip figure, debuts in television syndication.

October 14 — Johnny Weissmuller brings his movie character "Jungle Jim" to syndicated television through the courtesy of Screen Gem Productions.

October 15 — "Fury," the story of a horse and a boy who loves him, makes its Saturday morning debut over the NBC network. It becomes the first children's action-adventure series to encourage prosocial themes in contrast to violence.

December 10 — "The Mighty Mouse Playhouse" premieres on CBS as the first in a long line of animated television series for Saturday mornings.

1956:

February 10 — "My Friend Flicka," another horse opera, debuts on CBS.

June 1 — After nine years of being featured on weekday afternoons, "The Howdy Doody Show" is moved to Saturday mornings.

June 13 — Hosted by comedian Dick Van Dyke, the "CBS Cartoon Theater" debuts as television's first animated prime-time series.

September 10 — The theatrical animated shorts of "Popeye the Sailor" and "Little Lulu" from Paramount Studios debuted in over 61 local television markets.

September 23 — "Circus Boy," a turn-of-the-century Western from Screen Gems, premieres on Sunday nights on NBC.

October 14 — Paul Terry's wacky magpies "Heckle and Jeckle" are sold to CBS's cartoon production company, where they begin a long Saturday morning run on the network.

November 3 — The 1939 film classic *The Wizard of Oz* makes its first in a series of annual television appearances.

December 10 — The adventures of "Gerald McBoing-Boing" debut on CBS on Saturday afternoons from U.P.A. Productions.

1957:

August 5 — "American Bandstand" debuts on ABC weekday afternoons as the first music and dance program for teens. It becomes the network's longest running program.

August 30 — "Kukla, Fran, and Ollie" is canceled by ABC in favor of more sophisticated juvenile fare.

September 3 — The theatrical adventures of "Woody Woodpecker" debut on ABC on Thursday evenings, with creator Walter Lantz as host.

October 4 — "Leave It to Beaver" premieres over CBS for one season. It will be presented throughout the entirety of its remaining five years, beginning with the following season, on ABC.

October 10 — "Zorro" debuts from the Walt Disney Studios on the ABC Thursday night schedule.

December 14 — "Ruff and Reddy" debuts on the NBC Saturday morning lineup as the first made-for-the-network animated series. It was also the first of many successful television shows for creators William Hanna and Joseph Barbera.

1958:

January 12 — Shirley Temple premieres on an irregular basis as hostess and occasional star of the series, "Shirley Temple's Storybook."

February 17 — Several dozen "Three Stooges" theatrical shorts from Columbia Pictures are sold to television through distributor Screen Gems.

September 29–October 3 — Kellogg's Cereals presents "The Kellogg's Variety Pack," a week of programs, new and vintage, sponsored by Kellogg's in an effort to promote their newest cereals on the market. The shows were presented in this order: Monday, "The Adventures of Superman"; Tuesday, "The Adventures of Sir Lancelot"; Wednesday, "The Adventures of Wild Bill Hickok"; Thursday, "The Huckleberry Hound Show" (Hanna and Barbera's second animated series); Friday, "The Adventures of William Tell."

1959:

February 2 — "Bozo the Clown" cartoons become available to local stations across the country.

June 6 — Actor George ("Superman") Reeves is found dead in his home shortly after 3:00 A.M., an alleged suicide.

September 29 — "Quick Draw McGraw" replaces "Superman" as part of the Kellogg's weekly variety pack. It becomes the third animated series created by the team of William Hanna and Joseph Barbera.

October 3 — "Sky King" returns to television on Saturday mornings, sponsored by the Nabisco Company on CBS.

— Soupy Sales returns to ABC on Saturday afternoons in "Lunch with Soupy Sales."

October 4 — Hank Ketcham's "Dennis the Menace" comes to life over the CBS network on Sunday nights.

October 11 – "Matty's Funday Funnies" premieres over the ABC network through the courtesy of Mattel Toys and Harvey Comics.

November 7 – "American Bandstand" host Dick Clark is asked to testify before the congressional committee investigating radio's payola scandal.

November 19 – "Rocky and His Friends" is first presented over the ABC network. Created by Jay Ward, it becomes the first cartoon show with sophisticated adult humor.

December 29 – Kellogg's Cereals ends the decade as the largest manufacturer of children's consumer products.

1960:

September 18 – "Shirley Temple Theater" returns as a weekly series.

September 24 – "Howdy Doody" ends its long association with NBC in a final hour-long telecast.

September 30 – "The Flintstones" premieres on the ABC Friday night schedule. Created by William Hanna and Joe Barbera, it becomes the first successful animated sitcom series aimed at attracting an adult audience.

October 1: Ventriloquist Shari Lewis replaces "Howdy Doody" with her own series, "The Shari Lewis Show."

– Illusionist Mark Wilson debuts on the CBS Saturday morning lineup in "The Magic Land of Alakazam."

October 11 – "The Bugs Bunny Show" debuts in prime time over the ABC network with new introductions to the Warner Brothers shorts of the 1940s and 1950s.

October 15 – "King Leonardo and His Short Subjects" replaces the "Ruff and Reddy" program. Sponsored by General Mills, it is the first animated network series created by Leonardo Productions and Total Television.

November 9 – The animated theatrical shorts of "Mr. Magoo" are syndicated nationally through U.P.A. Productions.

1961:

January 30 – "Yogi Bear," formally a segment of "The Huckleberry Hound Show," becomes a 30-minute series of its own.

September 17 – *The Red Balloon*, a prize-winning French film, is first televised on the CBS "General Electric Theater," hosted by Ronald Reagan.

September 24 – "The Bullwinkle Show," a spinoff of "Rocky and His Friends," premieres on the NBC Sunday evening schedule.

September 27 – Hanna-Barbera's "Top Cat" premieres in prime time on ABC. It runs for one season before reverting to Saturday morning reruns.

October 4 — "The Alvin Show" premieres for one season in prime time over the CBS network. It is rerun for several seasons on Saturday mornings.

October 8 — Gerry Anderson's "super-marionation" technique comes to television in his premiere puppet-action series, "Supercar."

October 14 — The complete 48-film "Bowery Boys" package becomes available for television syndication by its distributor, Allied Artists.

1962:

February 10 — "Davey and Goliath," a religiously oriented claymation puppet series formerly available to a few local stations, is syndicated nationally on Sunday mornings.

April 7 — "The Bugs Bunny Show" moves to Saturday mornings. It becomes the longest running cartoon series of all time, shown at various times on both CBS and ABC.

September 23 — "The Jetsons" debuts on prime-time Sunday evenings from the studios of Hanna-Barbera. It becomes the ABC network's first color series.

October 1 — "Discovery" debuts as a weekly educational series.

1963:

January 6 — Zoologist Marlin Perkins is the creator and host of "Wild Kingdom," premiering over the NBC network and sponsored by Mutual of Omaha.

September 21 — "The Jetsons," after one season in prime time, begins its long Saturday morning run at various times over each of the commercial networks.

September 28 — The CBS Saturday morning lineup begins with reruns of such old favorites as "Quick Draw McGraw" and "The Alvin Show." Total Television's "Tennessee Tuxedo" also debuts. It is the first comical cartoon series to include educational inserts.

October 15 — "Fireball XL-5" arrives on the NBC Saturday morning schedule. It is the second puppet action series to feature Gerry Anderson's super-marionation technique, and the first for network broadcast.

November 3 — The irregularly scheduled "NBC Children's Theater" debuts.

1964:

January 11 — "Magilla Gorilla" debuts in weekly syndication, from Hanna-Barbera Productions.

September 18 — "The Adventures of Jonny Quest" makes its prime-time debut over the ABC network. Created by Hanna and Barbera, it is their first in a long line of animated science fiction 30-minute thrillers.

September 24 — "The Munsters" debuts on CBS in prime time for adult audiences. It will eventually become a huge children's favorite when rerun in syndication.

September 26 — "The Famous Adventures of Mr. Magoo" is featured as a regular weekly series (an introduction to the program was presented the previous week on September 19, on NBC).

— "Gilligan's Island" premieres over the CBS network on Saturday nights. Its childish nature will eventually gain the attention of children nationwide, who will keep the show alive in syndication.

October 3 — "Underdog" the third and most popular series from Total Television's Leonardo Productions, makes its debut on Saturday mornings on NBC.

1965:

September 12 — Hanna and Barbera present a 60-minute parody of the espionage films presently in vogue with "The World of Secret Squirrel and Atom Ant." Both become regular 30-minute series the following week on NBC's Saturday morning lineup.

— NBC initiates its first season of all color programs.

September 25 — After providing years of entertainment in theaters and in television syndication, "Tom and Jerry" debuts as a regular Saturday morning series for CBS.

— An animated version of the popular British group the Beatles appears in a 30-minute series on ABC.

December 9 — "A Charlie Brown Christmas" is presented on CBS as a prime-time network special. It not only becomes an annual favorite, but begins a long string of other Charlie Brown specials created by Charles Schulz.

1966:

January 12 — "Batman" debuts in the second half of ABC's 1965–66 prime-time season.

September 10 — Animated adventures of popular live heroes "Superman" and "The Lone Ranger" appear on the CBS Saturday morning lineup.

— "The Road Runner," formerly a segment of "The Bugs Bunny Show," debuts with its own series on CBS Saturday mornings.

December 18 — The Dr. Seuss special "How the Grinch Stole Christmas" begins its annual yuletide airing over the CBS network.

1967:

January 2 — Fred Rogers begins his long run as the kindly Mister Rogers over the national educational channel.

January 7 — "The Flintstones" begins its long Saturday morning run, beginning on the NBC network. It will eventually be featured on every network as well as in syndication.

February 5 — Kukla, Fran, and Ollie return to television as hosts of an irregular series of foreign films for children on CBS entitled "The CBS Children's Film Festival."

February 26 — Animation and live action are blended for the Hanna-Barbera NBC special, "Jack and the Beanstalk."

September 9 — CBS continues its monopoly on popular comic book action heroes with the Saturday morning debut of "Aquaman." ABC follows suit with "The Fantastic 4" and "Spiderman."

— "George of the Jungle" premieres on Saturday mornings on ABC. The animated series created by Jay Ward is an attempt to attract adult audiences.

September 10 — Network cartoons come to Sunday morning, premiering on NBC with reruns of Hanna-Barbera's "Atom Ant."

1968:

March 25 — The Children's Television Workshop becomes established through the courtesy of the Ford Foundation for the Public Broadcasting Systems a revised version of the Educational Television Channel.

September 15 — The cartoon/comic strip adventures of "Archie" debut on CBS Saturday mornings.

November 17 — "The NBC Children's Theater"'s presentation of "Heidi" preempts the final few minutes of the New York Jets and Oakland Raiders game, and the Raiders' two winning touchdowns are never shown.

1969:

September 6 — NBC leads the way into the new Saturday morning schedule with "The Pink Panther Show" and "H.R. Puf-n-stuf," the latter the first in a series of shows created by Sid and Marty Krofft.

September 13 — William Hanna and Joseph Barbera return comedy animation to Saturday mornings with the CBS debut of "Dastardly and Muttley and Their Flying Machines," "The Perils of Penelope Pitstop," and "Scooby-Doo, Where Are You?"

November 10—The newly developed PBS network premieres with "Sesame Street," a production of the Children's Television Workshop.

November 12—Comedian Bill Cosby serves as host to an NBC prime-time animated special entitled "Hey, Hey, It's Fat Albert" based loosely on the adventures of Cosby and his childhood playmates.

1970:

September 12—The animated adventures of "The Harlem Globetrotters" debut on CBS. Produced by Hanna and Barbera, it becomes the first cartoon series to feature black characters in a starring role.

—CBS develops "In the News," a series of 60-second inserts of news and information between Saturday morning programs.

1971:

September 11—ABC debuts its fall Saturday morning season with "The Jackson Five," the second animated series presenting blacks in a starring role.

—"Curiosity Shop" premieres, consisting of both animation and live action, with educational tidbits.

September 12—"Make a Wish," a public affairs program, debuts on the ABC Sunday morning schedule.

October 25—"The Electric Company" debuts over the PBS network. It is the second series produced by the Children's Television Workshop.

1972:

January 9—"Zoom" premieres over the PBS network as another creative effort to reinforce children's values.

August 31—Buffalo Bob Smith and Howdy Doody return in an hour-long special designed to introduce the new NBC fall children's lineup.

September 9—Scooby Doo goes from a 30- to a 60-minute format in "The New Scooby-Doo Movies," which feature weekly guest stars in animated form.

—Yogi Bear, Huckleberry Hound, and many other Hanna-Barbera favorites from the past are featured together in the 60-minute premiere of the new "ABC Saturday Morning Movie."

—"Fat Albert and the Cosby Kids" debuts on CBS on Saturday mornings. It becomes the first all-black cartoon series to examine social themes with informative values.

October 4—The first in a series of monthly weekend specials appears on ABC on Saturday afternoon.

1973:

September 8 — A new version of the "Yogi Bear Show" comes to ABC for the first time as "Yogi's Gang."

October 27 — "The CBS Festival of Lively Arts for Young People" begins a trend of irregularly scheduled presentations.

1974:

September 7 — Live-action programming returns to Saturday mornings with the network's debut of "Shazam" (CBS), "Land of the Lost," and "Run Joe Run" (NBC).

October 1 — Peggy Charren, president of Action for Children's Television since 1968, begins a crusade against violence in children's television.

1975:

September 6 — Live-action programming begins a second season on Saturday mornings. CBS continues the current, revival with "The Secrets of Isis," "The Ghost Busters," and "Far Out Space Nuts."

1976:

September 11 — "The Pink Panther" is featured in a new 90-minute format. It is the first animated series in such a format.

— Over 40 percent of children's Saturday morning programs are now presented in a live-action format. Although highly creative and inspiring, these shows will eventually lose revenue, forcing the networks to return to animation.

1977:

September 10 — "The ABC Weekend Specials" become a regular part of Saturday morning programming, consisting at various times of both live action and animation.

November 20 — The "CBS Bugs Bunny/Road Runner Show" goes from 60 to 90 minutes, with many of the cartoons edited for violence.

1978:

September 9 — "Popeye the Sailor" comes to network television for the first time in a new series for CBS Saturday mornings produced by William Hanna and Joseph Barbera in association with the King Features Syndicate Corporation.

October 6 — "The Muppet Show" begins its third season. It is now considered the most watched show in syndication.

1979:

September 8 — Filmation Industries revives Paul Terry's "Heckle and Jeckle" and "Mighty Mouse" for new adventures on Saturday mornings on CBS.

November 10 — "Sesame Street" celebrates its tenth season on the PBS network.

1980:

January 14 — "3-2-1 Contact" debuts over the PBS network as another production of the Children's Television Workshop.

November 22 — "The Flintstones" goes to 90 minutes on NBC Saturday mornings in a revised version of the program entitled "The New Flintstones Comedy Show."

1981:

September 12 — "Smurfs" premieres on the NBC Saturday morning fall schedule. Produced by the Hanna-Barbera studios, the cartoons are based on the work of Belgian cartoonist Peyo Culliford.

1982:

September 13 — Commercially related cartoon shows such as "My Little Pony" and "G.I. Joe" are criticized by Peggy Charren's Action for Children's Television group.

1983:

April — "Reading Rainbow" debuts on the PBS daily schedule as an innovator in encouraging children's reading habits.

October 1 — The Walt Disney cable network is established.

1984:

September 3 — After three decades on CBS, "Captain Kangaroo" is forced off the air to make room for an additional hour of morning news.

1985:

September 7 — Comedian Richard Pryor comes to CBS Saturday mornings in his own innovative 30-minute children's series, "Pryor's Place."

September 8 — After 30 years of being featured at various times on each of the commercial networks, "The Walt Disney Show" goes to syndication.

1986:

September 13 — "Pee Wee's Playhouse" debuts on CBS. It returns the live children's host to Saturday mornings.

September 15 — Edited versions of "Captain Kangaroo," broadcast on CBS from 1982 to 1984, premiere in reruns on the PBS daily schedule.

1987:

November — Buffalo Bob Smith, Howdy Doody, and Clarabell are featured along with several other original cast members of "The Howdy Doody Show" in a special syndicated two-hour reunion program.

1988:

October — The Playmate Company's toy-related characters the Teenage Mutant Ninja Turtles come to syndication in their own animated new series, presented daily.

1989:

November 15 — "Sesame Street" celebrates its twentieth year on PBS with a prime-time special featuring the memories of several of the show's original cast members.

1990:

September 20 — "The Simpsons," an animated new series with adult themes, makes its debut in prime time over the new Fox network.

Appendix C: Children's Series Appearing in Prime Time

Series	Network
The Abbott and Costello Show	Syndicated
The Alvin Show	CBS
American Bandstand	ABC
Batman	ABC
Brave Eagle	CBS
The Buccaneers	ABC
Buck Rogers in the 25th Century	ABC
The Bugs Bunny Show	ABC
The Bullwinkle Show	NBC
Calvin and the Colonel	ABC
The CBS Cartoon Theater	CBS
Champion, the Wonder Horse	CBS
The Charlie Brown Specials	CBS
Circus Boy	NBC/ABC
Circus Time	ABC
Daktari	CBS
Daniel Boone	NBC
Dennis the Menace	CBS
The Dr. Seuss Specials	CBS/NBC/ABC
The Flintstones	ABC
Flipper	NBC
The Garfield Specials	CBS
The Gene Autry Show	CBS
Gentle Ben	NBC
The Green Hornet	ABC
The Hardy Boys/Nancy Drew Mysteries	ABC
Hopalong Cassidy	NBC
International Showtime	NBC
The Jetsons	ABC
Jim Bowie	ABC
Jonny Quest	ABC
Kukla, Fran, and Ollie	NBC
Land of the Giants	ABC
Lassie	CBS

Leave It to Beaver	CBS/ABC
The Littlest Hobo	Syndicated
The Lone Ranger	ABC
Lost in Space	CBS
Mattie's Funday Funnies	ABC
Maya	NBC
Mr. Magoo	NBC
My Friend Flicka	CBS
National Velvet	NBC
The New Adventures of Huck Finn	NBC
Off to See the Wizard	ABC
The Paul Winchell and Jerry Mahoney Show	NBC
Picture This	CBS
Quiz Kids	NBC/CBS
Rin Tin Tin	ABC
Robin Hood	CBS
Sergeant Preston of the Yukon	CBS
The 77th Bengal Lancers	NBC
Shelley Duvall's Fairie Tale Theater	PBS
Shirley Temple Theater	NBC/ABC
The Simpsons	FOX
Swiss Family Robinson	ABC/CBS
Top Cat	ABC
Wait Until Your Father Gets Home	Syndicated
Walt Disney	ABC/NBC/CBS/Syn.
West Point	ABC
Where's Huddles?	CBS
Wild Kingdom	NBC/Syndicated
Wonder Woman	ABC/CBS
Zorro	ABC

Appendix D: Live-Action Shows Originating in Radio or Movies

Series	Origin
The Abbott and Costello Show	NBC radio
Batman	Syndicated radio
The Bowery Boys	Film Series–Monogram/Allied Artists, 1946–58
Captain Midnight	CBS radio
Flipper	MGM film release, 1963
The Gene Autry Show	CBS radio
Hopalong Cassidy	Film Series–Paramount, 1935–48
Jungle Jim	Film Series–Columbia, 1948–55
Lassie	MGM film release, 1942
The Little Rascals/Our Gang	Roach/Pathé/MGM short film series, 1922–43
The Littlest Hobo	United Artist film release, 1958
The Lone Ranger	WXYZ–Detroit Radio syndication
Robin Hood	Warner Brothers film release, 1938
Sergeant Preston	CBS radio
The Singing Lady	ABC radio
Smilin' Ed's Gang	NBC radio
Superman	ABC radio
Tales of the Texas Rangers	CBS
Terry and the Pirates	Columbia film release, 1941
The Three Stooges	Columbia short film series, 1934–58

Index